# Foundations of Doctrine

# FOUNDATIONS OF DOCTRINE

## In Scripture and Experience

## A Students' Handbook on Holiness

*by*

**HARRY E. JESSOP, D. D.**

President Emeritus of Chicago Evangelistic Institute

*Published by*
CHICAGO EVANGELISTIC INSTITUTE
University Park, Iowa

First printing, April, 1938
Second printing, November, 1938
Third printing, 1940
Fourth printing, 1943
Fifth printing, 1944
Sixth printing, 1946
Seventh printing, 1949—5,000
Eighth printing, 1954—3,000
Ninth printing, 1958—3,000

Printed in U. S. A.

*To those esteemed servants of God,*

DR. IVA DURHAM VENNARD

founder and president of the Chicago Evangelistic Institute
who, at much personal cost, has stood through the years
as the exponent of full salvation truth in the
field of education

*and*

REV. JOSEPH H. SMITH

stalwart of the faith, who for more than six decades has faithfully labored in the cause of holiness and has rejoiced
to carry the message throughout this
and other lands
this Students' Handbook is gratefully dedicated.

# Preface

THIS book, as its subtitle indicates, is a series of studies on full salvation truth. Its purpose is to place before students a clear presentation of what we as holiness people believe. The writer therefore disclaims originality except in the method of presentation.

The lessons were prepared solely for the writer's personal use in class work in The Chicago Evangelistic Institute. He has sought to place before the students, as concisely as possible, a general idea of Second Blessing holiness as taught in the Word of God and in the literature of the church. Upwards of a hundred books are quoted and duly acknowledged, as the accompanying list will show.

As will be readily seen, considerable use has been made of Rev. J. A. Wood's book "Perfect Love." This has been a valuable help in locating many suitable quotations, although whenever these have been used they have, wherever possible, been verified and often considerably extended.

If we have transgressed any copyright it has been done inadvertently and we ask the owner's indulgence. We are conscious of many limitations, and our readers will doubtless discover more.

We gratefully acknowledge the splendid work of Mr. William Vennard in arranging the text for book form, and the untiring efforts of the office staff in its preparation.

Chicago, 1938.                                           H. E. J.

# Contents

# Full Salvation

## A STUDY IN HOLINESS TERMINOLOGY

WHEN we speak of "full salvation" we mean full only as related to the present life, and that only in relation to sin. The term is not to be confused with:

(a) That maturity of Christian character which can be known only through spiritual development by growth in grace.

There is a perfection as to quality which admits of unbounded development in quantity, and is therefore capable of unlimited expansion and increase. See 2 Pet. 3:17, 18; Eph. 3:14-21.

(b) That experience altogether future to which believers of all ages have looked forward, which will consummate Christ's redemptive work for His church, namely, "the redemption of our bodies." This will take place as:

      1.   The godly dead are raised,

      2.   The living saints are raptured,

at the second advent of the Lord Jesus Christ. See Rom. 8: 18-25; 1 Cor. 15: 35-58; Phil. 3: 7-14; 2 Tim. 2: 18.

If, in our thinking, these two facts are clearly recognized, we may with Scriptural accuracy speak of "full salvation" as a present possible experience. This is implied in our holiness hymnology. Take, for instance, the following:

> "Full salvation! Full salvation!
>   Lo! the fountain, opened wide,
> Streams thru every land and nation
>   From the Savior's wounded side.
> Full salvation! Full salvation!
>   Streams an endless crimson tide.
>
> "Oh, the glorious revelation!
>   See the cleansing current flow,
> Washing stains of condemnation
>   Whiter than the driven snow.
> Full salvation! Full salvation—
>   Oh, the rapturous bliss to know!
>
> "Love's resistless current sweeping
>   All the regions deep within;
> Thought and wish and senses keeping
>   Now and every instant clean!
> Full salvation! Full salvation!
>   From the guilt and power of sin."

Numerous terms are used to indicate this experience, some of which are the express words of Scripture, while others are the accumulation of spiritual coinage within the church, being the outcome of this experience as it has applied itself to the individual consciousness. While no expression is to be rejected if it correctly expresses revealed truth, it is better that exact Bible terms be more frequently used, as these tend to give an authoritative tone to the testimony; other terms well authenticated by general usage may then be used as supplementary expressions. Among these terms are:

1. *Biblical:* Sanctification, see Lev. 21:8; John 17: 17-19; 1 Thess. 4:3; 5:23; holiness, see Luke 1:75; 2 Cor. 7:1; Eph. 4:24; 1 Thess. 4:7; Heb. 12:10, 14; 1 Pet. 1: 15, 16; a clean heart, see Psa. 51:10; 73:1; a pure heart, see Psa. 24:4; Matt. 5:8; the baptism with the Holy Ghost

and with fire, see Matt. 3:11; circumcision of heart, see Deut. 30:6; Col. 2:11; perfection, see Gen. 17:1; Matt. 5:48; 2 Cor. 13:9; Heb. 6:1; perfect love, see 1 John 4:17, 18; the fullness of God, see Eph. 3:19.

These are but representative expressions and Scripture references, to which more may be added by a study of the Word of God.

2. *Extra Biblical:* "The Second Blessing." "The Higher Life." "The Rest of Faith." "The Full Assurance of Faith." "The Fullness of the Blessing."

These are but samples of expressions which will be found throughout the range of holiness literature. Some expressions seem to have established themselves in current usage, while others become irregular and almost die.

Discussing the terms "Sanctify," "Sanctification," "Perfection," "Holy," "Holiness," etc., Rev. J. A. Wood says:

"These terms are synonymous, all pointing to the same precious state of grace. While they denote the same religious state, each one of them indicates some essential characteristic, and hence these terms are significantly expressive of full salvation.

"The word *'sanctification'* has the double meaning of consecration and purification—the Old Testament sense of setting apart to a sacred service, and the New Testament sense of spiritual purification. The word 'sanctify' and its derivatives occur in the Scriptures, with reference to men and things, over one hundred times.

"The term *'perfection'* signifies completeness of Christian character; its freedom from all sin, and possession of all the graces of the Spirit, complete in kind. The word 'perfection' and its relatives occur one hundred and one times in the Scriptures. In over fifty of these instances it is predicated of human character under the operation of grace.

"The term *'holiness'* is more generic and comprehensive than the others, including salvation from sin, and the possession of the image and spirit of God. To be holy is to be whole, entire, or perfect in a moral sense, and in ordinary use is synonymous with purity and goodness. The word 'holy' and its derivatives occur not less than one hundred and twenty times in their application to men and things, while the word 'justify' and its derivatives occur only seventy-four times in regard to men; and the word 'pardon' and its derivatives, in their application to penitent sinners, occur only seventeen times.

"The phrase 'perfect love' is expressive of the spirit and temper or moral atmosphere, in which the wholly sanctified and perfect Christian lives. 'He that dwelleth in love dwelleth in God, and God in him' and 'herein is our love made perfect'" *(Perfect Love, pp. 9, 10).*

Dr. John Paul has stated some definitions as follows:

"It will be borne in mind that this grace has several different names, which imply the same thing. The definition of each term will throw light on the experience it contains for the individual.

*"Sanctification*—The act of God's grace by which a man, having consecrated himself, is made holy. This gives us a view of the experience as a work of God, but requiring human co-operation. It is a strong term.

*"Holiness*—Complete moral and spiritual purity. Wholeness, perfect soul health. This is a comprehensive term, implying godlikeness of character.

*"Perfect Love*—The Spirit of Jesus filling the heart to the exclusion of all inward sin. This title represents the sweet side of the sanctified life and implies freedom from selfishness. It is a very heavenly title.

*"Perfection*—The presence of all the graces, unimpaired by depravity, implying freedom and preservation from all sin.

*"Circumcision of the Heart*—The removal from the soul of God's child of a something that came into the world with

him, and from which he ought to be free, since freedom from it insures supreme love to God (Deut. 30 : 6).

*"The Baptism of the Holy Ghost*—The promised Paraclete, whom the world cannot receive. A washing with the Spirit of heaven. It implies purity, power, and comfort.

*"The Fullness of the Blessing*—The full benefit of the Atonement of Jesus, which saves completely from sin, and furnishes an abundance of living and dying grace.

*"Heart Purity*—A term that implies that, although the Prince of this world cometh, he findeth nothing in us. Total deliverance from inward sin. An expression of the negative state of Christian perfection.

*"Full Salvation*—An experience of salvation from all sin, held intact by a fullness of the abounding grace of God.

*"The Second Blessing*—The more abundant life that is instantly realized when the soul receives the purifying baptism of the Holy Ghost. The word 'blessing' here, as appropriated by theology, does not have merely its ordinary meaning as we use it in speaking of refreshing showers, temporal benefits, or ordinary spiritual refreshings. The sophist would say that he has had the fourth, fifth, and thousandth blessing; but this is merely a play upon words, in order to avoid an issue. Those who seem opposed to the Second Blessing are usually more opposed to the standard it represents than they are to the innocent term.

*"The Higher Life*—A term equivalent to Paul's expression, 'A more excellent way.' It is understood to mean that improvement on the inner life brought about by the baptism of the Spirit. It does not refashion the outer life of God's child. It simply adds transparency to a life that is already good" (*Scriptural Holiness—The More Excellent Way*).

## QUESTIONS ON THE TEXT

1. Explain the meaning of the term "full salvation."

2. State the numerous Biblical terms used to indicate this experience, and give a Scripture passage for each.

3. State the extra-Biblical terms used to indicate this experience.

4. Define the numerous terms indicating full salvation.

# The Problem

**THE FACT OF HUMAN SIN
(1) THE FALL AND ITS EFFECT ON THE RACE. (2) THE
TWOFOLD NATURE OF SIN. (3) CARNALITY WITHIN
THE BELIEVER. (4) PAULINE PORTRAITURES OF IN-
DWELLING SIN.**

---

**(1) The Fall and Its
Effect on the Race**

UMANITY has problems
many and various, but its cardinal problem is the fact of
human sin. Sin is the foulest monster that ever entered the
fair universe of God. It is the root of every other ill. It
originates in the devil. Its first cause was human disobedience. Its end is death (Rom. 6:23).

Sin is a Biblical term and has to do with man in his relationship Godward. All else of difficulty in the human race
has its roots there. The law speaks of crime; society is
familiar with vice; but the Word of God brings us face to
face with the awful fact of sin.

For its sin, the Bible never regards the human race as
merely unfortunate, although of course there are indications on all its pages of the divine pity. The Bible always
treats of man as guilty, and distinctly culpable, therefore
destined to punishment.

　1.　*The fact of sin's presence is attributed to the fact of*

[7]

*a fall.* See Gen. 3; Rom. 5: 12-21; 1 Cor. 15: 21, 22; 1 Tim. 2: 13-15. The first of these Scriptures records the awful fact, while the other three emphasize the fact and indicate the wider result.

2. *The effect of that fall is regarded as extending to the entire race.* See Gen. 5: 3; 6: 5; 8: 21; Job 14: 1-4; 15: 14; Psa. 51: 5; Prov. 22: 15; Jer. 17: 9; Matt. 15: 19; Mark 7: 21-23; John 3: 6; Rom. 5: 19; Rom. 8: 5-8; Gal. 5: 16-21; Eph. 2-3. This depravity is seen in more detailed fashion as follows:

The understanding is darkened (Eph. 4: 18; 1 Cor. 2: 14).

The heart is deceitful and desperately wicked (Jer. 17: 9).

The mind and conscience are defiled (Gen. 6: 5; Titus 1: 15).

The will is enslaved (Rom. 7: 18).

The race is in bondage to Satan, sin, and death (John 8: 31-36; Heb. 2: 14, 15).

In view of all this, we face the problem, how may a fallen and depraved soul find its way into favor with, and likeness to, God?

## QUESTIONS ON THE TEXT

1. Why may the fact of sin be termed the cardinal problem of humanity?

2. Distinguish between "sin," "crime," and "vice."

3. Show that the fact of human sin is attributed to a "fall."

4. Show that the fact of the Fall is to be regarded as extending to: a. The entire race. b. The entire man.

## (2) The Twofold Nature of Sin

ACCORDING to the plain teaching of the Word of God, the nature of sin is twofold, being first an inward defilement from which acts of transgression spring; then an act of transgression having its source in the evil nature within.

The order of human recognition when the soul is seeking deliverance is, of necessity, inverted: the transgressor, naturally being burdened with the thought of acts of sin committed for which he feels guilty, seeks forgiveness. Ere long, however, the emphasis shifts to something interior, namely, the inward nature, for it is by reason of the corrupt inward nature that the outward acts were produced, and it will continue to produce more sinful acts unless some adequate provision can be made to the contrary.

The cry of the penitent sinner is—"I have done . . ." The cry of the convicted believer is—"I am . . ." Examples of this may be seen in:

(a) Psalm 51. Read carefully the entire Psalm, remembering its background (*i. e.,* 2 Sam. 11, 12). After a whole year of soul darkness the prodigal king is finding his way back to God, and this Psalm is to be regarded as the spiritual pathway which he trod. Note the contrasted confessions of verse 4 and verses 5-10. One is the confession of sin committed, while the other is the confession of sin inherited.

(b) Isaiah 6. Read the first eight verses, remembering that before us here is not an ungodly man bemoaning his lost condition, but a prophet of the Lord who has already been made conscious of some measure of divine grace. He is now brought face to face with the inward corruption of his nature; hence he gives his despairing confession, verse 5, "I am undone . . . I am unclean . . ."

With the prophet now it is not a question of sinful action

but of inward condition; that corrupt nature which not even the forgiving grace of God can remove.

Sin, then, is to be viewed in a twofold aspect which for want of a better expression, has been termed actual and original.

The Salvation Army is definite in its teaching here, being careful to insist on this dual presentation of evil. Say they:

"Man is sinful in two ways:

"He has a sinful nature. He is born with an inclination or tendency to evil. His heart is wrong; he prefers his own way to God's way. This depravity or disposition to sin affects every part of man's being, and it renders him unable, by his own efforts, to deliver himself (Psa. 51:5; Rom. 7:17; Eph. 2:3).

"He commits sinful acts. Those, although the outcome of his sinful nature, are yet done by his own choice. All men are thus themselves guilty of transgressing God's law (Rom. 3:12, 23)" (*Handbook of Salvation Army Doctrine,* p. 53).

1. Sin is an *outward manifestation,* that is, the act of sin committed. Sin is committed in one of three ways:

We may think—sinning in thought. We may speak—sinning in word. We may act—sinning in deed. A person cannot commit actual sin except in one of these three directions. The same may be said of sins of omission; they could be omissions only in one of these three ways.

Actual sin, being the result of inbred sin, is related to it as the fruit is related to the root; or as an eruption on the skin is related to a poisoned blood stream; it is the effect of an underlying cause. Hence, in general Scripture usage, actual transgression is set forth in plural nouns, such as "sins," "iniquities," etc., in contrast with the singular nouns "sin" and "iniquity," except where the context is so plain that their importance could not possibly be misunderstood.

2. Sin is an *inward quality,* that is, sin inherited. That inward condition which has resulted from the fall of our first parents from original righteousness, and, as a corruption of nature, has come down from Adam to his posterity.

This corruption is therefore as old as the race itself and is to be regarded as a unit of moral evil.

The acts of sin which are termed "the works of the flesh" (Gal. 5: 19-21) are many and diverse, but all are seen to come from one and the same root (see Mark 7: 21-23; James 1: 15).

For centuries numerous theological names have been used for this inward sin principle, such as "original sin," "inbred sin," and "indwelling sin." These are not the exact phraseologies of Scripture; yet they come as near as possible to it, and may be regarded as embodying in convenient fashion what the Scriptures have to teach.

### QUESTIONS ON THE TEXT

1. According to the plain teaching of the Word of God, the nature of sin is twofold. Explain this.

2. Show the teaching of Psalm 51 and Isaiah 6.

3. What is meant by the terms actual and original when discussing sin?

4. Show sin as an outward manifestation.

5. Show sin as an inward quality.

### (3) Carnality
### Within the Believer

THAT the terms "original sin," "inbred sin," etc., are not exact Scriptural phrases we have already seen; yet as convenient expressions they are not to be rejected since they come to us having the sanction of long general usage within the church.

As we continue the study of the principle which they represent, it soon becomes clear that this baneful thing which contaminates the inner nature of the sons of Adam, producing such disastrous results, is not confined to the soul without saving grace, but even after conversion is found within the regenerate also. In every unsanctified believer lurks the germ of indwelling sin.

We quote from Wesley: "Is there, then, any sin in him that is in Christ? Does sin remain in one that believes in Him? Is there any sin in them that are born of God, or are they wholly delivered from it? . . .

"By sin I understand inward sin; any sinful temper, passion, or affection, such as pride, self-will, love of the world, in any kind or degree; such as lust, anger, peevishness; any disposition contrary to the mind which was in Christ. . . .

"As this position 'There is no sin in a believer, no carnal mind, no bent to backsliding,' is thus contrary to the Word of God, so it is to the experience of His children. These continually feel a heart bent to backsliding; a natural tendency to evil; a proneness to depart from God and cleave to the things of earth. They are daily sensible of sin remaining in the heart—pride, self-will, unbelief; and of sin cleaving to all they speak and do, even their best actions and holiest duties. Yet at the same time they know they are of God; they cannot doubt it for a moment. They feel His Spirit clearly witnessing with their spirit that they are children of God. They rejoice in God through Jesus Christ, by whom they have now received the Atonement. So that they are equally assured that sin is in them, and that Christ is in them the hope of glory.

"But can Christ be in the same heart where sin is? Undoubtedly He can, otherwise it could never be saved therefrom. Where the sickness is, there is the physician, 'Carrying on the work within, striving till He cast out sin.'

"Christ indeed cannot reign where sin reigns; neither will He dwell where it is allowed. But He is and dwells in the heart of every believer who is fighting against all sin: although it be not yet purified according to the purification of the sanctuary" (*Sermon, "On Sin in Believers"*).

This teaching of Mr. Wesley on remaining sin within the justified believer is the emphatic pronouncement of the Word of God, and this pronouncement is emphasized through the centuries by the creeds of the churches, which we shall quote.

1. *The Scriptures plainly teach that there is remaining carnality in the justified child of God.* This is implied in the numerous records of individuals who have found God's saving grace, as later we shall see; but meanwhile we call attention to some outstanding Scripture passages which set forth this truth in a distinct and more general sense.

In the Pauline Epistles, written not to worldlings but to believers, expressions such as the following are used:

"Sin," a singular noun, is used in Rom. 6 at least seventeen times; "our old man," "the old man"—Rom. 6:6; Eph. 4:22; Col. 3:9; "the body of sin"—Rom. 6:6; "the body of the sins of the flesh"—Col. 2:11; "sin that dwelleth in me"—Rom. 7:17; "the body of this death"—Rom. 7:24; "the law of sin and death"—Rom. 8:2; "the carnal mind"—Rom. 8:7; "the flesh"—Rom. 8:8, 9, 12,13; Gal. 5:17; "filthiness"—2 Cor. 7:1.

But Paul is not the only Scripture writer to recognize this indwelling evil within the believer and to give it distinctive names, for its slimy trail may be traced in other portions of the Word of God:

"Iniquity"—Psa. 51: 5; Isa. 6: 7; "sin"—Psa. 51: 5; Isa. 6: 7; "filthiness"—Ezek. 36: 25; "bent to backsliding"—Hos. 11: 7; "the stony heart"—Ezek. 36: 26; "unrighteousness"—1 John 1: 9; "the sin which doth so easily beset us"—Heb. 12: 1; "superfluity of naughtiness"—James 1: 21; "ye double minded"—James 4: 8.

Added to these expressions, which the student should memorize, are the following passages which should be carefully read: Psa. 51: 6-10; Isa. 6: 5-7; 1 Cor. 3: 1-4; Gal. 5: 16-21.

2. *Universal experience confirms this.* We offer here two proofs of this general statement:

(a) From the creeds of the churches. So evident is this fact of retained carnality within the believer that practically all the churches, whether Catholic or Protestant, admit it in their creeds.

The Council of Trent (1546), Roman Catholic Church. "But this Holy Synod confesses and is sensible that in the baptized there remains concupiscence, or an incentive to sin."

The Helvitic Confession (1566), Swiss churches. "But even in the regenerate there remains some infirmity. The flesh strives against the Spirit to the end of life (Rom. 7: 14; Gal. 5: 17)."

The Formula of Concord (1580), Lutheran; Reformed Church of Germany. "And they that believe, according to the spirit of their mind, have perpetually to struggle with their flesh; that is, with the corrupt nature; which inheres in us till death."

The Heidelberg Catechism (1563), German. "The sinful nature with which I have to struggle all my life long."

The Confession of the Church of France. Prepared by Calvin. "Even after baptism it is still of the nature of sin.

... It is a perversity always producing fruits of malice and rebellion" (Art. XI).

The Belgic Confession (1561), Churches of the Netherlands. "Nor is it [original sin] by any means abolished or done away in baptism, since sin always issues from this woeful source as water from a fountain."

The Church of England (Art. IX). "And this infection of nature doth remain, yea, in them that are regenerate."

The Church of Scotland (Art. XIII). "And from this comes that continual battle between the flesh and the Spirit in God's children."

The Irish Church (Art. XXIV). "This corruption of nature doth remain, even in those that are regenerated."

The Baptist Church. Dr. Augustus Hopkins Strong of the Rochester Theological Seminary may be considered a good representative. He declares: "Although in regeneration the governing disposition of the soul is made holy, there still remain tendencies to evil which are unsubdued" (*Systematic Theology,* p. 869).

The Presbyterian Church. The Westminster Confession of Faith: "There remaineth still some remnants of corruption in every part, whence arises a continual war."

The Salvation Army "We believe that after conversion there remains in the believer inclination to evil and roots of bitterness" (*Handbook of Salvation Army Doctrine,* p. 2).

The Church of the Nazarene. This may be taken as representative of the holiness bodies in general today: "We believe that original sin, or depravity, is that corruption of the nature of all the offspring of Adam, by reason of which everyone is very far gone from original righteousness, or the pure state of our first parents at the time of their creation, is averse to God; is without spiritual life; and is inclined to evil, and that continually; and that it continues to exist with the new life of the regenerate . . ." (*Manual of the Church of the Nazarene*).

(b) From the testimonies of men. Personal experience, and the experience of our immediate acquaintances, will confirm this without going farther afield.

### QUESTIONS ON THE TEXT

1. Such terms as "original sin" and "inbred sin" are not exact Scriptural phrases. What shall we do with them?

2. Show that the Scriptures plainly teach that there is remaining carnality in the justified child of God.

3. Give other proof of this.

### (4) Pauline Portraitures of Indwelling Sin

WE have already noted the Scripture passages which will form the basis of the present study and shown them as being peculiar to Paul, but purpose to take them up again with a view to entering more intelligently into the Pauline conception of indwelling sin by noting the various figures which he uses concerning it.

Sin, to Paul, is no plaything. It is regarded as foul and loathsome, and foreign to our nature, yet in such absolute possession that unless some method can be found for its removal there is no hope for the race. His epistles give us a sevenfold portraiture of it.

1. Sin as a *dominating tyrant*. "S-i-n," a singular noun of three letters, in contrast to "s-i-n-s," the plural noun of four letters (Rom. 6, 7). Read through these two chapters and note the dominating fact of indwelling sin producing

the despairing cry of chapter 7: 14-20. Here "sin" is personified and regarded as a tyrant, possessing, indwelling, outworking, and driving to despair. Note by way of contrast the indwellers of Rom. 7: 20 and Gal. 2: 20, and the respective results. On the one hand we have sin as master, a tyrant in control; while on the other hand we have Christ living within the soul by purchased right and as the fruit of love.

2.   Sin as a *hereditary evil*. "Our old man," "the old man" (Rom. 6: 6; Eph. 4: 22; Col. 3: 9). This expression is distinctly Pauline. Only by Paul, and only in these three passages, is the expression used. This intruder into our nature is declared to be "old." This may be for two reasons:

(a)   From the fact of its age. It is far older than the individual. It is "ours" because it was born with us (Psa. 51: 5); it has entrenched itself in our personality and worked its wickedness through us (Rom. 7: 17). Nevertheless, its origin reaches far back, for it is as old as the race itself (Rom. 5: 12). "Coeval with our being, and as old as the fall" (*Notes on New Testament,* Rom. 6: 6, Wesley).

Here, then, is a hereditary transmission from our fallen first parents through each successive generation. It is a racial contamination in which every child of Adam is involved.

(b)   From the fact of its nature. It is a strong and impressive way of representing that depravity which has spread itself through our entire humanity, leaving no part unaffected.

3.   Sin as a *unitary evil*. "The body of sin" (Rom. 6: 6). "The body of the sins of the flesh" (Col. 2: 11). Here is another expression of Pauline origin, having reference not to the human body but to the sin principle in its totality. Paul had a high estimate of the human body, and regarded it as being destined, not for "destruction," as is this "body

of sin," but for "redemption" (Rom. 8:23), and meanwhile to be "the temple of the Holy Ghost" (1 Cor. 6:19, 20; 2 Cor. 6:16).

This "body of sin," however, is deeper. It is the "body" in the sense that it is the totality, the root cause, the source of evil. All evil in any life, whether of thought, word or deed, is from the same central source.

"For from within, out of the heart of men, proceed evil thoughts, adulteries, fornications, murders, thefts, covetousness, wickedness, deceit, lasciviousness, an evil eye, blasphemy, pride, foolishness: All these things come from within . . ." (Mark 7:21-23). They are the outward stream from that inward source, "the body," or totality of indwelling sin. Consequently, sin is to be viewed as an unitary principle which was injected into human nature and must be removed from the nature, if it is ever to be removed at all, by a single, decisive act.

4. Sin as a *body of death*. "O wretched man that I am, who shall deliver me from the body of this death" (Rom. 7:24).

As has been pointed out by other writers, the allusion here is to one of the modes of capital punishment in the Roman Empire. The Romans were cruel people and had no pity for their criminals. Various modes of execution were practiced.

(a) That of crucifixion, which has become familiarized by the death of our Lord.

(b) That of impalement, the throwing of the doomed man onto a huge spike.

(c) That of the attachment of the corpse. The condemned man was fastened to the dead body and made to inhale the death stench as decomposition worked itself out.

Each of these figures the Apostle Paul uses and spiritualizes. As to crucifixion, "I am crucified with Christ" (Gal. 2:20). As to impalement, "And lest I should be exalted above measure through the abundance of the revelations, there was given to me a thorn in the flesh . . ." or more literally, "an agony of impalement" (2 Cor. 12:7).

But here he used the third figure and shows how carnality is like the corpse fastened to the man. It is not actually a part of him, and yet it clings to him. It is a body of death from which he longs to be free.

5. Sin as a *downward drag*. "The law of sin and death" (Rom. 8:2). That downward drag in the nature which is contrary to "the law of the Spirit of life."

6. *Sin as an inward enmity*. "The carnal mind" (Rom. 8:5-8; 1 Cor. 3:1-4). Here are strangely repulsive words, having about them something decidedly unwholesome. The word "mind" indicates a propensity, a principle, or a disposition. The word "carnal" means fleshly. It is not only characterized by the vulgar, coarse and vile, but also by the thought of earthliness and weakness in contrast to the mind of the Spirit. Therefore it is a propensity, a disposition, a tendency working within man, having the weakness of human degeneracy and the wickedness of Satanically wrought depravity. Concerning this carnal mind, the apostle states that it is "enmity against God: for it is not subject to the law of God, neither indeed can be." Carnality is an ungovernable rebel which even the law of God cannot control.

7. Sin as a *corruption of the moral nature*. "The flesh" (Rom. 8:8; Gal. 5:16-21). Concerning this word flesh there has been much controversy. Bible dictionaries and lexicons give the word as having at least six different meanings.

(See, for example, Young's *Analytical Concordance; The International Standard Bible Encyclopedia;* Hasting's *Dictionary of the Bible; Biblico-Theological Lexicon,* etc.). The word will be seen to have numerous definitions until finally this is reached: "The seat and vehicle of sin"; or, "the sinful condition of human nature in and according to its bodily manifestations"; or, "applied to the carnal nature."

By a mere glance at these books of reference, two things will be seen concerning this word:

(a) That in the original, more than one word is used for the word which has been translated flesh.

(b) That in the Epistles Paul takes one of these words and uses it to indicate a distinct and emphatic meaning.

Writing on the word "flesh" as it occurs in Gal. 5:17, "The flesh lusteth against the Spirit, and the Spirit against the flesh," one writer says:

"The word 'flesh' does not mean the body. The word in the Greek is *sarx,* signifying the carnal mind. It has been observed that Paul adopts the word *sarx* to describe carnality; and the word *soma* to speak of the body. In this instance it is *sarx* and not *soma.* A strong proof of this interpretation is seen in the fact that God has no quarrel with the body. The Spirit does not lust against the body. Sin is not in the body, as it does not exist in any form of matter."

Here, then, is our problem—sin, inherited and committed. If it were only our problem we should be despairing indeed, but God has made it His own. He and He alone can solve the problem of human sin, and what a glorious solution He has found. Hallelujah!!!

### QUESTIONS ON THE TEXT

1. St. Paul gives a sevenfold portraiture of indwelling sin. Name the seven points before reading the other questions.

2. Show sin as a dominating tyrant.

3. Show sin as an hereditary evil.

4. Show sin as a unitary evil.

5. Show sin as a body of death.

6. Show sin as a downward drag.

7. Show sin as an inward enmity.

8. Show sin as a corruption of the moral nature.

# The Provision

## GENERAL STATEMENT. THE ENTIRE GODHEAD IS INTERESTED IN THE WORK.

THE work of human redemption is essentially a divine provision, for man in his fallen condition and left to his own devices neither would nor could have found his way back to God. By reason of the Fall and the consequent severed relationship from God, four terrible effects must be recognized now:

Death—Gen. 2:17; Rom. 5:12; Eph. 2:1-3; dread—Gen. 3:10; Psa. 139:7-12; Rev. 6:12-17; distance—Gen. 3:23, 24; Eph. 2:12; disinclination—Gen. 6:5; Eph. 4:18, 19.

Apart from a direct divine intervention the entire race was irrevocably doomed, hence the glory of redemption.

In this redeeming work the whole Trinity is involved. It was by the direct fiat of that Trinity in council that the race was first created (see Gen. 1:26); and it is by the operation of that same Trinity that the race is redeemed. Under the caption "The Covenant of Grace," Dr. A. A. Hodge says: "First, it is evident that as God is an infinite, eternal, and immutable intelligence He must have formed, from the beginning, an all-comprehensive and unchangeable plan of

[21]

all His works in time, including creation, providence, and redemption.

"Second, a plan formed by and intended to be executed in its several reciprocal distributed parts by Three Persons, as Sender and Sent, as Principal and Mediator, as Executor and Applier, must necessarily possess all the essential attributes of an eternal covenant between those Persons" (*Outline of Theology*, p. 367).

1. It is by the Father. In Him we have the expression of the divine purpose. It must never be imagined that the Father's part in the great work of Atonement is that of demanding sacrifice, and in a detached manner standing aside and sending the Son to suffer. The Father is to be regarded as suffering with, and in an inexplicable manner in, the Son, for in their redemptive qualities their natures can never be separated (see John 3: 16; 16: 27; Rom. 8: 3, 32; 2 Cor. 5: 19-21; Gal. 4: 4, 5; 1 Thess. 4: 3; 1 John 4: 10-14; Jude 1: 1).

2. It is by the Son. Through Him we see the outworking of the divine purpose (see Matt. 1: 21; Gal. 2: 20; Eph. 5: 25-27).

(a) His Calvary work (see Matt. 20: 28; John 1: 29; Gal. 1: 4; 3: 13; 6: 14; Eph. 1: 7; 2: 13; 5: 25-27; Col. 1: 20; 2: 14, 15; 1 Tim. 2: 6; Tit. 2: 14; Heb. 2: 14, 15; 9: 26; 10: 10; 13: 10-12; 1 Pet. 1: 18-20; 2: 21-25; 3: 18; 1 John 3: 8).

(b) His throne work (see Matt. 28: 18; Acts 1: 9; 2: 22-36; Heb. 1: 3, 4; 1 John 2: 1, 2.

The Book of the Revelation will be found to ring with the thought of the enthroned and exalted Lamb. There the designation "Lamb" is used concerning Jesus at least twenty-six times. It is John's favorite word for his Lord.

3. It is by the Holy Spirit. By Him we realize the application of the divine purpose.

(a) In the Pentecostal outpouring. (1) Promised (Isa.

44:3; Joel 2:28, 29).  (2) Fulfilled (Acts 1:4, 5; 2:1-21, 33).

(b) In the age-long outworking (John 7:39; 14:16, 17, 26; 15:26, 27; 16:7-15).

This outworking is seen in its beginnings in the Book of the Acts.

It thus becomes clear that the ground of our redemption is not human merit, neither is it divine pity, as such, but a satisfied justice for a broken law by a holy life first lived, then sacrificed, and finally exalted. This is seen to be the work of the entire Godhead in a magnificent unity, the Father, the Son, and the Holy Spirit.

## QUESTIONS ON THE TEXT

1.  State the four outstanding consequences of the Fall.

2.  Prove that the whole Trinity is involved in the works of creation and redemption.

3.  Show the place of the Father in the work of Atonement.

4.  Show the place of the Son in this great provision for mankind.

5.  Show the place of the Holy Spirit in this great work.

6.  What, then, is the ground of our redemption?

# 4

## The Method

### TWO WORKS OF GRACE

THE great results of the divine redemption work are to be made real in the personal experience of the child of God; and this, according to the plain teaching of Scripture and the testimony of reliable witnesses, by two distinct spiritual crises, which, for the sake of convenient expression, we shall call being *justified freely* and *sanctified wholly*.

The Scriptures teach a distinction between these two works of grace. See John 1:12, 13, with John 17:14-19; Acts 1:2-5; Acts 8:5-8, 14-17; 19:1-7; 26:18; 1 Cor. 3: 1-4; Eph. 1:13; 1 Thess. 4:1-8; 5:22, 23; 1 John 1:9.

The Christian church, and especially that section known as Methodism, recognizes this distinction.

Dr. T. C. Upham writes: "The gospel evidently contemplates, in the case of every individual, a progress from the incipient condition of mere forgiveness and acceptance, immensely important as it is, to the higher state of interior renovation and sanctification throughout. . . . The distinction which is made in the Scriptures between the two is regarded as so obvious and incontrovertible by most writers

that it has naturally passed as an established truth into trea-
tises of theology" (*Principles of the Interior or Hidden Life,*
pp. 17, 174).

Rev. J. A. Wood, answering the question, "Does the Meth-
odist Church teach such a distinction?" replies (*Perfect
Love,* pp. 21-24) : She does very clearly in her Discipline,
Catechism, hymn book, and by all her standard authorities.
(Rev. Wood is referring to the older editions).

"The Discipline recognizes a state of entire sanctification as attainable subsequent to regeneration and previous
to death.

"Every minister of the Methodist Episcopal Church has
affirmed, by his ordination vows, that entire sanctification
is a distinct work, subsequent to regeneration. In the Discipline, Part II, sec. 11 are the following questions : 'Have
you faith in Christ? Are you going on unto perfection?
Do you expect to be made perfect in love in this life? Are
you groaning after it?' These questions suppose that 'perfection' or 'perfect love' is distinct from and subsequent to
regeneration.

"The official Catechisms of the Methodist Church were
revised by Bishop Hedding, Nathan Bangs, Stephen Olin,
and Joseph Holdich, and then examined and indorsed by
the General Conference in 1852. These Catechisms define
regeneration—'The new birth of the soul in the image of
Christ, whereby we become the children of God'; and entire
sanctification—'The state of being entirely cleansed from
sin, so as to love God with all our heart and mind, and soul
and strength.'

"The hymn book teaches a distinction. Every edition from
the first has contained a specific class of hymns on sanctification. These hymns, more numerous than those on any
other subject, were written principally by the Wesleys to
define, defend, and promote entire sanctification in early
Methodism when it was greatly controverted. In the changes

made in the hymn book from time to time during the past century many sweet and clearly defined hymns on this subject have been left out; still our hymnal contains a beautiful and choice selection.

> " 'Speak the second time, "Be clean."
> Take away my inbred sin;
> Every stumbling-block remove;
> Cast it out by perfect love.'

> " 'The seed of sin's disease,
>     Spirit of health, remove,
> Spirit of finished holiness,
>     Spirit of perfect love.'

> " 'Refining fire, go through my heart,
>     Illuminate my soul;
> Scatter thy life through every part,
>     And sanctify the whole.'—*Charles Wesley.*

"All the leading writers and standard authorities of Methodism teach a distinction. Mr. Wesley might be quoted very largely; we will insert only a few lines from him. He says: 'Sanctification begins in the moment a man is justified. Yet sin remains in him, yea, the seed of all sin, till he is sanctified throughout' (*Works,* vol. vi, p. 496. See *Plain Account —Sermons,* vol. i, p. 124; also vol. i, p. 119).

"Rev. Richard Watson: 'That a distinction exists between a regenerate state and a state of entire and perfect holiness will be generally allowed' (*Institutes,* Part II, chap. 29).

"Rev. John Fletcher: 'We do not deny that the remains of the carnal mind still cleave to imperfect Christians. This fault, corruption or infection, doth remain in them who are regenerated' (*Last Check,* p. 507-541).

"Dr. Adam Clarke said to a friend who had been misinformed in regard to his views of entire sanctification: 'As to the words which you quote as mine, I totally disclaim them.

I never said, I never intended to say them. I believe justification and sanctification to be widely distinct works.' He used the term justification as including regeneration (*Everett's Life of Dr. A. Clarke.*)

" 'Regeneration also, being the same as the new birth,' says Bishop Hedding, 'is the beginning of sanctification, though not the completion of it, or not entire sanctification. Regeneration is the beginning of purification; entire sanctification is the finishing of that work' (*Address* at New Jersey Conference).

"Bishop Hamline: 'That this perfect love, or entire sanctification, is specifically a new state, and not the mere improvement of a former state, or of regeneration, is plainly inferred from the Bible' (*Beauty of Holiness,* 1862, p. 264).

"Bishop Foster: 'Regeneration is not entire sanctification; the merely regenerate are not sanctified; they are not entirely free from sin; they are not perfect in love' *(Christian Purity, p.* 69*)*.

"Dr. George Peck: 'The doctrine of entire sanctification, as a *distinct work* wrought in the soul by the Holy Ghost, is the *great distinguishnig doctrine* of Methodism. This given up, and we have little left which we do not hold in common with other evangelical denominations. The position that justification and entire sanctification take place at one and the same time, and that regeneration and entire sanctification are identical, is clearly contrary to the position taken by our standard theologians' (*Christian Perfection,* p, 363).

"Rev. William McDonald: 'Regeneration and entire sanctification are not received at one and the same time, except, perhaps, in a few extraordinary cases, if, indeed, the case ever occurs' (*New Testament Standard,* p. 44).

"Bishop Thomson, at the West Virginia Conference, in his last clerical address a few days before his death said: 'The justified and regenerate discover in themselves the remains of the carnal mind. If you accept the theory that you are sanctified when you are justified, if you find the remains of sin after you experience regeneration, you will be led to a melancholy conclusion. The opposite view, that we cannot be made pure, is equally pernicious.'

"Dr. Raymond: 'Entire sanctification is not usually, if ever, contemporary with regeneration. Regeneration is, in most cases of Christian experience, if not all, initial sanctification, not complete, perfect renewal. The regenerated person is not, at the moment of regeneration, wholly sanctified. (*Systematic Theology, Article on Sanctification,* Vol. 2, p. 375).

"Dr. Lowrey: 'The position is supportable on Scripture grounds, that true believers, born of the Spirit, and loving God, may be, and ordinarily are, the subjects of a residuum of inherent sin' (*Positive Theology,* p. 234).

"Bishop M. Simpson: 'Sanctification is not regeneration. . . . Methodism differs from Moravianism in that it does not hold regeneration and entire sanctification to be identical' (*Christian Perfection, in Encyclopedia of Methodism*)."

To this already lengthy list given by Rev. Wood, we append the following:

Bishop William Taylor: "It is not optional with a believer to go on to perfection or not. It is his imperative duty just as fast as the Holy Ghost gives him light and applies the command to his conscience. After the soul is established in the grace of pardon wherein he stands, the Holy Sanctifier sheds increasing light into the heart of the young believer and reveals its inherent depravity to an alarming degree. . . . Our only safety is to obey God and go on to perfection."

Dr. Asa Mahan (president of Oberlin College): "Both blessings, justification and entire sanctification, stand distinctly revealed in the Word of God as available on the same conditions, and for the same identical reasons; they are objects of faith and expectation, and the individual who professes to have received the one blessing makes no more incredible profession than he who professes to have received the other. Through faith, it is the privilege and duty of every believer to be saved to the uttermost, sanctified wholly, and his spirit and soul and body be preserved blameless; for after regeneration, there awaits the faith of the believer 'the promise of the Father,' the Holy Ghost."

Dr. A. J. Gordon: "Logically and chronologically, the gift of the Spirit is subsequent to repentance."

Bishop Mallalieu: "From the very first years of my ministry I have held with Adam Clarke, Richard Watson, John Fletcher, and John Wesley that regeneration and sanctification are separate and distinct one from the other and therefore received at different times. They are both received by faith, and the last one is the privilege of every believer as the first is of every penitent."

Bishop Wilson T. Hogue: "But what is complete sanctification? and wherein does it differ from the experience of regeneration? Entire sanctification is deliverance from all inward sin—from evil thoughts and evil tempers. It is a state in which no wrong tempers, dispositions, or affections remain in the soul; but in which all the thoughts, words and actions are governed by pure love.

"Regeneration is a work of grace within the heart which effects a change of our moral state and character, emancipating us from the dominion and love of sin, planting the principle of obedience in the heart, and restoring the soul to the image of God" (*The Holy Spirit—A Study,* pp. 267, 268).

Dr. Jesse T. Peck: "Now here are two things totally distinct from each other, as much so as a fact and a quality of a fact, a thing and an accident of a thing can be; and here are two terms, of entirely different import, completely adapted to represent these two things respectively—regeneration, the production of spiritual life; sanctification, the treatment of the soul spiritually alive—neither of which can, without violence to the laws of language, perform the office of the other. We humbly submit, therefore, that they ought not to be used interchangeably, and that attempts so to use them have caused nearly all the confusion which has embarrassed these great points of theology" (*The Central Idea of Christianity,* p. 16).

Rev. Thomas Cook: "Regeneration is holiness begun. Whatever is of the essence of holiness is found in germ in all who are children of God. But though all the elements of holiness are imparted, the work of inward renewal is only begun, not finished, by regeneration. . . . Regeneration is the beginning of purification. Entire sanctification is the finishing of that work" (*New Testament Holiness,* pp. 33-35).

Commissioner S. L. Brengle: "The Son of God came into the world, and lived, and toiled, and taught, and suffered, and died, and rose again, in order to accomplish a twofold purpose. The Apostle John explains this twofold purpose. In 1 John 3: 5, speaking of Jesus, he says, 'Ye know that he was manifest to take away our sins.' That is justification and regeneration, which are done for us and in us. In verse eight he adds, 'For this purpose the Son of God was manifested, that he might destroy the works of the devil.' That is entire sanctification, which is a work done in us. First, the sinner needs to get rid of his own sins and have a new principle of life planted in him. . . .The man is born of God and receives what Paul calls the washing of regeneration, which washes away all man's guilt and the sin for which he is responsible. . . . .He soon finds that sin's disease is deeper and more deadly than he thought, and that behind and below his own sins are the works of the devil that must be destroyed before the grace of God in his soul can be complete. . . . God does not admit that we get rid of this at conversion, for all His teachings and exhortations concerning it are addressed to Christians" (*Heart Talks on Holiness*, pp. 1-5).

Dr. Samuel Chadwick: "The baptism of the Holy Spirit is a definite and distinct experience, assured and verified by the witness of the Spirit. . . . The experience is distinct from that of regeneration. Of those who had believed and been baptized in the name of the Lord Jesus, it was said they had not yet been baptized with the Holy Ghost. It is evident, therefore, that a man may be born again of the Spirit and not be baptized with the Spirit" (*The Way to Pentecost*, p. 37).

Dr. R. Newton Flew: "It is for such a life as this that Paul directs his intercessions to God. For the Thessalonians he prays that God may 'fix' or establish their 'hearts in holiness, " (*The Ideal of Perfection in Christian Theology*, p. 55).

### QUESTIONS ON THE TEXT

1. By what twofold method are the results of the divine redemption work to be made real in the child of God?

2. Give Scriptural proof of the distinction between the two phases of the redemption method.

3. The Christian church, and especially that section known as Methodism, recognizes this distinction. Give proof of this.

## Two Works of Grace
(Continued)

"BUT," inquires some per-
plexed soul, "why this stress of difference between these two
divine works? Could not an almighty God bestow a full salvation all at once without dividing it into two sections? Do
not some, even Christian teachers, ridicule the idea of 'a
Second Blessing,' insisting that they have had a third blessing, and a fourth, and in fact thousands of blessings?"

Such sneering remarks are often made, but they indicate
one of two things, namely: ignorance concerning the teaching of the second work of grace, or deliberate desire to mis-
represent it.

No well-informed person who sincerely desires to present
the case as it really is will talk about *"a second blessing,"* as
though there could be a third, a fourth, a fiftieth, and so on.
It is rather, "The Second Blessing," each word being cap-
italized to indicate its nature as being entirely different
from all other blessings. Just as when the risen Lord commanded His disciples to wait for "The Promise of the
Father" (Acts 1:4) they immediately understood that such
an expression did not indicate that they were never to expect
the fulfillment of any other promise, but rather that here
was a promise of a totally different nature from the rest,
and while there "are given to us exceeding great and precious promises: that by these we might be partakers of the
divine nature," this *"Promise of the Father"* was to be distinguished from all others, and in a peculiar way sought and
received; hence the happenings on the Day of Pentecost.

In answer to the question we reply: "No! not even an
almighty God, things being constituted as they are, could
bestow this full salvation without two works of grace."
Here are reports of experts on the subject:

Rev. J. A. Wood: "In all our acquaintance with many
thousands of the purest and best Christians in all the vari-

ous churches we have yet to find a clear case of entire sanctification at conversion. While multitudes claim that their souls have been cleansed from all sin subsequent to their justification, we do not recollect a single instance of a distinct witness of entire sanctification at conversion" (*Perfect Love,* p. 25).

John Wesley: "But we do not know of a single instance, in any place, of a person's receiving in one and the same moment remission of sins, the abiding witness of the Spirit, and a new and clean heart" (*Plain Account of Christian Perfection*).

In giving an account of Grace Paddy, who was convicted of sin, converted, and purified within twelve hours, he says: "Such an instance I never knew before; such an instance I never read; a person convinced of sin, converted to God, and renewed in love within twelve hours! Yet it is by no means incredible, seeing one day is with God as a thousand years."

Adam Clarke: "I have been twenty-three years a traveling preacher, and have been acquainted with some thousands of Christians during that time, who were in different states of grace; and I never, to my knowledge, met with a single instance where God both justified and sanctified at the same time" (*Everett's Life of Dr. A. Clarke*).

The plain statements of the Word of God and the testimonies of an ever-increasing number of God's people leave no doubt in an honest mind which is prepared to think things through, that between these two works of grace there is not only a verbal distinction but also a vital difference.

1.    There is a difference in the *recipients*. Being totally different experiences, they are for totally different classes. The first is for a perishing world, while the second is for a polluted church.

The "Second Blessing" is not a "patch" wherewith to mend a faulty first experience. God is not in the tinkering business. Each experience is complete and perfect within its own limits, but it can be appropriated only by the peculiar class for whom it is designed.

a. That the first of these two blessings is designed for and offered to a perishing world, all evangelical Christians are agreed. On it the Word of God is exceedingly clear. See such Scriptures as John 3:16; 5:24; 10:9; Luke 19:10.

b. That the second of these two blessings is designed for and may be received only by those who are already in possession of the first is also clearly shown in the Word of God. See John 7:39; 14:17; Acts 8:14-17; 19:1-7; Eph. 1:13; Eph. 5:25-27; 1 John 1:9.

2. There is a difference in their *representation*. The words used to describe them are always definite and clear and cannot be mistaken the one for the other.

The first crisis, which concerns the sinner, is referred to in differing terms according to the aspect from which it is viewed, but it is never confused with the terms which are used to designate the later experience. The repentant sinner is spoken of as being:

(a) "Justified." That is, the judicial aspect; the adjustment of the penitent in his legal relationships, bringing him into harmony with the law of God and thereby securing peace. See Rom. 5:1, 9, 16; 8:33; Gal. 2:16; Tit. 3:7.

(b) "Forgiven." That is, the sovereign aspect; heaven's Monarch showing mercy to the rebel. See Acts 26:18; 1 John 1:9.

(c) "Born again." That is, the parental aspect; the believer is "begotten again" by an act of divine grace and power and receives "newness of life." See John 3:1-8; 1 Pet. 1:23.

(d) "Adopted." That is, the family aspect; God taking the repentant soul as His own child. See Rom. 8:15; Gal. 4:5; Eph. 1:5.

To these great spiritual facts the Holy Spirit bears witness within the believer. That "witness" is the birth certificate of the soul. See Rom. 8:16; Gal. 4:6; 1 John 5:10.

The second crisis, which concerns only the child of God, is also stated in differing terms according to the aspect from which it is viewed, but its designations are always distinct from the above. The soul wholly sanctified is spoken of as: having been "baptized with the Holy Ghost and with fire" (Matt. 3:11); having "the body of sin destroyed" (Rom. 6:6); being "crucified with Christ" (Gal. 2:20); being "dead unto sin" (Rom. 6:11); being "sanctified wholly" (1 Thess. 5:23); being "pure in heart" (Matt. 5:8); having "a clean heart" (Psa. 51:10); having "iniquity taken away" (Isa. 6:7); being "cleansed from all filthiness" (Ezek. 36:25; 2 Cor. 7:1); being "cleansed from all unrighteousness" (1 John 1:9).

Other expressions are also used for this "Second Blessing," as a careful reading of the Word of God will show, but here are enough to prove to any thoughtful mind the difference of the divine representation between the two works of grace. The designations are always kept clearly apart, and the classes addressed are always recognized.

3.   There is a difference in their *results*. Rev. C. W. Ruth has set forth twenty-three distinctions, each of which will be seen to indicate this difference:

"In justification there is life:
In sanctification there is life more abundant.
"In justification there is love:
In sanctification there is perfect love which casteth out fear.
"In justification the 'old man' is repressed:
In sanctification the 'old man' is destroyed.
"In justification there is 'peace with God':
In sanctification there is 'the peace of God.'
"Justification destroys the 'shoots' of sin:
Sanctification destroys the 'roots' of sin.

"Justification gives the right to heaven:
Sanctification gives the fitness for heaven.

"In justification we 'put on the new man':
In sanctification we 'put off the old man with his deeds.'

"In justification there is joy—intermittent joy:
In sanctification there is fullness of joy—abiding joy.

"Justification includes pardon, which is a judicial act:
Sanctification includes a cleansing, which is a priestly function.

"Justification is obtained by surrender, repentance, and faith:
Sanctification is obtained by obedience, consecration, and faith.

"Justification delivers from guilt and condemnation:
Sanctification delivers from unholy tempers and abnormal appetites.

"Justification comprehends adoption; making us children of God:
Sanctification comprehends anointing, making us kings and priests unto God.

"Justification is illustrated by the rescue of the sinking man from the water:
Sanctification is getting the water out of the lungs of the drowning man.

"Justification is conditioned on confession of sin (1 John 1:9):
Sanctification is conditioned on walking 'in the light as he is in the lgiht' (1 John 1:7).

"Justification has to do with sin as an act—sins committed:
Sanctification has to do with sin as a principle—the sin nature we inherited.

"Justification comes by the birth of the Spirit—when the repentant sinner is born again:

Sanctification comes by the baptism with the Spirit—when the believer has a personal pentecost.

"Justification restores to us the favor of God which we had lost through our own disobedience:

Sanctification restores to us holiness or the moral likeness of God, which we had lost through Adam's disobedience.

"Justification is the impartation of a spiritual nature, bringing us into possession of eternal life:

Sanctification is the crucifixion and destruction of our carnal nature, making us dead indeed unto sin.

"Justification separates us from the world, so we are no longer of the world:

Sanctification takes the world out of us; worldly desires and ambitions.

"Justification makes us free—free from outward sin and condemnation:

Sanctification makes "free indeed." Gives the "deed" to our freedom with all the mortgages paid off. Freedom from fear, doubt, pride, etc.

"In justification we are united to Christ as the branch to the vine:

In sanctification we receive the purging promised to the living, fruitful vine, that we may "bring forth more fruit" (John 15:2).

"In justification the experience is a "well of water" (John 4:14). A well is for personal use.

In sanctification there is a fullness of blessing so that out of our inward parts "shall flow rivers of living water" (John 6:38, 39). A river cannot be confined to personal use, but will bless and fructify wherever it flows" (*Entire Sanctification a Second Blessing,* pp. 31-34).

## QUESTIONS ON THE TEXT

1. "Second blessing indeed! I have had thousands." Deal with this remark.

2. "Could not an almighty God bestow a full salvation all at once without the necessity of dividing it into two sections?" Deal with this inquiry.

3. Show how God describes the recipients of each of these blessings.

4. Show how God represents each of these blessings.

5. Show the difference in the results of each of these blessings.

# The First Work of Grace

**ITS FOURFOLD ASPECT.
(1) SOVEREIGN—FORGIVENESS. (2) JUDICIAL—JUSTI-
FICATION. (3) PARENTAL—REGENERATION. (4) FAM-
ILY—ADOPTION.**

---

**(1) Sovereign
(2) Judicial**

By general usage, we have come to speak of the two outstanding crises of spiritual experience as being "saved" and "sanctified," but under both of these general terms must be grouped numerous Biblical and theological conceptions, each having its own distinctive emphasis. Under this first great experience the outstanding aspects are: sovereign, the act of forgiveness; judicial, the fact of justification; parental, the work of regeneration; family, the position of adoption.

1. The *sovereign* aspect. The act of *forgiveness*. In this, God is to be regarded as Sovereign, dealing with a rebel. The rebellion has been broken and the rebel sues for mercy. This is granted on Calvary ground, and the soul receives a pardon which is abundant, full, and free (see Isa. 55: 7; Eph. 4: 32, b).

> "Great God of wonders! all Thy ways
>   Are matchless, godlike, and divine,
> But the fair glories of Thy grace
>   More godlike and unrivaled shine:
> Who is a pardoning God like Thee?
> Or who has grace so rich and free?

"Such dire offenses to forgive,
  Such guilty, daring worms to spare;
This is Thy grand prerogative,
  And in this honor who can share:
Who is a pardoning God like Thee?
Or who has grace so rich and free?

"In wonder lost, with trembling joy
  We take the pardon from our God;
Pardon for sins of deepest dye,
  A pardon sealed with Jesus' blood:
Who is a pardoning God, like Thee?
Or who has grace so rich and free?"

—*Samuel Davies*, 1723-61.

2. The *judicial* aspect. The fact of *justification*. Justification has to do with the sinner in his legal relationships. The word at once carries us into the Court of Divine Justice, before which he is arraigned, and wonder of wonders, the verdict goes in his favor and he is honorably discharged, although he has been proved guilty and has confessed to all the charges laid against him. What ,then, is the secret here? See Acts 13: 38, 39; Rom. 1: 17; 3: 19-31; 5: 1; 8: 33, 34; 1 Cor. 6: 11; Gal. 2: 16; 3: 11, 24. On the basis of these and other Scriptures the doctrine may be stated thus:

Justification is that judicial act by which God, on account of a new faith relationship to Jesus Christ, declares the sinner to be no longer exposed to the penalty of a broken law, but restored to the divine favor. It is a reversal of the divine attitude, bringing the sinner into harmony with the law of God, and thereby securing peace.

Justification presupposes some preliminary facts, namely:

a. Concerning the past. A radical repentance, with all that this involves. A complete renunciation. The sinner has now turned his face in an opposite direction, and refuses even to consider the things left behind (see Gal. 2: 17, 18).

A willing restitution. If wrongs toward others existed, he has made an honest effort to make them right (see Luke 19: 1-10).

A full reliance on the Calvary work of Jesus (see Rom. 3:25, 26).

b. Concerning the present. An honesty of purpose as to daily walk with God.

Justification cannot be obtained while there is a background of unconfessed sin (see Psa. 32:5; 1 John 1:9).

Justification cannot be retained while there is a conscious present committing of sin (Gal. 2:17, 18; 1 John 3:8). Conscious sinfulness and Divine favor never coexist.

Rev. J. A. Wood: "No state of grace admits of committing sin. A state of justification implies freedom from the guilt of sin by pardon, and freedom from the commission of sin by renewing, assisting grace. The lowest type of Christian sinneth not and is not condemned. The minimum of salvation is salvation from sinning. The maximum is salvation from pollution—the inclination to sin.

"The conditions of receiving justification and of retaining it are the same. Christ is received by penitential submission and faith. 'As ye have received Christ Jesus the Lord, so walk ye in him.' Justification cannot be retained with less consecration and faith than that by which it was received.

"Conscious confidence and conscious guilt cannot coexist in the same heart. There is a vital union between justifying faith and an obedient spirit. While obedience makes faith perfect, disobedience destroys it. Salvation is by appropriating faith, and such faith or trust can be exercised only when there is a consciousness of complete surrender to God. A justified state can exist only in connection with a serious, honest intention to obey all the commands of God.

"The standard of justification is too low among many professors of religion. It should be ever borne in mind that believers cannot commit sin without forfeiting justification and laying the foundation for repentance from dead works.

There must be a continued obedience to all the known will of God if we would retain His favor" (*Perfect Love,* pp. 12-14).

Justification has been stated as being fivefold in its aspect: The spring of our justification is grace (Rom. 3:24). The principle of our justification is faith (Rom. 5:1; Gal. 3: 24-26). The ground of our justification is "His blood" (Rom. 5:9). The guarantee of our justification is His resurrection (Rom. 4:25). The outcome of our justification is good works (James 2:21-26).

> "Jesus, Thy blood and righteousness
> My beauty are, my glorious dress;
> Midst flaming worlds, in these arrayed,
> With joy shall I lift up my head.
>
> "Bold shall I stand in that great day;
> For who aught to my charge shall lay?
> Fully through these absolved I am,
> From sin and fear, and guilt and shame.
>
> "The holy, meek, unspotted Lamb,
> Who from the Father's bosom came,
> Who died for me, even me, to atone,
> Now for my Lord and God I own.
>
> "Lord, I believe Thy precious blood,
> Which at the Mercy-Seat of God
> For ever doth for sinners plead,
> For me, even for my soul was shed.
>
> "Lord, I believe were sinners more
> Than sands upon the ocean shore,
> Thou hast for all a ransom paid,
> For all a full atonement made.
>
> "When from the dust of death I rise
> To claim my mansion in the skies,
> Even then this shall be all my plea,
> Jesus hath lived, hath died for me."
> —*Count Zinzendorf,* 1700-1760.

## QUESTIONS ON THE TEXT

1. Name the four great aspects of the first work of grace.
2. Show God in His position as Sovereign.
3. Discuss the judicial aspect of salvation.
4. Show what justification presupposes.

**(3) Parental**
**(4) Family**

IN our previous study, we named the four outstanding aspects of the first work of grace, and dealt with the first two. We now take up the others.

3. The *parental* aspect. The work of *regeneration.* Thus far we have dealt with divine "acts" on the sinner's behalf, having to do with his standing before God. These, however, are not wrought alone, but are complementary to a divine operation within the soul itself, by which the believer is "begotten again." It is called being "born again," "quickened," also "passing from death unto life" (see John 1: 13; 3: 1-8; 5: 24; Eph. 2: 1; Tit. 3: 5; 1 Pet. 1: 3, 23; 1 John 3: 14; 5: 4, 13.

Defining regeneration the following quotations will be helpful:

Dr. Luther Lee: "Regeneration is a renewal of our fallen nature by the power of the Holy Spirit, received through faith in Jesus Christ, whereby the regenerate are delivered from the power of sin which reigns over all the unregenerate. . . . Regeneration reverses the current of the affections, and so renews the whole soul that all the Christian graces exist. . . . The power of sin is broken; the principle of obedience is planted in the heart" (*Theology,* pp. 194-200).

Bishop Foster: "With respect to regeneration, that is a work done in us, in the way of changing our inward nature; a work by which a spiritual life is infused into the soul, whereby he (the regenerate) brings forth the peaceable fruits of righteousness, has victory over sin, is enabled to resist corrupt tendencies, and has peace and joy in the Holy Ghost; a radical change by which the preponderating tendencies of the soul are turned towards God, whereas they were previously from Him—by which the love of sin is destroyed, its dominion broken, and a desire and relish for and longing after holiness implanted" (*Christian Purity,* p. 43).

Rev. J. A. Wood: "Regeneration is the impartation of spiritual life to the human soul, in which God imparts, organizes and calls into being the capabilities, attributes and functions of the new nature. It is a change from death to life, from the dominion of sin to the reign of grace, and restores the spiritual life which was lost by the fall. It is instantaneously wrought by the Holy Spirit, and always accompanies justification" (*Perfect Love,* p. 17).

Rev. John Wesley: "From hence it manifestly appears what is the nature of the new birth. It is that great change which God works in the soul when He brings it into life; when He raises it from the death of sin to the life of righteousness. It is the change wrought in the whole soul by the almighty Spirit of God when it is 'created anew in Christ Jesus'; when it is renewed after the image of God in righteousness and true holiness; when the love of the world is changed into the love of God; pride into humility; passion into meekness; and hatred, envy, malice, into a sincere, tender, disinterested love for all mankind. In a word, it is that change whereby the earthly, sensual, devilish mind is turned into the 'mind which was in Christ Jesus.' This is the nature of the new birth: 'so is everyone that is born of the spirit'" (*Sermon on "The New Birth"*).

This experience of the new birth is set forth in John's first epistle as having seven decided characteristics: A righteous life (2:29); victory over sin (3:9); brotherly love (3:14); a compassionate spirit (3:17); recognition of the Lordship of Jesus (5:1); victory over the world (5:4); the Spirit's inward witness (5:10).

> "Soon as my all I ventured on the atoning blood,
> The Holy Spirit entered, and I was born of God;
> My sins are all forgiven, I feel the blood applied,
> And I shall go to heaven if I in Christ abide."

4. The *family* aspect. The position of *adoption*. The thought behind the position of adoption is the putting of a stranger in the place of a son. Its relation to regeneration differs from that of justification, although, like justification, it is a legal idea. In the case of justification the thought is that of the criminal being treated as righteous, whereas in adoption it is the stranger being treated as a son. This is the legal privilege of the second birth, the heritage of saving grace.

Here we have a spiritual counterpart of what was frequently happening among men in Bible times: *e. g.*, Mordecai adopted Esther as his own daughter (Esther 2:7). The daughter of Pharaoh adopted Moses as her own son (Ex. 2:10).

This "adoption" was familiar among both Greeks and Romans at the period at which the New Testament was penned, and Paul, ever on the lookout for current illustrations of the gospel which he preached, seized upon the fact as illustrative of that act of free grace whereby the soul, pardoned, justified, and twice born, becomes a member of the divine family and is made an heir of God by faith.

The term "adoption" is found five times in the Pauline Epistles, but nowhere else in the entire Scriptures. It is distinctly a revelation of God to the Apostle Paul. See Rom. 8:15, 23; 9:4; Gal. 4:5; Eph. 1:5.

Here, then, under four great aspects we have this magnificent "first work of divine grace." The soul's relation to sin is now such that most extraordinary figures are used to express it. They are pardoned, forgiven, covered (Psa. 32:1; Isa. 55:7; Jer. 33:8; 1 John 1:9); removed as far as the east is from the west (Psa. 103:12); cast into the depth of the sea (Mic. 7:19); cast behind God's back (Isa. 38:17); blotted out (Isa. 44:22, 23); sought for and not found (Jer. 50:20); and remembered no more (Jer. 31:34).

> "Now I have found the ground wherein
>   Sure my soul's anchor may remain,
> The wounds of Jesus, for my sin
>   Before the world's foundation slain;
> Whose mercy shall unshaken stay,
> When heaven and earth are fled away.
>
> "O Love, thou bottomless abyss,
>   My sins are swallowed up in Thee!
> Covered is my unrighteousness,
>   No spot of guilt remains on me,
> While Jesus' blood, through earth and skies,
> Mercy, free, boundless mercy cries.
>
> "With faith I plunge me in this sea;
>   Here is my hope, my joy, my rest;
> Hither, when hell assails, I flee,
>   I look into my Savior's breast;
> Away, sad doubt and anxious fear!
> Mercy is all that's written there.
>
> "Fixed on this ground will I remain,
>   Though my heart fail and flesh decay;
> This anchor shall my soul sustain,
>   When earth's foundations melt away:
> Mercy's full power I then shall prove,
> Loved with an everlasting love."
>                     —*Johann Andreas Rothe*, 1688-1756.
>                         Trans. by John Wesley

### QUESTIONS ON THE TEXT

**1.** What do we mean when we speak of the work of regeneration? Show this from Scripture.

**2.** Give the seven characteristics of the new birth as found in John's first epistle.

**3.** Explain and illustrate the teaching of adoption.

**4.** Name the seven figures which God uses to express His dealing with our sins.

# 6

# The Second Work of Grace

**ITS FOURFOLD ASPECT**
**(1) NEGATIVE—PURIFICATION. (2) POSITIVE—THE INDWELLING GOD. (3) ETHICAL OBLIGATIONS. (4) PROGRESSIVE—GROWTH AND DEVELOPMENT.**

**(1) Negative—Purification**

AS with the first experience, so with the second, it will be found that in order to obtain a clear idea as to its content we must analyze its parts, which again may be stated as fourfold, namely: Negative, the work of purification; positive, the fact of the indwelling God; ethical, some matter of fact obligations; progressive, the growth and development of a sanctified soul.

No more fitting introduction to this section could be found than the utterance by Rev. J. M. Pike: "The Methodist Church, claiming to be Scriptural in its origin and design, is based upon this fundamental fact of the Christian faith—the holiness of God's people.

"John Wesley says, 'In 1729 my brother Charles and I, reading the Bible, saw we could not be saved without holiness, followed after it, and incited others to do so. In 1737 we saw that holiness comes by faith. In 1738 we saw that men are justified before they are sanctified; but still holiness was our object—inward and outward holiness. God then thrust us out to raise up a holy people.'

"After he had preached the doctrine for half a century, and had seen thousands brought into the experience, two years before his death he wrote, 'This doctrine is the grand depositum which God has lodged with the people called Methodists; and for the sake of propagating this chiefly He appears to have raised us up.'

"The distinctive mission of Methodism was recognized by the bishops of the Methodist Episcopal Church in 1824, and in the address to the General Conference they said, 'If Methodists give up the doctrine of entire sanctification, or suffer it to become a dead letter, we are a fallen people. Holiness is the main cord that binds us together; relax this, and you loosen the whole system. This will appear more evident if we call to mind the original design of Methodism. It was to raise up and preserve a holy people. This was the principal object that Mr. Wesley had in view. To this end all the doctrines believed and preached by Methodists tend' " (Sermon on Psa. 93: 5, *The Double Cure,* 1887, pp. 3-4).

The work of purification is the groundwork of all else. Carnality must be removed from the nature. Our humanity must be made pure. See Psa. 51: 7, 9; Isa. 6: 5-7; Ezek. 36: 25; Matt. 3: 11; Acts 15: 8-9; Rom. 6: 6; 2 Cor. 7: 1; Eph. 5: 25-27; 1 Thess. 4: 3-8; 5: 23, 24; Tit. 2: 11-14.

The literature of the church is rich in its teaching on this subject, as the following excerpts will show:

Rev. John Wesley: "Both my brother Charles and I maintain that Christian perfection is that love of God and our neighbor which implies deliverance from all sin.

"It is the loving God with all our heart, mind, soul, and strength. This implies that no wrong temper, none contrary to love, remains in the soul; and that all the thoughts, words, and actions are governed by pure love.

"It is nothing higher and nothing lower than this—the

pure love of God and man. It is love governing the heart and life, running through all our tempers, words, and actions. Certainly sanctification, in the proper sense, is an instantaneous deliverance from all sin." (*Wesley's Works*).

Rev. John Fletcher: "It is the pure love of God and man shed abroad in a faithful believer's heart by the Holy Ghost given unto him, to cleanse him and to keep him clean, 'from all the filthiness of the flesh and spirit,' and to enable him to 'fulfill the law of Christ,' according to the talents he is intrusted with, and the circumstances in which he is placed in this world" *(Last Check to Antinomianism,* p. 567).

Dr. Adam Clarke: "What, then, is this complete sanctification? It is the cleansing of the blood, that has not been cleansed; it is washing the soul of a true believer from the remains of sin" (*Clarke's Theology,* p. 206).

Rev. Richard Watson: "We have already spoken of justification, adoption, regeneration and the witness of the Holy Spirit, and we proceed to another as distinctly marked and as graciously promised in the Holy Scriptures. This is the entire sanctification, or the perfected holiness of believers. Happily for us, a subject of so great importance is not involved in obscurity. By which can only be meant our complete deliverance from all spiritual pollution, all inward depravation of the heart, as well as that which, expressing itself outwardly by the indulgence of the senses, is called 'filthiness of the flesh'" (*Biblical and Theological Institutes,* Vol. II, p. 450).

"Sanctification is that work of God's grace by which we are renewed after the image of God, set apart for His service, and enabled to die unto sin and live unto righteousness. ... Sanctification in this world must be complete; the whole nature must be sanctified; all sin must be utterly abolished, or the soul can never be admitted into the glorious presence of God" (*Biblical and Theological Institutes*).

Rev. Joseph Benson: "To sanctify you wholly is to complete the work of purification and renovation begun in your regeneration" (*Com.,* 1 Thess. 5:23).

Dr. Jesse T. Peck: "To do less for man than to make him holy would be, in effect, to do nothing for him; and to do this is to do all. Holiness is therefore the central sun which pours its glorious light through every part of the system. . . . Remove it, and all is as black as midnight" (*Central Idea of Christianity,* p. 19).

Dr. Asbury Lowrey: "It is sanctification from all sin, in opposition to a partial or inceptive work. It is obvious that a man cannot be wholly sanctified so long as any sin remains in him. We conclude, therefore, that entire sanctification signifies deliverance from all sin, internal and external; that is, from all indwelling sin, as well as from its outward manifestations; not from its uprisings and guilty motions merely, but from its contaminations and inherent existence" (*Possibilities of Grace,* p. 270).

Dr. Thomas N. Ralston: "Whenever we comply with the conditions prescribed in the gospel, that is, whenever we exercise the requisite degree of faith, be it one day or ten years after conversion, that moment God will cleanse us from all unrighteousness" (*Elements of Divinity,* p. 468).

Dr. Amos Binney: "It is called holiness, sanctification, purity. . . . What is meant by these expressions is that participation of the divine nature which excludes all original depravity or inborn sin from the heart. . . . Entire sanctification is that act of the Holy Ghost whereby the justified soul is made holy" (*Theological Compend,* pp. 128, 129).

The Methodist Catechism: "What is entire sanctification? The state of being entirely cleansed from sin."

Dr. William Bert Pope: "Sanctification in its beginning, process, and final issues is the full eradication of sin itself which, reigning in the unregenerate, co-exists with the new

life of the regenerate, is abolished in the wholly sanctified"
(*Compendium of Christian Theology,* Vol. II, p. 64).

Dr. Daniel Steele: "That inward holiness which the altar
ritual of the Hebrews, with their interminable repetitions,
was unable to produce, has been rendered possible to every
believer through the offering of the adorable God-man once
for all. While the Atonement sanctified no one, it renders
possible the entire sanctification of every offspring of Adam
who will trust in Christ for this purchased blessing" (*The
Gospel of the Comforter,* p. 121).

"What evidence does the Greek Testament afford that sin
may be destroyed? (1) The absence of all terms expressive
of mere repression; (2) the use in Paul's Epistles of such
words as 'crucify,' 'cleanse,' 'destroy' (Gk. *Katargeo—i. e.,*
annihilate, abolish. See Cremer and Thayer), 'circumcision
without hands,' 'mortify' or 'kill' " (Col. 3:5). (3) If this
is not the doctrine of the New Testament, Christ's mission
is a stupendous failure, because He does not destroy the
works of the devil, and perfect holiness is impossible either
in this world or that to come" (*Steele's Answers,* p. 85).

Dougan Clark, M.D.: "But what does this expression
'purifying their hearts' mean? It means the removal of the
remains of their carnality. It means the creation of a clean
heart, and the renewal of a right spirit. It means the crucifixion of the flesh. It means the destruction of the body of
sin. It means the casting out of the strong man, who was
only bound in conversion. It means entire sanctification.
. . .Sanctification is that act of divine grace whereby we are
made holy" (*The Offices of the Holy Spirit,* pp. 51, 67).

Rev. Seth C. Rees: "One of the most evident effects of the
work of fire is purification. Many things can be cleansed by
the application of water, especially if the impurity is external, but it takes the powerful heat of fire to thoroughly
cleanse anything in which the baser part is mixed all
through that which needs purification. All precious metals

are fired again and again until they are made fit for use. Thus the inspired writer uses a vivid figure to illustrate the radical and cleansing work of the Holy Ghost in His Pentecostal capacity. Just as the smelter of precious metals subjects them to the intense heat of the furnace, so, says the Scriptures, does the Lord of heaven subject the heart of the believer to the cleansing process of the furnace of the Upper Room" (*Fire from Heaven*, p. 16).

Dr. Edward F. Walker: "This is the sanctification Jesus prayed His disciples might have—a personal cleansing from sin, in order to a holy life. Made pure in order to sustained devotion to God. A pure heart full of holy love. Beyond this we cannot go in this world; but short of this we ought never to rest. Perfect purity plus perfect love in the heart by the efficiency of Christ and the power of the indwelling Spirit equal personal sanctification" (*Sanctify Them*, pp. 46, 49).

Rev. Isaiah Reid: "Sanctification or cleansing is for depravity, and is met by cleansing, not by pardon" (*Holiness Bible Readings*, p. 61).

Dr. Asa Mahan: "I hear instructions given to believers seeking this 'rest of faith,' instructions of which I cannot approve. They are told that Christ will not take away their evil propensities, and prevent their acting within the mind, but will enable believers to resist and hold in subjection such promptings. The apostle, on the other hand, tells us that for the purpose that we should not serve sin, 'our old man is crucified with Christ' and 'the body of sin is destroyed.' In express view of this fact, he requires us to 'reckon ourselves dead indeed unto sin, but alive unto God through Jesus Christ our Lord.' As long as our lusts are left to 'war in our members' there may be expected to be 'wars and fightings' in the churches and lapses and backslidings in the membership. Christ 'takes away our sins' by taking away the evil dispositions within us that prompt us to sin, and in the place of these dispositions giving us 'a divine nature' which will prompt us to 'love, joy, peace, longsuffering, gentleness, faith, meekness, temperance'" (*Out of Darkness into Light,* p. 154).

Rev. M. L. Haney: "The work of sanctification brings its subject into a state a thousand times more important than a blessing. The soul may or may not be filled with joyful emotions when it is wholly sanctified. It may, at frequent periods, pass ordeals of unspeakable sorrow; but that does not affect its state. The idea that sanctification means simply a fit of rapture, or a baptism of joy, should be at once and forever excluded from the common sense of mankind. No, beloved, 'the act of God's free grace whereby we are made holy' is worth more than the joy of a lifetime without it. Having exercised faith in Jesus' cleansing blood to wash out all the stains of inbred sin, the Holy Ghost has made the application, and eternal power has swept from the whole domain of your nature everything that is out of harmony with God. There is not a root or seed of sin remaining. Entire sanctification, therefore, brings you into a state of moral purity. Hitherto the evils of your heart were held in check by a power implanted that was greater than they; now these evils are destroyed, and the whole man becomes the temple of God" (*Inheritance Restored,* pp. 126, 127).

Rev. James Caughey: "It is clear, also, that so long as sin remains in us, we cannot be holy as God is holy, nor perfect as He is perfect, nor pure as Jesus is pure; nor can we love God with all our heart so long as sins and unholiness divide it. . . .It may not be the will of God that we should be rich, or great, or noble, but it is the will of God that we should be holy.

"But does God desire us to be holy now? to be perfect now? pure now? to love Him with all our heart now—this moment? Most certainly. To suppose the contrary would be to set God a trifling with us, and us trifling with God!

. . .'The blood of Jesus Christ His Son cleanseth us from all sin.' Cleanseth, which cannot surely mean in the future, but the present; and from all sin, which cannot mean a part; then, by the help of God, I will preach the doctrine of present salvation from all inward as well as outward sin, with the same assurance as I would preach on the Godhead of Christ or the day of judgment" (*Earnest Christianity,* pp. 260, 261).

The Salvation Army: "We believe that it is the privilege of all believers to be 'wholly sanctified,' and that the whole spirit and soul and body may be preserved blameless unto the coming of our Lord Jesus Christ. That is to say, we believe that after conversion there remain in the heart of the believer inclinations to evil, or roots of bitterness, which unless overpowered by divine grace produce actual sin; but that these evil tendencies can be entirely taken away by the Spirit of God, and the whole heart, thus cleansed from everything contrary to the will of God, or entirely sanctified, will then produce the fruit of the Spirit only. And we believe that persons thus entirely sanctified may, by the power of God, be kept unblamable and unreprovable before Him" (*Handbook of Doctrine,* pp, 2, 122).

"An entirely sanctified person is without sin—freed from sin (Rom. 6: 7). He is delivered from all sin; his disposition is entirely purified; inward sin is done away with or destroyed" (*Handbook of Doctrine,* p. 125).

Commissioner S. L. Brengle: "The great hindrance in the hearts of God's children to the power of the Holy Ghost is inbred sin—that dark, defiant, evil something within that struggles for the mastery of the soul, and will not submit to to be meek and lowly and patient and forbearing and holy as was Jesus; and when the Holy Spirit comes, His first work is to sweep away that something, that carnal principle, and make free and clean all the channels of the soul. Peter was filled with power on the day of Pentecost; but evidently the purifying effect of the baptism made a deeper and more lasting impression on his mind than the empowering effect" (*When the Holy Ghost is Come,* pp. 44, 45).

Rev. G. A. McLaughlin: "A clean heart is one that has nothing in it that ought not to be there. Every good affection is in it and no evil affection. If there is one evil affection, it causes the heart to be unclean. A clean heart, in other words, is a heart that is the home of every good affection and has none of the evil actions in it. It is 'A heart from sin set free' " (*A Clean Heart,* p. 2).

Dr. Samuel Chadwick: "As pardon abounds over guilt so sanctification abounds over the presence of sin in the soul. Forgiveness without cleansing would not cover man's need. The work of grace must be co-extensive with the work of sin. Where sin had its seat His throne is established. The will is surrendered, the heart cleansed, the desire changed and the nature renewed. Sin disturbed the true order of man's nature and defaced the divine image within him, grace creates him anew after the image of God in righteousness and true holiness. No man need continue in sin, for grace has abounded unto complete salvation" (*Humanity and God,* pp. 36, 37).

"Carnality needs to be purged out. Entire sanctification completes the work of regeneration, pervading every part of the renewed creature. . . .It is entire, complete, and without restriction. Every part is cleansed, perfected, and pervaded with the energy of the divine presence. The fleshly is eradicated and the spiritual prevails. In this state of entire sanctification man is preserved without blame" (*Humanity and God,* pp. 70, 71).

"Delivered from the flesh, he lives in the Spirit. . . . Guilt is purged, sin is cleansed away, and carnality is destroyed."

"The heart is cleansed from sin and made perfect in love."

"The nature is cleansed from sin. The carnal mind, the

body of sin, is done away. This is the Bible word for what happens—sin is done away" (*The Way to Pentecost*).

Mr. Paget Wilkes: "Salvation from the presence and inbeing of sin! It is deliverance from the presence of sin in the heart, the clearing of the soul from 'indwelling sin,' 'the evil heart of unbelief,' 'the carnal mind,' 'the body of sin,' 'the superfluity of naughtiness,' 'all unrighteousness.' . . .In the wounds of Jesus there is a perfect healing; in His cross a perfect destruction of the body of sin; and in His blood a perfect cleansing from its taint, as applied to our hearts by the Holy Ghost" (*The Dynamic of Service*, pp. 236, 237).

Dr. H. C. Morrison: "The baptism with the Holy Ghost casts out the 'old man.' And the casting out of the 'old man,' the plucking up of the 'root of bitterness,' the destruction of the 'body of sin,' the eradication of the 'carnal mind,' the purging out of the 'sin that dwelleth in me,' are all one and the same thing, which is accomplished by the instantaneous baptism with the Holy Ghost, purifying the heart by faith. This is entire sanctification" (*The Baptism with the Holy Ghost*, p. 35).

Dr. Z. T. Johnson: "By heart purity is meant the extermination of inbred sin, the eradication of the depraved nature and the infilling of the heart with perfect love for God and for humanity. The inner disturbances resulting from inbred sin, which come to every Christian after conversion, are no longer manifest.

"God does not try to control the carnal nature. If God cannot suppress it, we cannot. But God can completely eradicate it. He can fling it out of our souls; He can purge it; He can eliminate it and purify our hearts. The Son of God was manifested to destroy the works of the devil; and even though He cannot control it, He can destroy it. The destructive process is far more satisfactory"( *What is Holiness?* pp. 10, 81).

Rev. Joseph H. Smith: "The Christian man, though truly justified from all his past sins and now at peace with God, has still a great and grave problem awaiting settlement. The provisions of Christ's death, the promises of God's Word, and the power of the Holy Spirit furnish a complete solution of the believer's sin problem" (*Pauline Perfection,* p. 47).

Dr. Iva Durham Vennard: "The negative side is completed in the destroying of carnality.

"The gift of the Holy Ghost was accompanied by the purifying of the hearts.

"The sanctification of the believer has in it the thought of being set apart, which the Old Testament sanctification of vessels and animals typifies; but it includes also the moral element of heart cleansing, for the believer has this moral capacity and hence this need which the irresponsible vessel or animal has not.

"It has been the will of God from the beginning that we should be holy. It is not an afterthought by which it is hoped to patch up our conversion. Regeneration is in itself a perfect work, planting within the soul the germ of eternal life.

"Sanctification is entirely distinct, removing from the heart-soil all roots of bitterness, that the divine germ implanted at regeneration may develop in perfect symmetry.

"We are to be cleansed not only from actual sins committed, but from the filthiness of sin in our hearts" (*Heart Purity,* pp. 15, 17, 18, 19, 35).

"What was it that died in Saint Paul? It was the carnal nature, the man of sin, that malefactor that is enmity against God, that is not subject to the law of God, neither indeed can be. . . .Thank God that the old man can be put off; the carnal nature can be crucified. Dear hearts, let us follow the Pauline plan and be crucified, killed out, in the carnal nature.

"If it is true that carnality is still present in your heart, then the integrity of the promise is your security that it can be destroyed, and you can be, by an uttermost consecration and appropriating faith in the Blood, cleansed from all sin" (*Upper Room Messages,* pp. 40-42).

To some this long list of quotations may have become tedious, but they will, if conscientiously perused, become far more valuable than at first sight they appear to be. They will give to the student a general acquaintance with holiness literature; but more than this, they will prove to any thoughtful mind that the emphasis placed on holiness of heart is not the insistence of a few narrow-minded people, but the emphasis of reliable religious teachers, both ancient and modern. In making our selection our embarrassment has been in the wealth of literature that has offered itself. Volumes could be filled with such quotations.

### QUESTIONS ON THE TEXT

1. Name the four aspects of the second work of grace.
2. Why is the work of purification known as the negative aspect of entire sanctification?
3. Give Scripture evidence for the divine work of purification.
4. Having read through the quotations given in this section, write your own statement on the negative aspect of the second work of grace.

## (2) Positive—The Indwelling God

IT is important to remember that this experience we call "entire sanctification" is much more than the mere negative fact of the absence of sin. It is essentially the positive fact of the indwelling God. When we say this, we do not mean a blessing from God, nor the influ-

ence of God upon our souls, however sweet and sacred this
may be. We mean, rather, the personal presence of the eternal God Himself, made real within the believer by the
indwelling Holy Ghost (see John 14:16,17). Such an
indwelling has many results; among them are the following:

1. An abundant *life*—indwelling and overflowing (see
John 10:10; Rom. 8:11; John 7:37-39).

2. An enduement of *power* (see Acts 1:8). "Power"
here is not the "authority" of John 1:12 and Luke 10:19.
It is the introduction of an inward, spiritual dynamic. It
is the word from which we get our English word dynamite.
Lit.: "Ye shall become spiritually endynamited, the Holy
Ghost coming upon you."

3. An inward *illumination* (see John 14:26; 1 John 2:
20,27). Bishop Wilson T. Hogue writes:

"The presence of the indwelling Comforter secures to
believers in Christ a clearer understanding of spiritual
things. . . .

"By nature men are in a stage of spiritual darkness. . . .
It is impossible to educate men out of their spiritual blind-
ness and darkness. Nor does conversion bring entire
deliverance from it, though it begets in some degree an
understanding of the mysteries of grace. Conversion intro-
duces the soul into a state of spiritual childhood—a state in
which spiritual life and perceptions are begotten and manifested. But in this state the soul's conceptions of spiritual
things are more or less crude and imperfect, and are intermixed with many carnal views and ideas. The fullest
apprehension of the oracles of God cannot be realized in the
absence of that spiritual purity and sensitiveness which
result alone from the sanctifying baptism of the Holy
Ghost. This sanctifying, illuminating agency of the indwelling Comforter is the divine safeguard against the numerous
perils which would otherwise attend the entrusting of the
Scriptures to the perusal of the unlearned—the key which

enables the plain man, the uncultured but reverent student of the Word of God, to unlock its hidden treasures of wisdom, truth and grace, to lay hold upon and enrich himself with its most comforting promises, to penetrate the deeper meaning of its numerous prophecies, and to take a firmer grasp upon the rock of Bible truth than the more cultured students of Scripture who have not experienced the baptism with the Holy Spirit. This is 'the anointing which abideth' and which 'teacheth' those who receive it of all things (1 John 2: 27), and without which those who apply themselves to the most critical study of the divine oracles cannot discern their true spirituality" (*The Holy Spirit,* pp. 112-117).

4. A perfection of *love* (see 1 John 2: 5, 6; 4: 16-21). Dr. J. G. Morrison writes:

"When entire sanctification is come, then love becomes perfect. With hatred gone, and envy no more, and jealousy driven away, and pride cast out, and anger transformed and malice removed, and unholy ambition sanctified, and self-seeking banished, and avarice nailed to the Cross, and covetousness clean gone forever, the heart, now released from its bondage to moral corruption, swells with ecstasy of perfect love to God, perfect fellowship with God's children, and a tender compassion for the lost members of Adam's race."

> " 'Tis as easy now for the heart to be true,
> As for the grass to be green and the skies to be blue,
> 'Tis the natural way of living."
> —*Our Lost Estate,* p. 107.

5. A perfect *peace* (Isa. 26: 3). This peace is the outcome of soul poise, a rest of heart.

6. An unbroken *communion* (see 1 John 1: 3-7). Harmon A. Baldwin writes:

"Jesus Christ, in His own divine personality, really and

truly enters the trusting, believing soul; and, having entered, He so sheds abroad the heavenly fragrance of His presence as to cause to spring up a burning 'hope of glory.' Yea, more, this indwelling Christ is Himself the hope of glory. Consequently, when we have Him we have 'the Hope of glory,' we have a foretaste of glory, we have a measure of the ineffable splendor of the upper world, not in its radiations or drippings, but in its glorious cause. Christ is the Flower whose matchless fragrance floats o'er the hills and vales of Paradise; He is the Sun whose shining so illuminates the heavenly courts that there is no need of sun, or moon, or candle to dispel the gloom; He is the Anointing Horn from which flow rivers of oil over every ravished soul; He is the Joy Spring from which bubble streamlets of salvation which, swelling to majestic rivers, reach the utmost boundaries of infinite blessedness; He is the Fountain of Life that flows from the throne of God and causes heaven's glorified millions to live forever; and this Christ, Himself, proposes to enter your soul, and mine, and shed abroad His joy, His sweetness, His light, His life. Thank God for the fulness of grace" (*The Indwelling Christ,* p. 68).

7. A sacrificial *devotion* (see Rom. 12:1, 2). Rev. Oswald Chambers writes:

"By the discipline of obedience, I come to the place Abraham reached and see God as He is. The promises of God are of no use to me until by obedience I understand the nature of God. . . .

"The more we have to sacrifice for God, the more glorious is the reward presently. We have no right to choose our sacrifice. God will let us see where the sacrifice is to come, and it will always be on the line of what God has given us, our 'Isaac,' and yet He calls us to sacrifice it. God is always at work on the principle of lifting up the natural and making it the spiritual one, and very few of us will go through with it. We will cling to the natural when God wants us to

put a sword through it. If you go through the transfigura-
tion of the natural you will receive it back on a new plane
altogether. God wants to make eternally our own what we
only possessed intermittently.

"No language can express the ineffable blessedness of the
supreme reward that awaits the soul that has taken its
supreme climb, proved its supreme love, and entered its
supreme reward. What an imperturbable certainty there is
about the man who is in contact with the real God! Thank
God, the life of the Father of the Faithful is but a specimen
of the life of every humble believer who obediently follows
the discipline of the life of faith. What a depth of trans-
parent righteousness there must be about the man who
walks before God, and the meaning of the Atonement is to
place us there in perfect adjustment to God" (*Not Knowing
Whither,* pp. 128, 129).

### QUESTIONS ON THE TEXT

1. What do we mean when we speak of
"the indwelling God"?

2. Name from memory the seven results of
the indwelling God as given in this study.

3. Having named the seven results of the
indwelling God, take up each in turn and explain its meaning, giving Scripture authority
for what you say.

### (3) Ethical Obligations

THE experience of full salvation has its ethics as well as its thrill. Here is a danger point at which many have run aground. Forgetting that the experience sought is distinctly ethical in its content, they have occupied themselves with the emotional aspect to the neglect of the practical, and so have made shipwreck of faith.

Dr. J. R. Miller: "A great deal of our talk about consecration is vague and visionary. Our trouble is that the consecration we aim at is emotional rather than practical" (*Week Day Religion*).

There, in less than thirty words, Dr. Miller has gone to the very heart. It is possible to be highly emotional, yet decidedly impractical, and even unethical. This may not always be manifest in our actions, but may be there in our intentions. A real experience of full salvation will correct both.

1. Concerning our *actions*. Full salvation lays upon the believer some unequivocal demands. The God of the Sinai thunder did not retire in favor of the God of the Pentecostal flame. The Two are one and the same God; for while it is unmistakably true that we are now "not under law but under grace," it is also true that the indwelling God of grace keeps through His people the requirements of the law. Not one of these great moral requirements has been abrogated. Our Lord came, not to destroy but to fulfill, and that fulfillment is still going on through the spirit-filled believer by the Holy Spirit, for "love is the fulfilling of the law." See Matt. 5: 17, 18; Rom. 8: 3, 4; 10: 4; 13: 8-10; Heb. 8: 10, 11; 10: 16, 17.

This experience has its social implications.

a. In common honesty. It seems almost a slur on the experience that such a thing should be even mentioned. Good moral men are honest. And yet, there have been professors of this exalted experience of full salvation who have not been scrupulously careful in the payment of debts and the meeting of obligations.

b. In general courtesy. While this experience will not impart a knowledge of the rules of etiquette, it will at least manifest the indwelling of Him who is the most gentle Person in God's great universe, the Holy Spirit Himself; and it is wonderful how quickly a Spirit-filled soul anticipates in action what it later learns through books.

A sanctified man, whatever his restrictions, is never a boor. There is no refining influence like the indwelling of the Holy Spirit.

This experience has its personal responsibilities. There are responsibilities toward God and the house of God. There are also responsibilities toward home and those who reside there. There are times when we should be on our knees in prevailing prayer, but there are times when it would be more glorifying to God to be kneeling with a brush and pail. There are times for communion, but there are also times to darn socks. There are times for the Bible and hymn book, but there are times for the cash book and ledger. It is just as sinful to steal an employer's time for prayer as it is to take it to play baseball. Nothing but scrupulous honesty will suffice.

The following little poem may help us in our estimate of the mere matter-of-fact duties:

"Lord of all pots and pans and things, since I've no time to be
A saint by doing lovely things, or watching late with Thee,
Or dreaming in the dawnlight, or storming heaven's gates,
Make me a saint by getting meals, and washing up the plates.

"Although I must have Martha's hands, I have a Mary mind;
And when I black the boots and shoes, Thy sandals, Lord, I find.
I think of how they trod the earth, what time I scrub the floor;
Accept this meditation, Lord, I haven't time for more.

"Warm all the kitchen with Thy love, and light it with Thy
        peace;
Forgive me all my worrying, and make all grumbling cease.
Thou who didst love to give men food, in room or by the sea,
Accept this service that I do—I do it unto Thee."

2. Concerning our *intentions*. One of the steadying
factors in the experience of John Wesley throughout his
entire lifetime was his acquaintance while at Oxford with
such literature as William Law's work, *A Serious Call to a
Devout and Holy Life*, and Jeremy Taylor's *Rules and
Exercises of Holy Living and Holy Dying*. In Dr. Taylor's
work he was especially helped by the section on "Purity of
Intention."

It was in those historic Oxford days, when John and
Charles Wesley, with George Whitefield, William Morgan
and others, formed themselves into what became known as
"The Holy Club" for the avowed purpose of Bible study and
serious searching after the things of God, that this type of
literature so powerfully influenced Wesley's thinking. At
that time, although an earnest seeker, he was not aware of
the way of faith and consequently found in such literature
a ground of serious mental conflict and almost of despair.
It became the schoolmaster to help bring him to Christ.
Once he knew the way of faith, however, such teaching was
not lost. It was on the basis of his Oxford reading that his
later evangelical revelation swung with such fine poise.
Wesley's faith never even skirted the borders of presumption, and he owed his magnificent balance to such teaching
as Taylor's on the purity of intention, an excerpt of which
we give below.

"That we should intend and design God's glory in every
action we do, whether it be natural or chosen, is expressed
by St. Paul, 'Whether ye eat or drink, do all to the glory of
God' (1 Cor. 10:31). Which rule, when we observe, every
action of nature becomes religious, and every meal is an act

of worship, and shall have its reward in its proportion, as well as an act of prayer. Blessed be that goodness and grace of God which, out of infinite desire to glorify and save mankind, would make the very works of nature capable of becoming acts of virtue that all our lifetime we may do Him service.

"This grace is so excellent that it sanctifies the most common actions of our life; and yet so necessary that without it the very best actions of our devotions are imperfect and vicious. For he that prays out of custom, or gives alms for praise, or fasts to be accounted religious, is but a Pharisee in his devotion, and a beggar in his alms, and a hypocrite in his fast. But a holy end sanctifies all these, and all other actions which can be made holy, and gives distinction to them, and procures acceptance.

"For as to know the end distinguishes a man from a beast, so to choose a good end distinguishes him from an evil man Hezekiah repeated his good deeds upon his sick-bed, and obtained favor of God; but the Pharisee was accounted insolent for doing the same thing; because this man did it to upbraid his brother, the other to obtain a mercy of God. Zacharias questioned with the angel about his message, and was made speechless for his incredulity; but the blessed Virgin Mary questioned, too, and was blameless, for she did it to inquire after the manner of the thing; but he did not believe the thing itself; he doubted of God's power, or the truth of the messenger; but she only of her incapacity. This was it which distinguished the mourning of David from the exclamation of Saul, the confession of Pharaoh from that of Manasses, the tears of Peter from the repentance of Judas; 'For the praise is not in the deed done, but in the manner of its doing. If a man visits his sick friend, and watches at his pillow for charity sake and because of its old affection, we approve it; but if he does it in the hope of a legacy, he is a vulture, and only watches for the carcase. The same things are honest and dishonest; the manner of doing them and the end of the design makes the separation' (Seneca).

"Holy intention is to the actions of a man that which the soul is to the body, or form to its matter, or the root to the tree, or the sun to the world, or the fountain to the river, or the base to the pillar; for without these the body is a dead trunk, the matter is sluggish, the tree is a block, the world is darkness, the river is quickly dry, the pillar rushes into flatness and ruin, and the action is sinful or unprofitable and vain. The poor farmer that gave a dish of cold water to Artaxerxes was rewarded with a golden goblet, and he that gives the same to a disciple in the name of a disciple shall have a crown; but if he gives water in despite when the disciple needs wine or a cordial, his reward shall be to want that water to cool his tongue" (*Holy Living,* pp. 9, 10). See Matt. 5; Rom. 12-14; Eph. 4:17 to 5:21; Tit. 2:11-14.

### QUESTIONS ON THE TEXT

1.  Show the difference between an ethical obligation and an emotional urge.

2.  What does Dr. Miller mean when he speaks of consecration that is "vague and visionary"?

3.  A real experience of full salvation will correct both actions and intentions. Discuss this.

4.  Give Scripture proving that the experience of full salvation has its social implications.

5.  Discuss the experience of full salvation with regard to "intentions" and show how Mr. Wesley was influenced here.

## (4) Progressive

D r. Phineas F. Bresee said: "A sanctified man is at the bottom of the ladder. He is now to learn; to grow; to rise; to be divinely enlarged and transformed. The Christ in him is to make new and complete channels in and through every part of his being— pouring a stream of heaven through his thinking, living, devotement and faith. The divine battery—His manifest presence—is to be enlarged. The truth of God is to be revealed, and poured through the soul and lips, with holy fire and divine unction more and more aboundingly. A lack of personal realization that I, myself, must stir myself up, has brought wreck and ruin to many. God will stir him up who stirs up himself, until he comes 'unto the measure of the fullness of the stature of Christ'" (*A Prince in Israel,* biography by E. A. Girvin).

It is impossible to grow into this experience, as later we shall see; but once the experience becomes a realized fact, growth is both natural and essential. See Psa. 1:3; 72:7; 92:12, 13; Prov. 12:12; Hosea 14:5-9; John 15:1-16; Acts 9:22; 1 Cor. 13:11; 14:20; 2 Cor. 9:10; Eph. 3:14-21; 4:11-16; Col. 1:9-11; 2:19; 1 Thess. 3:12; 4:10; 2 Thess. 1:3; Heb. 5:14; 1 Pet. 2:2; 2 Pet. 1:5-8; 3:17, 18.

Concerning this growth in grace Rev. J. A. Wood will speak: "Christian perfection does not exclude growth in grace. The pure in heart grow faster than any others. We believe in no state of grace excluding progression, either in this world or in heaven, but expect to grow with increasing rapidity forever. It is the same with the soul wholly sanctified as with the merely regenerate: it must progress in order to retain the favor of God and the grace possessed. Here many of both classes have fallen.

"There is no standing still in a religious life, nor in a

sinful life. We must either progress or regress. If living according to our light and duty, we are growing, no matter what our gracious state may be, or however largely we may have partaken of the Holy Spirit—if neglecting present duty, we are backsliding, whatever our attainments may have been.

"Holiness cannot be retained without growth in grace. It can only be retained by a steady progress in the divine life. The conditions of obtaining holiness and of retaining it are the same; and the conditions of obtaining and retaining it are those by which the soul is to grow and mature in holiness. Hence a violation of the conditions of increase and growth in holiness forfeits the state of holiness itself.

"Again, our capacities and powers are improvable and expansive, and we must proportionately grow in holiness or incur guilt and fall from grace.

"Holiness may be perfect and yet progressive. Perfection in quality does not exclude increase in quantity. Beyond entire sanctification there is no increase in purity, as that which is pure cannot be more than pure; but there may be unlimited increase in expansion and quantity.

"After love is made perfect, it may abound more and yet more. Holiness in the entirely sanctified soul is exclusive, and is perfect in kind or in quality, but is limited in degree or quantity. The capacities of the soul are expansive and progressive, and holiness in measure can increase corresponding to increasing capacity. Faith, love, humility, and patience may be perfect in kind, and yet increase in volume and power, or in measure harmonizing with increasing capacity. A tree may be perfectly sound, healthy, and vigorous in its branches, leaves, and fruit, and yet year by year increase perpetually its capacity and fruitfulness. Analogous to this is a wicked life. The Church has always held the doctrine of total depravity, and yet believed in acquired depravity, and in aggressive depravity.

"Growth in grace is chiefly subsequent to sanctification. A vast majority of church-members appear to think, between regeneration and entire sanctification must be a lifetime of growth in grace. This is a serious mistake, and we fear has overthrown millions. It is unscriptural to teach growth as a substitute for cleansing. Entire sanctification is the divine preparation of heart for the growth or development of all the fruit and graces of the Holy Spirit (Eph. 4: 12, 16).

"A soul entirely sanctified can grow in grace more rapidly than others. Holiness does not put a finality to anything within us, except to the existence and practice of sin.

"Because all the internal antagonisms of growth are excluded from the heart. Indwelling sin is the greatest hindrance to growth in grace. When this evil principle is destroyed, with all its real, living, stirring, inward evils, the chief hindrance to our growth is removed. When the weeds in a garden are exterminated, the vegetables will grow the more rapidly.

"Because the purified heart has stronger faith, clearer light, is nearer the fountain, and dwells in a purer atmosphere than before it was cleansed.

"Because after the Holy Ghost has cleansed the heart, He has a better chance than before to enlighten, enrich, adorn, and renew it, with more and more of love and power. The cleansing blood, having removed all the interior obstructions to the Holy Spirit's most gracious operations, affords more room for the Christian graces to grow and flourish.

"Because the death of sin gives free scope to the life of righteousness. The purified heart is a pure moral soil, where the plants of righteousness, the graces of the spirit, have an unobstructed growth. In the very nature of the case, in the pure heart, the Christian virtues are less impeded, and their growth more rapid, uniform and solid.

"It should be borne in mind that growth in grace appertains to the positive in Christian life, to the graces of the Spirit, and is not a process of separating sin from the soul, either before or after entire sanctification. There is no growing out of sin from the vicious to the virtuous, or from defilement to purity. Growth in a Christian has respect to the expansion and development of the moral features or virtues of the life in Christ.

"Because the powers and capacities of the entirely sanctified soul increase and expand more rapidly than before, and with this increasing capacity there is a corresponding increase in the volume and power of the graces of the Spirit. Indwelling sin degenerates, blinds, cripples, and enervates the soul, while holiness quickens, invigorates, and secures the best possible foundation for its expansion and development.

"Because it perfects the conditions of the most thrifty and symmetrical growth possible in this life. Holiness is spiritual health. 'By his stripes we are healed.' All disease and deformity obstruct growth, while health is its most essential condition. A child in perfect health will grow in stature and strength more rapidly than if possessed of some constitutional disease.

"Grace has the best possible chance in an entirely sanctified soul to achieve its grandest results. The very conditions of retaining purity are the precise conditions of the most rapid, healthful, and beautiful growth in love, knowledge, and holiness" (*Perfect Love,* pp. 55-59).

Rev. John Wesley: "One perfected in love may grow far swifter than he did before" (*A Plain Account of Christian Perfection*).

Dr. Luther Lee: "When the embarrassments are thus removed out of the soul itself, progress will be more rapid; every virtue may increase in strength and brightness" (*Theology,* p. 25).

Rev. John Fletcher: "A perfect Christian grows far more than a feeble believer whose growth is still obstructed by the shady thorns of sin, and by the draining suckers of iniquity" (*Last Check,* p. 499).

Bishop Hamline: "The heart may be cleansed from all sin, while our graces are immature, and the cleansing is a preparation for unembarrassed and rapid growth" (Sermon, *Beauty of Holiness,* 1862).

## QUESTIONS ON THE TEXT

1. Show the difference between growing in and growing into this experience.

2. Give some Scripture passages on this subject.

3. Show that Christian perfection cannot be retained without growth in grace.

4. Show how it is possible to be perfect and yet progressive.

5. Show that growth is chiefly subsequent to sanctification.

# 7

# The Time Period

## HOW LONG BETWEEN THE TWO EXPERIENCES?

**B**ETWEEN the work of regeneration and the experience of entire sanctification there is such a distinction as to make necessary a time difference as to their reception. The question therefore arises, How much time must elapse between the two? In other words, how soon after regeneration may the soul be entirely sanctified?

Most Christians testify to an extended period of struggling and of frequent defeat, but we are persuaded that this is not God's perfect plan, neither is it the Scriptural way, as the following passages will show.

Acts 2:37-39: It is evident that in Peter's thinking on the Day of Pentecost, "the remission of sins" and the "gift of the Holy Ghost" were not far apart.

Acts 8:5-8, 14-17: It is evident that in the thinking of the Jerusalem authorities, the uppermost thought was, "The sooner these new converts receive the blessing, the better it will be."

Acts 9:17-19: It is evident that in the thinking of Ananias, Saul should receive the Holy Ghost without delay.

Acts 19:1-7: It is evident that in Paul's thinking these

[74]

Ephesian believers should not be allowed to go on indefinitely without being challenged as to their reception of the Holy Ghost.

1 Thess. 4:3; 5:23, 24: Although so recently converted from heathenism—converts probably little more than six months old—Paul urges them to seek the experience of entire sanctification.

Rev. J. A. Wood: "There is no time stated in the Scriptures which must elapse after conversion before the soul can be entirely sanctified. The only prerequisite to the seeking of holiness is the justified and regenerate state. Even 'babes in Christ' are exhorted to 'go on unto perfection'; and all believers are included in the command, 'Be ye holy, for I am holy.' The declaration, 'It is the will of God, even your sanctification,' is true of every believer, and was originally addressed to heathen converts who were but babes in Christ. Today, the present time, is the voice both of the Law and the Gospel in regard to our sanctification. It is the duty and privilege of all believers to have hearts cleansed from sin, and filled with love at once.

"When first converted, we should press on into this goodly land which flows with milk and honey. When the kingdom of God is first set up in our hearts, the course is short, the difficulties are comparatively few, and we cannot be too early, or too much in earnest, seeking purity.

"Ancient Canaan was a type of gospel privilege, and is frequently used in the Scriptures to illustrate truth and duty. As entire holiness is the objective point in the whole Christian system, so Canaan was the objective point to the Israelites when they left Egypt. After they left Horeb, on the shores of the Red Sea, they consumed only eleven days in reaching the borders of Canaan, in sight of the beautiful hills of that goodly land. Joshua, the faithful servant of God, seeing their privilege and duty, said to them: 'Let us go up at once and possess it: for we are well able to overcome it.' But the unbelieving Israelites remained forty years in the wilderness, with all their disabilities and sorrows, when they might have entered their long promised Canaan in less than a month.

"Are there not ten times six hundred thousand in the Christian church today who ought to pass over at once into the Canaan of perfect love? And some of these, we fear, have been more than forty years in the wilderness" (*Perfect Love*, pp. 30, 31).

Rev. John Wesley: "The next morning I spoke severally with those who believed they were sanctified. They were fifty-one in all—twenty-one men, twenty-one widows or married women, and nine young women or children. In one, the change was wrought three weeks after she was justified. In three, seven days after it; in one, five days; and in S. L., aged fourteen, two days only" (*Wesley's Journal*, August 4, 1762).

"I have been lately thinking a good deal on one point, wherein, perhaps, we have all been wanting. We have not made it a rule, as soon as ever persons are justified, to remind them of 'going on unto perfection.' Whereas this is the very time preferable to all others. They have then the simplicity of little children; and they are fervent in spirit, ready to cut off a right hand or pluck out the right eye. But if we once suffer this fervor to subside, we shall find it hard enough to bring them again even to this point" (Letter to Thomas Rankin).

"Every one, though born of God in an instant, yea, and sanctified in an instant, yet undoubtedly grows, by slow degrees, both after the former and the latter change. But it does not follow from thence that there may be a considerable tract of time between the one and the other. A year or a month is the same with God as a thousand. It is therefore our duty to pray and look for full salvation every day, every hour, every moment, without waiting until we have either done or suffered more" (*Wesley's Works*).

"Many at Macclesfield believed that the blood of Christ had cleansed them from all sin. I spoke to these forty in all, one by one. Some of them said they received that blessing ten days, some seven, some four, some three days, after they found peace with God, and two of them the next day" (*Wesley's Works*).

"With God one day is as a thousand years. It plainly follows that the quantity of time is nothing to Him. Centuries, years, months, days, hours and moments are exactly the same. Consequently, He can as well sanctify in a day after we are justified, as a hundred years. There is no difference at all, unless we suppose Him to be such a one as ourselves. Accordingly, we see, in fact, that some of the most unquestionable witnesses of sanctifying grace were sanctified within a few days after they were justified." No wonder that he exclaims, "Oh, why do we not encourage all to expect this blessing every hour from the moment they are justified?" (*Wesley's Works*).

To Freeborn Garrettson in 1785: "It will be well, as soon as any seekers find peace with God, to exhort them to go on unto perfection."

Rev. Luther Lee: "This progressive work may be cut short and finished at any moment, when the intelligence clearly comprehends the defects of the present state, and faith, comprehending the power and willingness of God to sanctify us wholly, and do it now, is exercised" (*Lee's Theology,* p. 214).

Rev. J. S. Inskip: "We are generally inclined to the opinion that between our justification and sanctification there must necessarily be an extended period of many months or years, or well-nigh a lifetime. This is a most grievous error" (*Methods of Promoting Perfect Love,* p. 14).

Dr. Jesse T. Peck: "They were not wholly sanctified

when they were justified. This they have learned by experience, if they did not from the Bible, where it is clearly taught; and they have argued that time is necessary for the completion of the work—how much they know not, but a long time, and at length; it has been, perhaps in many cases, unconsciously extended to the period of death. In this way, with a few, weeks and months; but with most, years, many long years have passed, and the time of their entire consecration has not yet arrived.

"But why might not the work have been sooner completed? . . . There is surely no time fixed in the Scriptures which must elapse before the work can be accomplished. The Savior prays for His disciples, 'Sanctify them through thy truth,' assuming that they were all at that time eligible to this great blessing. And in view of the same fact, Paul prays, 'The very God of peace sanctify you wholly.' Even 'babes in Christ' are exhorted to 'go on to perfection'; and all believers are included in the command, 'Be ye holy.' The want of time is not the difficulty. Alas, how many gracious privileges have been neglected! how long have most of us been called to holiness! what darkness and condemnation have we brought upon our souls by refusing the call or postponing attention to another period! All of which clearly shows that, had we given the subject suitable consideration, we might have been long since wholly saved from sin" (*The Central Idea of Christianity*, pp. 110, 111).

### QUESTIONS ON THE TEXT

1. Discuss the time limit between the two experiences.
2. Show from Scripture the necessity of the distinction between the two experiences.
3. Give the views of Mr. Wood and Mr. Wesley on this subject.

# 8

## Definitions of Sanctification

### HOLINESS IN THE DICTIONARY

F OR the purpose of breadth of outlook we leave for the moment the atmosphere of the theological treatise and turn to those very matter-of-fact volumes, the dictionaries.

On the subject of holiness in the dictionary, Rev. C. W. Ruth says: "Men speak of the subject of sanctification as though it were something so mysterious and incomprehensible that but very few could know its meaning. While its reality can only be known as the result of experience, the meaning of the word may be found by consulting almost any dictionary, just as one finds the meaning or definition of any other word.

"While different phases of the subject may be emphasized by different lexicographers, there is a most substantial agreement regarding the fact of this word having both a human and a divine aspect; the human aspect being a consecration and devotement to God and His service, and the divine work in sanctification a complete deliverance and purification from all sin. To use the word contradictory to these authenticated definitions is to do violence to the word

[79]

and make words meaningless. No man is at liberty to say
that light means darkness or darkness light" (*Entire Sanctification a Second Blessing,* p. 15).

On this subject also Rev. H. T. Heironimus writes:
" 'Rightly dividing the word of truth' is truly to know what
sanctification means as the dictionaries define it. The Word
of God, the dictionaries, the encyclopedias, and the theol-
ogies here quoted all agree that it has two meanings—one,
in consecration as setting aside for a sacred work, man's
part; the other, making pure and holy, God's part. The one
is a rite or ceremony, a sacred religious operation, an office
or performance, on the human side, a duty to ourselves and
to our God—a true fitting for service. The other is a divine
act that renovates the nature, that purifies the soul, that
makes clean and holy the heart and the life, that transforms
the affections, perfects the love, and lifts out of sin into
divine likeness and fellowship; a process of the Holy Spirit
to a believing, willing child of God—a thorough inward
purging and qualification for divine service.

"A man cannot be an unbiased student and scholar and
ignore sanctification, since even our secular dictionaries
have so clearly defined it. One cannot be truly educated,
either in sacred or profane writings, without giving this
subject a place in his thought" (*The Theme of the Ages,*
pp. 11, 12).

Here are nine dictionaries with their respective meanings, to which, doubtless, many more could be added.

*Webster's Dictionary.* "Sanctify.—1. To make sacred or
holy, to set apart to a holy or religious use, to consecrate by
appropriate rites, to hallow.

"2. To make free from sin, to cleanse from moral corruption and pollution, to purify (John 17:17). Esp.
(Theol.), The act of God's grace by which the affections of
men are purified or alienated from sin and the world, and
exalted to a supreme love to God."

*Century Dictionary.* "Sanctify.—1. To make holy or clean, either ceremonially or morally and spiritually; to purify or free from sin.

"2. In theology, the act of God's grace by which the affections of men are purified and the soul is cleansed from sin and consecrated to God . . . conformity of the heart and life to the will of God."

*Imperial Dictionary.* "Sanctify.—1. To make holy or sacred; to separate, set apart or appoint to a holy, sacred or religious use.

"2. To purify in order to prepare for divine service and partaking of holy things.

"3. To purify from sin, to make holy."

*Worcester's Dictionary.* "Sanctify.—1. To free from the power of sin; to cleanse from corruption; to make holy . . . sanctification; the act of sanctifying, or purifying from the dominion of sin.

"2. The act of consecrating or setting apart to a sacred end or office; consecration.

*Universal Dictionary.* "Sanctify.—1. To make holy or sacred; to consecrate.

"2. To make holy or godly; to purify from sin."

*Standard Dictionary.* "Sanctify.—To make holy; render sacred; morally or spiritually pure, cleansed from sin. . . . sanctification; especially in theology, the gracious work of the Holy Spirit whereby the believer is freed from sin and exalted to holiness of heart."

*The Encyclopaedic Dictionary.* "Sanctification. — State of being sanctified, purified, or made holy; conformity of heart and life to the will of God."

*Funk and Wagnall's Practical Standard Dictionary.* "Sanctify.—1. To make holy; purify, as from sin; in theology, to cause to experience sanctification.

"2. To set apart as holy, or for holy purposes; consecrate.

"3.   To render operative for, or productive of, holiness.
"4.   To give a sacred or inviolable character to . . ."

*New Standard Encyclopaedia.* "Sanctification.—In theology, the process by which the Holy Spirit renews in man the divine image, destroying within him the power of evil and quickening the life of holiness" (Vol. XXI, p. 452).

However theologians may quibble, the makers of our dictionaries are agreed that when plain English is needed, there can be no doubt as to the meaning of the words "sanctify" and "sanctification."

## QUESTIONS ON THE TEXT

1.   Show from the dictionary that God can make men holy.

# 9

## The Way Into the Blessing

**(1) IT MAY BE PERSONALLY KNOWN. (2) IT MAY BE INSTANTANEOUSLY KNOWN. (3) IT MUST BE PERSONALLY SOUGHT.**

**(1) It May be Personally Known**

HAVING said so much about this blessing, we now pause for a while before the entrance, so that the reader may consider the way in.

We begin by insisting that there is a way in. The teaching before us is not a fanciful mental plaything, but represents a distinct and definite spiritual experience to be personally enjoyed.

Concerning this, Rev. J. A. Wood says: "The essential facts of personal salvation are knowable—they may be known by experience. The fallen condition of man, with all his deplorable convictions, sufferings and degradation, is not more a matter of assurance and positive consciousness than their counterpart in the redemption of Christ—pardon, adoption, regeneration and sanctification. The latter come as clearly and fully within the purview of experimental knowledge as the former. We believe with Lord Bacon that 'experience should be the test of truth'; and with Dr. C. H. Fowler, 'Entire sanctification will, sooner or later, afford the best solution of any difficulties we may have on this subject.'

"There is philosophy as well as inspired truth in the declaration of Christ, 'If any man will do his will, he shall know of the doctrine.' Here is common ground, on which all may prove the power of Christ to save, and obtain freedom from doubts and uncertainty, in a conscious realization of personal salvation.

"Christian holiness, theoretically and experimentally, is no greater mystery than regeneration, neither is it removed any further from the laws of human thought, but is as plain as any other fact of consciousness. The provisions and the possibilities of grace in this regard are alike adapted to all, needed by all, and free to all. Christ 'by the grace of God tasted death for every man,' and every man may taste the joys and sweet delight of full salvation. There are three things that are distinct in this experience:

"1. There is a consciousness of inbred sin and moral deficiency after conversion, and the more devoted and faithful the justified soul, the clearer and stronger this conviction.

"2. There is conviction, in the light of gospel provisions, of the duty and privilege of being 'cleansed from all sin,' and made 'pure in heart.'

"3. It is prayerfully sought and experienced as an instantaneous cleansing by faith in the blood of Christ.

"These three items of experimental knowledge will be found in every clear case of entire sanctification" (*Perfect Love,* pp. 95, 96).

That this experience may be personally known may be argued from:

1. The commands and exhortations of the Bible: Gen. 17: 1; Ex. 22: 31; Lev. 11: 44, 45; 20: 7, 26; Deut. 10: 12; 18: 13; 1 Kings 8: 61; 1 Chron. 28: 9; 2 Chron. 19: 7, 9; Matt. 5: 48; 22: 37; 2 Cor. 6: 14 to 7: 1; 13: 11; Eph. 5:

18; 1 Tim. 1: 5; 5: 22; Heb. 6: 1; 12: 14; 1 Pet. 1: 15, 16.

2. The promises and declarations of the Bible: Deut. 7: 6; 14: 2, 21; 26: 19; 28: 9; 30: 6; 2 Chron. 16: 9; Psa. 130: 8; Jer. 33: 6-9; Ezek. 36: 25-27; Obad. 17; Zech. 13: 1; 14: 20, 21; Matt. 1: 21; Matt. 5: 8; Luke 1: 74, 75; John 1: 29, 33; 7: 37-39; Acts 1: 4, 5, 8; 2: 38; 15: 8, 9; 26: 18; Rom. 6; Eph. 5: 25-27; 1 Thess. 3: 13; 4: 3; 4: 7; 5: 22-24; 2 Tim. 2: 21; Tit. 2: 11-14; 3: 5, 6; Heb. 2: 11; 7: 25; 10: 10, 14; 13: 11-13; 1 Pet. 1: 16; 1 John 1: 5 to 2: 2; 3: 3-9; Jude 24.

3. The prayers of the Bible: 1 Chron. 29: 19; Psa. 5; Matt. 6: 10, 13; John 17: 15-23; Acts 20: 32; 2 Cor. 13: 9; Eph. 1: 15-23; 3: 14-19; Col. 4: 12; 1 Thess. 5: 23; Heb. 13: 20, 21.

4. The testimonies and examples of the Bible: Gen. 5: 23, 24; Heb. 11: 5, 6; Gen. 6: 9; 2 Kings 4: 9; 20: 3; 2 Chron. 15: 17; Job 1: 1-8; 2: 3; Psa. 101: 2; Luke 1: 5, 6; Acts 2: 1-4; 8: 14-17; 9: 17-19; 10: 44-48; 15: 8-9; 19: 1-7; Rom. 8: 3-4; Gal. 2: 20; Phil. 3: 15; 1 Thess. 2: 10; Heb. 2: 11; 1 Pet. 1: 2; 2 Pet. 1: 21; 1 Pet. 3-5; 1 John 4: 17, 18; Jude 1: 1.


### QUESTIONS ON THE TEXT

1. Give in your own words the gist of Mr. Wood's insistence that this experience may be personally known.

2. Show from the commands of the Bible that this experience may be personally known.

3. Show from the promises and declarations of the Bible that this experience may be personally known.

4. Show from the prayers of the Bible that this experience may be personally known.

5. Show from the testimonies and examples of the Bible that this experience may be personally known.

## (2) It May be
## Instantaneously Known

THE entrance into this experience is not by the slow process of growth but by the instantaneous method of faith. This is seen in

1. The *terms* used to describe it.

An act of *circumcision*. A divine operation on the heart (see Deut. 30: 6; Col. 2: 11).

A work of *purging*. A divine elimination of that which is unnatural from the nature (see Psa. 51: 7; John 15: 2).

An act of *cleansing*. A divine sweep of defilement from the life (see Psa. 51: 7; Ezek. 36: 25; 1 John 1: 9; Matt. 8: 1-4).

A work of *creation*. A divine word, calling into being something new (see Psa. 51: 10; Eph. 4: 24; Psa. 33: 9).

An act of *baptism*. A divine work, immersing the soul in God (see Matt. 3: 11; Rom. 6: 4).

An act of *crucifixion*. A divine work, bringing death (see Rom. 6: 6; Gal. 2: 20).

A work of *destruction*. A divine work, ridding the soul of sin's nature within (see Rom. 6: 6).

In view of this sevenfold decisive work, we are commanded to "Put off . . . the old man" (Eph. 4: 22) ; "put on . . . the new man" (Eph. 4: 24) ; "put away" whatever belonged to the old, because we are now acknowledging only the new.

2. The *tense* used in speaking of it.

Here we meet that Greek peculiarity which has become the unanswerable argument in instantaneous Second Blessing holiness.

Dr. Daniel Steele: "In this age of astonishing scientific progress, when the microscope applied to living tissues reveals whole continents of evidences of design in bioplastic life, and marvelously strengthens theism in it debate with atheism, we have applied the same instrument to the Greek Testament, in the aid of exegesis, in the interest of disputed truths, and for the refutation of certain doctrinal errors. Our microscope will be directed to a long-neglected field of research, the Greek tenses, not for the purpose of discovering new truths, but for the confirmation and clear elucidation of verities as old as revelation.

"Dean Alford and Bishop Ellicott, and other late sacred scholars, enrich their notes with gems of truth discovered by applying the microscope of modern learning. They call attention to the tenses of the Greek verbs used in the New Testament as conveying important truth. . . .

"That the English scholar may understand our argument and our illustrations, we give the following definitions:

"1. The present tense denotes what is now going on, and indicates a continuous, repeated, or habitual action, as 'I am writing.'

"2. The imperfect denotes the same continuity or repetition in the past, as 'I was writing.'

"3. The aorist indicative (says Goodwin) expresses the simple momentary occurrence of an action in time past, as, 'I wrote.'

"4. The perfect denotes an action as already finished at the present time, as 'I have written; my writing is just now finished.' It also expresses the continuance of the result down to the present time; as the formula, 'It is written,' is literally, 'It has been written,' and implies that it now stands on record.

"5. The pluperfect denotes an act which took place before another past act.

"6. The chief peculiarity lies in the aorist. We have in the English no tense like it. Except in the indicative, it is timeless, and in all the moods indicates what Krueger styles 'singleness of act.' This idea our translators could not express without a circumlocution in words having no representatives in the Greek. 'The poverty of our language,' says Alford, 'in the finer distinctions of the tenses often obliges us to render inaccurately and fall short of the wonderful language with which we have to deal."

"All exhortations to prayer and to spiritual endeavor in the resistance of temptation are usually expressed in the present tense, which strongly indicates persistence.

"Example: Matt. 7:7. 'Keep asking [pres.], and it shall be given you; seek [pres.] again and again, and ye shall find; knock persistently, and it shall be opened unto you.'

"The next thing that impresses us is the absence of the aorist and the presence of present tense whenever the conditions of final salvation are stated. Our inference is that the conditions of ultimate salvation are continuous, extending through probation, and not completed in any one act. A careful study of the Greek will convince the student that it is a great mistake to teach that a single act of faith furnishes a person with a paid-up, non-forfeitable policy, assuring the holder that he will inherit eternal life, or that a single energy of faith secures a through ticket for heaven. The Greek tenses show that faith is a state, a habit of mind, into which the believer enters at justification.

"But when we come to consider the work of purification in the believer's soul by the power of the Holy Spirit, both in the new birth and entire sanctification, we find that the aorist is almost uniformly used. This tense, according to the best New Testament grammarians, never indicates a continuous, habitual, or repeated act, but one which is momentary, and done once for all.

"E. g., Matt. 8:2, 3, 'And behold there came a leper, and he kept worshiping [imperfect] him, saying, Lord, if thou wilt, thou canst cleanse [aorist] me [once for all]. And Jesus, stretching out [aorist] his hand, touched [aorist] him, saying, I will, be thou instantaneously cleansed [aorist].'

"The leper prayed to be cleansed, not gradually, but instantly, and it was done at a stroke, according to his faith.

"John 17:17-19: 'Sanctify [aorist imperative] them [once for all] through thy truth [that is, through faith in the distinctive office and work of the Comforter.] ... And for their sakes I am consecrating [present] myself, in order that they in reality may be permanently sanctified.'

"The imperative aorist denotes an action either rapidly completed and transient, or viewed as occurring but once.

"Acts 15:9: 'Instantaneously purifying [aorist] their hearts by faith.' This verse is a key to the instantaneous sanctifying work of the Holy Spirit wrought in the hearts of believers on the day of Pentecost, since the words 'even as he did unto us' refer to that occasion. See Acts 10:45-47.

"Rom. 6:6: 'Knowing this, that our old man was crucified [aorist, once for all], that the body [being or totality] of sin might be destroyed [aorist, at a stroke], that henceforth we should no longer be serving [present] sin. For he who [once for all, aorist] died [unto sin] has been justified from sin.'

"The aorist here teaches the possibility of an instantaneous death-stroke to inbred sin, and that there is no need of a slow and painful process, lingering until physical death or purgatorial fires end the torment. Men are not crucified limb by limb, after one part is dead finding a hand or arm or finger alive, but the whole life is extinguished all at once.

"2 Cor. 7:1: 'Let us cleanse [aorist] ourselves [at a stroke] from every filthiness of the flesh and spirit, perfecting [present] holiness in the fear of the Lord.'

"The tenses used in connection with various metaphors and phrases employed to denote entire sanctification are significant.

"Example, Gal. 2:19, 20: 'For I through the law died [aorist, quite suddenly] to the law, that I might live unto God. I have been crucified [perfect] with Christ [and stay dead till now], and it is no longer I that live, but Christ that liveth in me.'

"Here is a perfect answer, in Paul's testimony, to the advocates of a lingering death of the old man, continuing up to the separation of soul and body. There was a time when Paul died to sin by a crucifixion—a short and sharp kind of death—and the old man lived no more.

"Eph. 1:13: 'After that ye believed [aorist], ye were sealed [aorist] with that Holy Spirit of promise.' Here the believing and the sealing are acts distinct, definite and completed.

"Eph. 3:16-19: Here are six aorists in four verses: 'Grant,' 'be strengthened,' 'dwell' (*i. e.,* take up his abode), 'may be able to comprehend,' 'to know,' 'be filled.'

"May we not infer that Paul chose this tense to convey most strongly and vividly the ability of Christ to do a great work in a short time, to save believers fully, and to endow them with the fullness of the Spirit?

"Eph. 4:22-24: 'That ye put off [aorist] the old man.' Here the aorist is used because the act of putting off is one and decisive. 'And that ye be renewed [present] in the spirit of your mind. And that ye put on [aorist] the new man, which after God is created [aorist, was instantaneously created] in righteousness and true holiness.'

"1 Thess. 5:23: 'And the very God of peace [once for all] sanctify [aorist] you wholly . . .' " (*The Tense Readings of the Greek New Testament, Milestone Papers,* pp. 52-86, which see for more complete treatment).

### QUESTIONS ON THE TEXT

1. By what method is the experience of entire sanctification to be realized?

2. Prove your answer to the previous question by stating and explaining the terms used to describe the experience.

3. What further argument has been advanced in favor of the instantaneous blessing? State the argument, and give Scripture proof.

## (2) Instantaneously Known (Continued)

To the other evidences of the fact that the blessing may be instantaneously known, there may be added a third:

3. The *teaching* of those who have received it. It will be noticed that we say "of those who have received it." We are aware that there is much teaching contrary to that of the instantaneous blessing, but those who speak thus admit that they know nothing about such an experience; they are therefore not safe guides here. We would not go to a butcher for a discussion on surgery, nor to a blind man for the description of a landscape. High scholastic attainments call for respect in the sphere in which they operate, but only those who have tasted of this grace are competent consultants concerning it.

Mr. Wesley: "Indeed, this is so evident a truth that well-nigh all the children of God, scattered abroad, however they differ in other points, yet generally agree in this: That although we may 'by the Spirit mortify the deeds of the body,' 'resist and conquer both outward and inward sin,' although we may weaken our enemies day by day, yet we cannot drive them out. By all the grace which is given at justification we cannot extirpate them. Though we watch and pray ever so much, we cannot wholly cleanse either our hearts or hands. Most sure we cannot, till it please our Lord to speak to our hearts again—to speak the second time, 'Be clean'; and only then the leprosy is cleansed. Only then the evil root, the carnal mind, is destroyed and inbred sin subsists no more. But if there be no such second change; if there be none but a gradual work of God (that there is a gradual work none denies), then we must be content, as well as we can, to remain full of sin till death" (*Sermons*).

"Inquiring [in 1761] how it was that in all these parts we had so few witnesses of full salvation, I constantly received one and the same answer: 'We see now we sought it by our works; we thought it was to come gradually; we never expected it to come in a moment, by simple faith, in the very same manner thus; as all who believe they are sanctified declare with one voice that the change was wrought in a moment.' I cannot but believe that sanctification is commonly, if not always, an instantaneous work.

"I have continually testified (for these five and twenty years), in private and public, that we are sanctified as well as justified by faith. And, indeed, the one of those great truths does exceedingly illustrate the other. Exactly as we are justified by faith, so are we sanctified by faith.

"You may obtain a growing victory over sin from the moment you are justified. But that is not enough. The body of sin, the carnal mind, must be destroyed. The old man must be slain or we cannot put on the new man. . . . and this is done in a moment. To talk of this being gradual would be nonsense, as much as if we talked of gradual justification" (*Christian Perfection*).

Rev. John Fletcher: "It is, I think, allowed on all sides that 'we are saved,' that is, sanctified, as well as justified 'by faith.' Now, that particular height of sanctification, that full 'circumcision of the heart,' which centrally purifies the soul, springs from a peculiar degree of saving faith, and from a particular operation of the 'spirit of burning,' a quick operation this, which is compared to a baptism of fire, and proves sometimes so sharp and searching that it is as much as a healthy, strong man can do to bear up under it" (*Last Check to Antinomianism*, p. 566).

Dr. Adam Clarke: "We are to come to God for an instantaneous and complete purification from all sin, as for instantaneous pardon. In no part of the Scriptures are we directed to seek the remission of sins seriatim—one now and another then, and so on. Neither in any part are we directed to seek holiness by gradation. Neither a gradation pardon nor a gradation purification exists in the Bible. . . . For as the work of cleansing and renewing the heart is the work of God, His almighty power can perform it in a moment, in the twinkling of an eye. And as it is this moment our duty to love God with all our heart, and we cannot do this till He cleanse our hearts, consequently He is ready to do it this moment, because He wills that we should in this moment love Him. . . . This moment, therefore, we may be emptied of sin, filled with holiness, and become truly happy" (*Clarke's Theology*, p. 208).

Rev. Richard Watson: "The attainment of perfect freedom from sin is one to which believers are called during the present life; and it is necessary to completeness of holiness and of those active and passive graces of Christianity by which they are called to glorify God in this world and to edify mankind. . . . All the promises of God which are not expressly, or from their order, referred to future time, are objects of present trust; and their fulfillment now is made conditional only by our faith. They cannot, therefore, be pleaded in our prayers, with an entire reliance upon the truth of God, in vain. To this faith shall the promises of entire sanctification be given, which in the nature of the case supposes an instantaneous work immediately following upon entire and unwavering faith" (*Theol. Inst.*, Vol. II, p. 455).

Rev. John Inskip: "I apprehend in all cases where any special success has been given to the teaching of this doctrine it has been where the instantaneous character of the work has been made very prominent" (*Method of Promoting Perfect Love*).

Rev. William McDonald: "The present is as the future with God, and they do not reckon wisely who conclude that tomorrow will be more abundant in privilege than today. There can be no want of power on the part of Christ; and as it is by faith and not by works, it requires but little time to believe. Whenever the soul sees its wants, and believes in Christ, the work is accomplished" (*New Testament Standard of Piety,* p. 167).

Dr. George Peck: "It will be remembered that we have found sanctification to imply both the death of sin and the life of righteousness. And when we speak of entire sanctification, as to the former part of it, we say it may be attained at once—it is an instantaneous work. . . . But in relation to the latter part of this great work, viz., the life of righteousness, embracing all holy affections and pious efforts, it is regarded as entirely progressive. . . . The destruction of sin in the soul, and the growth of holiness, are two distinct things. . . . The one is instantaneous, the other gradual; and hence it is that we sometimes say, with propriety, that the work of entire sanctification is both gradual and instantaneous" (*Christian Perfection,* p. 212).

One more quotation closing this section:

Rev. J. A. Wood: "The church generally hold that God instantaneously removes all indwelling sin from dying infants and from all justified believers who die suddenly like the dying thief, and it is reasonable to believe that He instantaneously sanctifies those who trust in the blood of Christ to have it done.

"Purity being God's work, and being by faith, is evidence that it is instantaneous, the same as its kindred blessings—pardon, adoption, and regeneration.

"The beautiful analogy in the conditions and experience of regeneration and entire sanctification teaches an instantaneous work similar to regeneration. The sinner, convicted of his guilt, believes in Christ for pardon, and is forgiven freely and fully. The Christian, convicted of impurity, believes in Christ for holiness, and his heart is made pure, entirely and instantaneously. The promise, 'Believe on the Lord Jesus Christ, and thou shalt be saved,' covers the latter case just as much as the former. Gradualism is not according to the analogy of the great work of God in spiritual regeneration. The instantaneous is.

"The commands, exhortations, and promises of the Bible teach that purity is instantaneous. God desires, commands, and expects instant obedience. This cannot be done if holiness is not instantaneous. God's command, 'Be ye holy,' plainly requires present holiness; 'Be ye filled with the Spirit,' 'Be ye therefore perfect,' enjoins perfection today. 'This is the will of God, even your sanctification,' means now. 'Thou shalt love the Lord thy God with all thy heart,' is a command enforcing perfect love today, if it means anything. Just as surely as God desires and commands us now to 'be holy,' now to 'be perfect,' now 'to be filled with the Spirit' and now to 'love him with all our hearts,' so surely is sin's destruction and heart purification instantaneous.

"All the commands, invitations, and promises of God in respect to holiness are in the present tense. They are as clearly and definitely so as those to the sinner in regard to repentance, obedience, justification, and regeneration. In point of time, their united language is, 'Behold, now is the accepted time; behold, now is the day of salvation.'

"One act of sin by Adam instantly corrupted human nature. Is it not reasonable to believe that Christ, our second Adam, can as instantly purify the soul when He is fully trusted to do it. Could Adam do in an instant, in corrupting the soul, what it must take our Lord Jesus Christ a lifetime to undo, and call in death in the end, as some think, to complete the work?

"If, as all believe, in a moment a work of such magnitude as regeneration is wrought, imparting spiritual life to a soul, dead in trespasses and sins, and removing its weight of guilt, grief, and doubt, may not the remains of impurity be washed out instantly by the inspiration of the Holy Spirit, that we may perfectly love and worthily magnify His holy name?'

"The fact that inborn sin is a unit, an evil principle or taint infecting our nature, and cannot be removed by parts, any more than its antagonism, the principle of life in Christ, can be imparted gradually in our regeneration, is evidence that sanctification is instantaneous.

"The efficacious, meritorious ground of purity is the atoning blood of Christ. The proximate, conditional source of purity is faith. The instrumental source is the Word of God. The grand efficient agent is the Holy Ghost—'sanctified by the Holy Ghost.' If the work of purification is thus wrought according to the Word of God, it must be instantaneous.

"The uniform experience of all who are clear in the light of personal holiness teaches that purification is instantaneous and not gradual. Experience has but one voice on this subject, *i. e.,* that it was sought by consecration and faith, and received the same as regeneration, by direct divine power. Gradualism does not accord with the experience of those who profess perfect love. The instantaneous does" (*Perfect Love,* pp. 90-92).


### QUESTIONS ON THE TEXT

1. Letting the mind travel back over the previous section and then linking up the present section, state the threefold argument for the instantaneous blessing.

2. Show from the teaching of those who have received it that the blessing may be instantaneously known.

### (3) It Must be Personally Sought

**H**ERE often is the danger point, especially to the studious mind. It is far easier to assent to a doctrine than to seek an experience; but in doing this the results are disastrous. We must not be content to endorse the teaching—we must seek the blessing.

Much has been said and written about the "how" of seeking, and some of these "instructions" would seem more likely to becloud than to clarify the issue.

Broadly speaking, these advisers may be divided into three groups which, for want of better designations, we might label: Takers, Diggers, and Waiters.

*The Takers.* Directing a seeker, their favorite expression is: "Just take it by faith, brother; that is all you need." That is a Scriptural truth (see Acts 15: 8, 9; 26: 18; Mark 11:24; Luke 11:9-13). There is no other way of obtaining this experience, except in the last analysis "taking it by faith." Yet every experienced worker has in mind the many shallow souls who with glib tongue and obvious lack of brokenness and passion will tell how they got it by "just believing." "Take it by faith" is a Scriptural truth, but in practice it is not complete.

*The Diggers.* How often do we hear it: "Keep digging, brother, you'll get through." And how necessary this digging is. Few feel that they have done too much. In foundation work it is surely deep digging that counts (see Luke 6: 48)—digging that unearths hindrances and uncovers hidden things (Joshua 7: 12; 1 Sam. 15: 6-23; Matt. 5: 23, 24). And yet even here there are dangers to be recognized:

(a) That of perpetual self-introspection. A vague, always going deeper, which never gets into the depths and consequently knows no final rest of soul. (b) That of emotional manifestation. A temperamental clutching at feelings which mistakes a momentary wave of emotion for the work of the Holy Ghost.

*The Waiters.* Among these brethren, Acts 1:4 is stressed: "Wait for the promise of the Father." Here also "signs" and manifestations are the order of the day. The fact of "manifestations" may be dismissed for the time being, as we shall meet it again and take it up in a more definite manner.

As to the "waiting," we distinguish between waiting on the Lord and waiting for the Lord in the matter of blessing. Every believer must learn to spend time waiting on God, but in the matter of seeking the experience of entire sanctification the "wait" of Acts 1:4 is distinctively pre-pentecostal and has no significance whatever for the present day. It was a dispensational command, which concerned only those to whom it was given, and stands in comparative value with the words "waiting" and "looked" in Luke 2:25, 38. Concerning the coming of the Savior, Simeon, Anna and others "waited" for the coming Christ, but that by no means put every seeker for salvation under obligation to wait for it. The fact that He has come put an end to all waiting. So with the Holy Ghost, after Pentecost we are never told to wait. The truth is that the ideal way takes in all these.

Summing up the instructions as to the method of seeking, it may be stated as being fivefold:

1. *A Conscious Sense of Need.* Catherine Booth said: "God never gave this gift to any human soul who had not come to the point that he would sell all to get it (*Aggressive Christianity*, p. 8).

Dr. R. A. Torrey declared: "No man ever got this blessing who felt he could get along without it" (*Addresses*).

The Bible aptly describes this need consciousness as "panting," "thirsting," "longing," "fainting," "the heart and flesh crying out," "the soul breaking with longing," "hungering and thirsting" (Psa. 42:1, 2; 63:1; 84:2;

119 : 20; Matt. 5 : 6). In these days such soul hunger is comparatively rare; but once it possesses the soul it is intensely real and, moreover, becomes amazingly resolute, as we shall see.

Hannah Whitehall Smith (Society of Friends): 'I began to long after holiness; I began to groan under the bondage of sin in which I was still held. My whole heart panted after entire conformity to the will of God and unhindered communion with Him" (*Forty Witnesses*).

Anna M. Hammer (noted temperance worker): "Finally a great hunger came upon me" (*Forty Witnesses*, p. 138)

David B. Updegraff (Society of Friends): "Along with this consciousness of depravity and desire for cleanness there came a great hunger and thirst to be filled with all the fullness of God. I longed for a clean heart . . ." (*Forty Witnesses*, p 29)

Dr. J. O. Peck (Methodist): "God never left me a single year without a gracious reward in which many souls were given as seals of my ministry . . . but in the summer of 1872 a deep heart hunger that I had never known began to be realized. I had not lost spirituality so far as I could judge my condition. I longed for I scarcely knew what. I examined myself and prayed more earnestly, but the hunger of my soul grew more imperious. I was not plunged in darkness or conscious of condemnation, yet the inward craving increased" (*Forty Witnesses*, p 296).

Amanda Smith (converted slave; converted, 1856, and twelve years after received the blessing): "I went home, but oh, this hunger and thirst after righteousness. I had no doubt about my acceptance with God. When I was converted it was a conviction of guilt, but now it was a conviction of want."

Thomas Cook (Methodist evangelist and later principal of Cliff College): "My experience was full of fits and

starts; changeable and uneven. I was conscious also of a
mighty want. There seemed a vacuum in my nature which
grace had not filled; a stranger sense of need, which I cannot describe but which all who love the Lord Jesus with less
than perfect love will understand" (*New Testament Holiness, p.* 174).

As we write, names multiply, but here are enough. Now,
for what is this hunger? What is this need? Both Scripture
and witnesses are clear:

It is "after righteousness" (Matt. 5 : 6) ; it is the consciousness of inward corruption and bent to sinning, driving the
soul to God to be made consciously clean. The thought
behind the word is that of straightness. It suggests having
the inward crook removed; the sinful bent straightened out;
and the spiritual nature made akin to God.

Hos. 11 : 7 : "My people are bent to backsliding."

Wesley: "Take away the bent to sinning."

It is "for God" (Psa. 42 : 1, 2 ; 63 : 1; 84 : 2 ; 119 : 20).
All tell the same story, *i. e.,* a conscious craving to possess
God. This will include: Possession of the nature of God
(2 Pet. 1 : 4) ; conformity to the will of God (Rom. 8 : 29) ;
conscious oneness with God (John 17 : 23).

2. *A candid confession of that need.* This is often far
more difficult than it seems, especially if the convicted one
has some reputation in the church.

Too often there is a shaving of corners by a substituting
of the plural for the singular and a confession of the general
instead of the particular.

John Fletcher: "All my righteousness is as filthy
rags. I am a very devil, though of an inferior sort, and if
I am not renewed before I go hence, hell will be my portion
to all eternity." (*Deeper Experiences, pp.* 189-190),

A congregation may say, "We have done those things we
ought not to have done," but a convicted soul seeking deliverance will ultimately cry, "Woe is me, for I am undone. . .

I am unclean . . ." Only a confession of utter bankruptcy and conscious corruption will bring the despairing soul to God. Dr. R. A. Torrey cried: "I cannot take another step in Christian service until I know I am baptized with the Holy Ghost."

3. *A removal of every known hindrance and an utter renunciation of every evil thing.* See Matt. 5 : 23, 24; Acts 5 : 3.

4. *A complete consecration of the whole being to God* (Rom. 6 : 13; 12 : 1, 2; 1 Cor. 6 : 19, 20; 2 Cor. 8 : 5).

This will include all else, both persons and things. Dr. A. M. Hills: "Consecration is the actual present surrender to God of the whole man and all that we possess. Consecration is not an act of feeling but of will" (*Holiness and Power, pp.* 242, 246).

Dr. Asbury Lowrey: "Consecration is a voluntary, unreserved and irrevocable dedication to God with all that pertains to us. It is in nature a repetition of the surrender we made when seeking justification, only it is now enlightened and comprehensive, and made for the attainment of a different and more specific object. A willing mind to be all the Lord's sweeps in everything. When we give all to God we make a summary transfer of ourselves to Him" (*Possibilities of Grace, p.* 310).

Dr. Dougan Clark: "Consecration is not to God's service; not to His work; not to a life of obedience and sacrifice; not to the church, not to the missionary cause, nor even to the cause of God, but to God Himself.

> " 'I am willing
> To receive what Thou givest,
> To lack what Thou withholdest,
> To relinquish what Thou takest,
> To suffer what Thou inflictest,
> To be what Thou requirest,
> To do what Thou commandest. Amen.' "

(Theology of Holiness, pp. 102-104).

Capt. R. Kelso Carter (Methodist) wrote: "Kneeling alone in my mother's room in Baltimore, I made a consecration that covered everything. I have never been compelled to renew it, for it covered all. To die at once—a young man; to live and suffer; to live and recover; to be, to do, to suffer anything for Jesus—that was my consecration. All doubtful things were swept aside and a large margin left on God's side. I knew in my soul I meant every word, and I have never had any doubts about it since" (*Forty Witnesses,* p. 123).

5. *A confident claim upon the resources and faithfulness of God* (Mark 11: 24; Luke 11: 13).

Dr. A. S. Keen: "Are you a child of God seeking full salvation? Seize upon some declaration of God's Word, such as 'The blood of Jesus Christ his Son cleanseth us from all sin.' Apply it to your own heart. Confess it to yourself, to Satan, and to God, that it is true to you, even you, because the Lord hath spoken it. Refuse to believe the lying voice of Satan that it is not so. Let no inward feeling or outward sign dissuade you from your voluntary choice to count God's Word true to yourself, and according to your faith it shall be done unto you. What every seeking soul needs most to know is that it can believe unto salvation if it will, and that choosing to count God's Word as true in the face of every temptation to distrust is faith. Have you given all to Christ? Are you longing to be fully saved? Are you persuaded that

> ' 'Tis the promise of God full salvation to give,
> Unto him who on Jesus His Son will believe.'?

"You may at once begin to sing:

> 'I can, I will, I do believe
> That Jesus saves me now.'

"Should we lose every other line from the volumes of sacred song not extant, and this later couplet remain, we could sing the world to pardon and the church to purity" (*Faith Papers,* pp. 38, 39).

Being now on believing ground, you cannot be refused. Here is your plea:

> "Come, O my God, the promise seal,
>    This mountain, sin, remove;
> Now in my gasping soul reveal
>    The virtue of Thy love.
>
> "I want Thy life, Thy purity,
>    Thy righteousness brought in;
> I ask, desire, and trust in Thee,
>    To be redeemed from sin.
>
> "For this, as taught by Thee, I pray,
>    And can no longer doubt;
> Remove from hence! to sin I say
>    Be cast this moment out.
>
> "Anger and sloth, desire and pride,
>    This moment be subdued!
> Be cast into the crimson tide
>    Of my Redeemer's blood!
>
> "Savior, to Thee my soul looks up,
>    My present Savior Thou!
> In all the confidence of hope,
>    I claim the blessing now.
>
> " 'Tis done! Thou dost this moment save,
>    With full salvation bless;
> Redemption through Thy blood I have,
>    And spotless love and peace."

## QUESTIONS ON THE TEXT

1. Show the difference between endorsing the teaching, and seeking the blessing.

2. Show three classes of advisers concerning the blessing, and point out where they fall short.

3. The method of seeking has been stated as fivefold. Explain this.

# 10

## The Abiding Blessing
### (1) EVIDENCES
### (2) THE SECRET OF GOING ON

**(1) Evidences**

WHILE the fact of our sanctification is in no way dependent on our fluctuating feelings—for feelings are physical, and the work of entire sanctification takes us into a far deeper realm—the blessing received becomes a fact of conscious enjoyment, for the indwelling Holy Spirit gives abundant evidence of His presence. This evidence is threefold:

1. The *witness* of the Spirit.

Answering the question, "What is the character of the evidence of a state of entire sanctification?" Rev. J. A. Wood replies: "It is just as strong, positive, and reliable as can be given to substantiate any fact. Indeed, it is the very strongest of all evidence.

"The testimony of consciousness. This testimony we can no more doubt than we can doubt our existence. No testimony is more certain than this. By it we know we live and breathe, love or hate, sit or stand, or walk, and that we are joyful or sorrowful, happy or wretched. The sanctified soul may be as clearly and fully conscious of purity as the unsanctified is of impurity. While on the one hand pride,

[104]

anger, unbelief, love of the world, are matters of positive consciousness, on the other hand love, peace, humility, patience, faith, are equally so. Indeed, conscience usually speaks louder and clearer in the latter case than in the former, because it has received more gracious energy. Sin paralyzes; grace quickens.

"The testimony of God—'The witness of the Spirit.' This testimony is divine, direct, and positive. The Holy Ghost is the witnessing Spirit.

"He speaks first to the sinner's heart. Every convicted sinner has the witness of the Spirit, testifying to his guilt, condemnation, and exposure to the displeasure of God.

"He speaks to every justified soul. Every truly regenerated soul has, or may have, the witness of the Spirit testifying that he is born of God, and in a state of justification.

"He speaks to every sanctified soul. Every truly sanctified soul has, or may have, the witness of the Spirit testifying that the blood of Jesus Christ hath cleansed him from all sin. Now while all this testimony is given by the infallible Spirit, the latter testimony is given under more favorable circumstances, and, consequently, is quite as clear and strong, if not more so, than either of the others.

"We sum up the testimony as follows:

"(1) The convicted penitent sinner may know by the testimony of his spirit, and the witness of the Holy Spirit, that he is guilty and unsaved. This testimony is stronger and clearer than in the impenitent.

"(2) The justified soul may know, and be equally certain, by the testimony of his spirit and the witness of the Holy Spirit, that God has regenerated his nature, and pardoned his sins. This testimony is stronger and clearer than that of the convicted sinner.

"(3) The sanctified soul may know with equal certainty by his spirit, and the testimony of the Holy Spirit, that God has cleansed his heart from all sin. This testimony is still clearer and stronger than that of the merely regenerated. The inferential and corroborating evidences are equally as strong for the fully sanctified as in either of the other cases" (*Perfect Love, pp.* 119, 120).

Rev. John Wesley: "But how do you know that you are sanctified, saved from your inbred corruption? I can know it no otherwise than I know that I am justified, 'Hereby know we that we are of God, in either sense, 'by the Spirit that he hath given us.' We know it by witness and by the fruit of the Spirit" (*Plain Account of Christian Perfection*).

Bishop O. C. Baker: "We have been accustomed to believe that our standard authors have presented the doctrine of Christian holiness in a very perspicuous light; and if they have never declared that it is the privilege of the sanctified believer to enjoy the direct witness of the Spirit, so far as their influence goes, it would check the panting soul from seeking after the direct evidence of internal purity. May God grant that we may know by happy experience that the doctrine is true, and that the pure in heart enjoy the comforting indwelling of the Holy Spirit, assuring us that sin in us is all destroyed" (*Letter in "Guide,"* 1844).

Dr. Jesse T. Peck: "As surely as the Holy Ghost is our Sanctifier, we may have satisfactory and reliable evidence that we are sanctified wholly, and that evidence must be the witness of the Spirit.

"The soul in which the work is wrought recognizes and understands the divine testimony. It has been aware of a supernatural agency, operating with silent power to produce a state of perfect purity and giving distinct assurance that the work is accomplished" (*The Central Idea of Christianity,* p. 252).

Defining the Witness of the Spirit:

Rev. J. A. Wood: "It is a sweet, inward persuasion of the Spirit that God, for Christ's sake, has either pardoned my sins and regenerated my soul, or that the blood of Jesus Christ has cleansed it from all sin" (*Perfect Love,* p. 121).

"When real faith is exercised, and the work of entire sanctification fully wrought, the witness of the Spirit may be expected, and it is usually apprehended then with greater or less distinctness. Although the witness of the Spirit is usually given in connection with saving faith, yet it may not always be distinctly apprehended as such at the time. It may please the Lord to withhold it temporarily sometimes, in order to teach important lessons and discipline and test the faith of the believer. St. John says, 'He that believeth on the Son of God hath the witness in himself'" (*Perfect Love,* p. 123).

Rev. John Wesley: "By the testimony of the Spirit I mean an inward impression on the soul, whereby the Spirit of God immediately and directly witnesses to my spirit that I am a child of God; that Jesus Christ hath loved me and given Himself for me; that all my sins are blotted out, and I, even I, am reconciled to God.

"Some have the testimony both of their justification and sanctification without any intermission at all, which, I presume, more might have did they walk humbly and closely with God.

"It is inevitably destroyed, not only by the commission of any outward sin, or the omission of any known duty, but by giving way to any inward sin; in a word, by whatever grieves the Holy Spirit of God" (Wesley's *Plain Account of Christian Perfection*).

Dr. R. S. Foster: "The method of the Spirit's witness we do not conceive to be by sensible signs. It may be accompanied by such, but not ordinarily; not by an audible voice, not by a visible manifestation, not by a sensible touch —not anything of this kind; and yet the witness is direct and assured, as much as though accompanied by outward manifestations. It is a consciousness wrought in the soul that a change is effected. The soul takes knowledge of itself, of its own state, and so bears witness to the change; the Spirit of God joins with ours, in that manner in which spirit can impress other spirit, and asserts also the same truth" (*Christian Purity*, p. 227).

Dr. Jesse T. Peck: "There is no audible voice through the outward ear. . . . nor would we call the state of mind produced by the witness of the Spirit an impression; for there is much which is misleading in the doctrine of impressions. . . . We prefer, however, to speak of the mental state produced by the witness of the Spirit as a divine persuasion or conviction of the truth communicated and under the authority of revelation, to a mind suitably prepared; there is no necessity of mistake. . . . God undertakes to make Himself understood and succeeds. . . . There is a spirit-voice to a spirit-ear and the communication is intelligible. . . . To reason ourselves into the belief that we are wholly sanctified in the absence of this witness would be wholly perilous" (*The Central Idea of Christianity*, pp. 252-273). We recommend the students to read the entire section from the book itself, Ch. 5, Section 8, "The Evidence Received").

Bishop W. F. Mallalieu: "It is equally clear and certain that the Holy Spirit does testify to the reality and actual possession of the fullness of the blessing.

"The Spirit witnesses just as definitely to the experience of sanctification as to that of adoption. By whatever name the experience may be called, it is found by the gracious help of the Holy Spirit, and the Spirit will bear witness to His own work.

"This witness may be delayed—it may not come in accordance with preconceived notions, it may not involve any anticipated manifestations, but it will come.

"Let it be clearly understood that the witness of the Holy Spirit does not involve the idea of anything that can be perceived by any or all of the five senses. It is surely not impossible to imagine that the Spirit might communicate with us in this way, and possibly He has done so in some instances; but no one has any good ground for supposing that such will be his experience" (*The Fullness of the Blessing of the Gospel of Christ,* pp. 58-60).

Rev. C. W. Ruth: "The witness of the Spirit is the divine assurance, the voice of God in the soul, that gives the conviction or knowledge to our inner consciousness that the blessing sought is now mine" (*Entire Sanctification a Second Blessing,* p. 93).

While not to be confused with mere emotionalism, the fact of such an experience is not likely to be entirely destitute of emotion.

Rev. J. A. Wood: "There is doubtless as great a variety as in justification and regeneration. Some are exercised in one way, some in another; some have one class of emotions, and some another. Sometimes there is an unusual illumination of soul. Sometimes a sweet resting and sinking into Christ. Sometimes great joy and ecstasy, though this is not the general experience. Sometimes there is an astonishing increase of faith, and assurance that all sin is gone. Sometimes an overwhelming sense of the divine presence. Sometimes the cleansing energy comes in a mighty torrent, and sometimes in a gentle breeze. Glory to God! although there is a diversity of operation both with respect to the divine and human spirit, yet the blessed results are the same. Let us never mark out a way for God, but seek the cleansing power of the Holy Ghost, until it comes, just as he is pleased to manifest it.

"Let the prayer of your heart be:

> 'Come as thou wilt—I that resign—
> But oh, my Jesus, come.'

"Sanctified souls are inclined to name the blessing after their principal sensations, harmonizing with their emotional experience.

"One person realizes principally a marked increase of faith, and he calls it 'the rest of faith.'

"Another is conscious of a deep, sweet resting in Christ, and he calls it 'resting in God.'

"Another is permeated with a sense of the divine presence, and filled with ecstatic rapture, and calls it 'the fullness of God.'

"Another feels his heart subdued, melted, refined and filled with God, and calls it 'holiness.'

"Another realizes principally a river of sweet, holy love flowing through the soul, and he calls it 'perfect love.'

"Another is prostrated under the power of the refining and sin-killing Spirit, and calls it 'the baptism of the Holy Ghost.'

"And another realizes principally a heaven of sweetness in complete submission to God, and he calls it 'entire sanctification.'

"While another may feel clearly and strongly conscious of complete conformity to all the will of God, and call it 'Christian perfection.' If genuine, the work wrought in each case is essentially the same" (*Perfect Love,* pp. 124, 125).

2. The *manifestation* of the Spirit. By "manifestation" here we do not mean anything in the nature of the spectacular. (The gifts of the Spirit will be dealt with elsewhere. We are rather concerned with that consistent outworking which betokens His perpetual indwelling, giving power in service, unction in prayer, and fragrance in the life (see John 7: 37-39).

3. The *fruit* of the Spirit. Says Rev. John Wesley, answering the question, "By what fruit of the Spirit may we know that we are of God?" "By love, joy, peace, always

abiding; by invariable longsuffering, patience, resignation; by gentleness triumphing over all provocation; by goodness, mildness, sweetness, tenderness of spirit; by fidelity, simplicity, godly sincerity; by meekness, calmness, and evenness of Spirit; by temperance, not only in food and sleep, but in all things natural and spiritual" (*Plain Account of Christian Perfection*). See Gal. 5:22, 23.

This "Fruit of the Spirit" is not the production of our natural energy but it is the spontaneous product of the divine life within the soul.

### QUESTIONS ON THE TEXT

1. What may be said to be the three-fold evidence of the Spirit's presence within the believer?

2. Show the difference between fluctuating feelings and the witness of the Spirit.

3. What do we mean when we speak of "the manifestation of the Spirit?"

4. Discuss the fruit of the Spirit.

## (2) The Secret of Going On

IT is one thing to start in the holy way, but quite another thing to endure.

1. A note of *warning*. This glorious blessing may be lost. We quote from Wesley. Numerous references to and illustrations of this vital fact are found in his writings which, for lack of space, we limit here to five:

a. Sermons. "It is a common thing for those who are sanctified to believe they can not fall; to suppose themselves pillars in the temple of God to go out no more. Nevertheless, we have seen some of the strongest of them, after a time, moved from their steadfastness. Sometimes suddenly, but oftener by slow degrees, they have yielded to temptation; and pride, or anger, or foolish desires have again sprung up in their hearts. Nay, sometimes they have utterly lost the life of God, and sin hath regained dominion over them.

"Several of these, after being thoroughly sensible of their fall and deeply ashamed before God, have been filled again with love, and not only perfected therein, but stablished, strengthened, and settled. They have received the blessing they had before with abundance."

b. *To Miss Jane Hilton* (1769) : "I rejoice to hear that you stand fast in the liberty wherewith Christ hath made you free; and the more because, although many taste of that heavenly gift, deliverance from inbred sin, yet so few, so exceedingly few, retain it for one year; hardly one in ten; nay, one in thirty. Many hundreds in London were made partakers of it within sixteen or eighteen months; but I doubt whether twenty of them are now as holy and happy as they were."

c. *To Mrs. Elizabeth Bennis* (1769) : "Some years since I was inclined to think that none who had once enjoyed and then lost the pure love of God must ever look to enjoy it again until they were just stepping into eternity. But experience has taught us better things; we have at present numerous instances of those who had cast away that unspeakable blessing, and now enjoy it in a larger measure than ever."

d. *To Miss Jane Hilton* (1770) : Two things are certain: the one, that it is possible to lose even the pure love of God; the other, that it is not necessary—it is not unavoidable; it may be lost, but it may be kept. Accordingly, we have some in every part of the kingdom who have never been moved from their stedfastness. And from this moment you need never be moved; His grace is sufficient for you. But you must continue to grow if you continue to stand; for no one can stand still" (*Journal*, July, 1774).

e.  "I went to Sheffield, and on Tuesday met the Select Society. But it was reduced from sixty to twenty; and but half of these retained all that they once received! What a grievous error, to think those that are once saved from sin can not lose what they have gained! It is a miracle if they do not, seeing all earth and hell are enraged against them."

2.  A Word of *Direction*—How this blessing may be retained. While it is evident that the soul has no ground for presumption, it is also clear that there is every reason for confidence. It is the will of God that we should enjoy an unbroken continuance of this glorious experience.

Five simple words will comprehend all that needs to be said concerning direction here:

a.  *Abide:* Remember, this experience is not primarily something you are to "live up to" but to "live in." It is a life, a sphere, a spiritual contact.

Read John 15: 1-10. Note the expressions "abide" and "in me." This continual abiding knows nothing of the need of periodical re-consecration, but steps into each new ray of light as it is given, and thus continually walks with God.

b.  *Obey:* Here let it be remembered that true obedience is not the sudden rush at some blind impulse, but the intelligent "Yes, Lord!" to the known will of God. When you know God's will, obey promptly, but if you are not sure then wait! Light will come.

c.  *Watch:* This word takes in far more than at first it seems, and covers every sphere. There will be that rigorous watch of oneself, which on the other hand must not be allowed to deteriorate into a morbid self-introspection.

"If you want to be discontented—look within.

"If you want to be distracted—look around.

"If you want to be delivered—look to Jesus."

Continual self-introspection is extremely unwise and is bound to end in disaster. Moods must not be allowed to regulate experience.

There is, however, a self-examination which will deepen our lives.

The following rules of the saintly John Fletcher, if faithfully practiced, can but result in great spiritual blessing.

1. Did I awake spiritual, and was I watchful in keeping my mind from wandering this morning?

2. Have I this day got nearer to God in prayer, or have I given way to a lazy, idle spirit?

3. Has my faith been weakened by a lack of watchfulness, or quickened by diligence?

4. Have I walked by faith, and have I seen God in all things?

5. Have I made the most of my time as I have had light, strength and opportunity?

6. Have I kept the issues of my heart in the means of grace, so as to profit by them?

7. What have I done this day for the souls and bodies of God's dear saints?

8. Have I laid out anything to please myself, when I might have saved money for the cause of God?

9. Have I governed well my tongue this day, remembering that "in the multitude of words there wanteth not sin"?

10. In how many instances have I denied myself this day?

11. Do my life and conversation adorn the gospel of Jesus Christ?

d. *Pray:* Let nothing crowd out the precious season which the soul loves to spend with its beloved. Have set prayer periods. Cultivate that underflow of constant communion.

e. *Witness:* Take care not to presume even here. Don't

make your "holiness talk" so cheap and light that people will be inclined to turn some other way rather than meet you. But on every suitable occasion as He leads, tell out the glorious witness to full salvation.

## QUESTIONS ON THE TEXT

1. Show that the experience of full salvation may be lost.
2. Show how this blessing may be retained.

# 11

## Distinctions

**(1) THE HUMAN VESSEL AND THE DIVINE INDWELLING. (2) THE PRESENCE OF TEMPTATION AND THE ABSENCE OF SIN. (3) THE PRESENCE OF INFIRMITY AND THE ABSENCE OF SIN. (4) PURITY AND MATURITY.**

**(1) The Human Vessel and the Divine Indwelling** THERE is a distinct human side to this experience of entire sanctification, for "we have this treasure in earthen vessels" (2 Cor. 4:7), and therefore we "groan in our earthly house" (2 Cor. 5:1, 2), "waiting for the redemption of our body" (Rom. 8:23), for we have not yet "attained unto the resurrection out from among the dead" (Phil. 3:11, 12). It is necessary, therefore, to maintain a clear balance of thought with regard to these things, recognizing the distinct limitations of the human side.

"We have this treasure"—That is the ground of our confidence.

"In earthen vessels"—That is the ground of our humiliation.

In fact, that is the designation of the English Revised

[116]

Version and the American Standard Version concerning our body—"The body of our humiliation" (Phil 3 : 21).

The "earthen vessels" are in contrast to the "treasure" which they contain. The figure is startling, *lit.*, "An earthenware jar filled with deity." The word used suggests the material of a terra cotta tile—clay; brittle; of the earth; yet in it is made to dwell the very treasure of God. The contrast is so marked that human pride is utterly abased, so that no one really God-possessed could ever say, "What a wonderful man am I," but would be bound to exclaim, "What a condescending God is He."

1.   Since we have this treasure in earthen vessels we are bound by *limitations*.

There are many things which we do not and cannot know. Holiness is not omniscience, nor even super-intelligence.

There are many things which we cannot do. Holiness is not omnipotence nor even super-ability.

There are many things which we do, which if at the time of doing them we could see all the far-reaching issues, we might do differently. Holiness is not immutability—nor even human par excellence. The Holy Spirit within does not turn a person into a wizard or a superman, but works through him according to the limitations of "a man in Christ Jesus."

2.   Since we have this treasure in earthen vessels we are subject to *temptations*. See Matt. 26 : 41; 6 : 13; Gal. 6 : 1; James 1 : 13-15; 1 Cor. 10 : 13; 2 Pet. 2 : 9; Heb. 2 : 18; 4 : 15; James 1 : 2, 3, 4, 12.

Rev. Thomas Cook: "It is a mistake to suppose that there is any state of grace this side of heaven which puts a Christian where he is exempt from temptation. So long as a soul is on probation it will be tested by solicitations to sin. It is true, when the heart is cleansed from all evil the warfare within ceases. The struggle with the flesh, or inbred sin, or depravity, by whatever name it may be called, comes to an end when all antagonisms to God are expelled from the soul and Christ reigns without a rival. But there are other enemies than those which exist within, against whom we shall have to fight strenuously to the end" (*New Testament Holiness,* p. 15).

On this question of temptation Rev. J. A. Wood asks and answers the following questions: "Does Christian perfection exclude a liability to temptation?

"It does not. Adam and Eve were tempted in Eden. Our Savior was tempted. Temptation does not imply any necessity to sin, nor necessarily any tendency in the mind to sin. The fact that a man is tempted is no proof that he is sinful, or inclined to sin. An unfelt trial is no trial, and pain of mind, in itself, is no more sin than pain of body. Even Jesus 'suffered being tempted' (Heb. 2:18). If temptation is incompatible with holiness, then He was unholy. He had a long and bitter siege of temptation during forty days in the wilderness. He was tempted even to kneel down and worship the devil. He was 'in all points tempted like as we are, yet without sin.' If temptation is inconsistent with holiness, then Adam and Eve were unholy before their fall. A liability to temptation is an unchangeable condition of probation. So long as we are in the world, so long as Satan goeth about as a roaring lion, seeking whom he may devour, so long as we have five senses which come in contact with a world abounding with evil, we may expect to be tempted. It is no sin to be tempted, provided proper caution has been used to avoid the occasions of temptation.

"Are the temptations of the entirely sanctified soul the same as those of persons merely regenerated?

"While they are essentially the same, yet the temptations of each are peculiar to themselves. The temptations of the entirely sanctified are usually sharper and shorter than others. They are also entirely from without; there being no foes within a sanctified heart, all is peaceful, friendly, and

right there. The temptations of a sanctified soul find no
favorable response from within, while those of the unsanctified do, more or less. In the one case, temptations find
corrupt inclinations in the heart in their favor; in the other,
they find none. An entirely sanctified soul is tempted just
as others are from without, and while his temptations tend
in common with temptations of those not entirely sanctified,
to the excitement of desires, he does not allow them to take
hold of the desires. His heart is in a moral condition where
he arrests them at this point, and successfully repels them.
He may be tempted as much intellectually, but certainly not
so much sensitively, as his passions and appetites are pervaded and purified by the presence and power of the divine
spirit, and the inward tendency is towards God. In the one
case temptation finds no inward sympathy or tendency to
evil; in the other, it may find more or less of desire or
inclination to side with it. An inclination to side with
temptation, if known to be an evil, or temptation, is evidence of indwelling sin, as that is the principal way
depravity is manifest—in wrong leanings or sinward inclinations.

"Wrong tendencies are the expression of a back-lying corrupt state, and when this corruption is cleansed away, the
tendency ceases" (*Perfect Love,* pp. 61, 62).

Dr. G. Peck: "The great difference between the temptations of those who are entirely sanctified and those who
are not is that the temptation, coming into contact with
the latter, often stirs the sediment of corrupion, while
assaulting with equal violence the former, it meets with uniform resistance, and leaves no trace behind but an increase
of moral power and the fruits of a new triumph" (*Christian Perfection,* p. 433).

3.   Since we have this treasure in earthen vessels we are
liable to *mistakes.* Mistakes arise from the infirmity of our
human nature, which is to be remedied only by the resur-

rection, and to this we have not "already attained," neither are we in this sense "already perfect" (see Phil. 3:12).

Yet we may be human without being sinful.

### QUESTIONS ON THE TEXT

1. Show the distinction between the "vessel" and the "treasure."

2. Show that since we are human we are bound by limitations.

3. Show that since we are human we are subject to temptations.

4. Show that since we are human we are liable to mistakes.

5. Show that limitations, temptations and mistakes may exist without sin.

### (2) The Presence of Temptation and the Absence of Sin

WE have already seen that since "we have this treasure in earthen vessels," we are always subject to temptation. This fact has baffled some, for they have not yet so clarified their thinking as to be able to distinguish between the two vitally different facts of temptation and sin. Hence in the conflict hour they slump and allow Satan to rob them of their confidence.

Two simple statements will help us to find solid ground here:

1. *Temptation is ever the lot of the holiest souls while in this mortal state; but sin may forever cease.*

That it is not a sin to be tempted is proved from these facts:

Our first parents were tempted in their original innocency (see Gen. 3). No condemnation came to them until they yielded to the tempter's snare.

Joseph was tempted in Egypt (see Gen. 39). Although only seventeen years of age, he stood the test and came out of the conflict with a soul as pure as when he went in.

Our Lord Himself was tempted in the wilderness, beside the fact of perpetual harassment from His subtle foe. But He never yielded, and for thirty-three years kept His soul free from sin (see Matt. 4:1-11; Heb. 7:26).

2. *There is a place, however, where temptation ends and sin, with all its dreadful condemnation, really begins.*

Rev. J. A. Wood: "No temptation or evil suggestion to the mind becomes sin till it is cherished or tolerated. Sin consists in yielding to temptation. So long as the soul maintains its integrity so that temptation finds no sympathy within, no sin is committed and the soul remains unharmed, no matter how protracted or severe the fiery trial may prove" (*Perfect Love*, p. 63).

Dr. G. Peck: "First, I suppose all will admit that when the temptation gains the concurrence of the will the subject contracts guilt. There can be no doubt here. Secondly, it is equally clear that when the temptation begets in the mind a desire for the forbidden object, the subject enters into temptation, and so sins against God. Thirdly, it is also clear that temptation cannot be invited or unnecessarily protracted without an indication of a sinful tendency toward the forbidden object, and consequently, such a course not only implies the absence of entire sanctification, but involves the subject in actual guilt" (*Christian Perfection*, p. 435).

Bishop Foster: "To this most difficult question we answer, sin begins whenever the temptation begins to find inward sympathy, if known to be a solicitation to sin. So long as it is promptly, and with the full and hearty concurrence of the soul, repelled, there is no indication of inward sympathy; there is no sin" (*Christian Purity*, p. 55).

Rev. Thomas Cook: "Some precious souls are in constant bondage because they have never been taught to discriminate between evil thoughts and thoughts about evil. They must discern between the things that differ. So long as we are in the world, and so long as we have five senses coming in contact with a world abounding with evil, Satan will be sure to use these as avenues of temptation. But no taint comes on the spirit from temptation which is at once and utterly rejected. It may and should be instantly repelled. Milton says:

> 'Evil into the mind of God or man
> May come and go, so unapproved, and leave
> No spot or blame behind.'

"It may seem difficult to some to ascertain whether certain states of mind are the result of temptation or the uprisings of evil in their own nature. But when suggestions of evil awaken no response and kindle no desire, when they cause a shudder and a recoil, when they are opposed to our usual inclinations and desires, and cause pain, we may safely conclude that they are from without and not from within, and no self-reproach need ensue.

"An evil thought springs from evil existing in the heart, but a thought about evil is a suggestion flashed upon the mind by what we see or hear, or by the law of association, or by the enemy of souls. Those who are holy have no evil within, consequently, no evil thoughts; but intruding thoughts and whispers of evil will often need to be resisted. These are an unchangeable condition of probation. Provided proper caution has been used to avoid occasions of temptation, 'no spot of blame' is left behind, any more than the shadow of a cloud passing over a beautiful lake disturbs or defiles it. It is not temptation, but the yielding to it, that is sinful, and there is a condition in which we may, with St. Paul, always triumph.

"Temptation is first presented to the intellect, flashed,

it may be in a moment, the thoughts are appealed to—this is the earliest stage of temptation. Thence it is transmitted to the sensibilities, in which region it operates upon the senses, appetites, passions, or emotions. There is a danger lest these be excited with a desire for gratification. A critical stage of temptation is now reached, but no guilt is necessarily contracted. In the case of those whose hearts are not entirely cleansed from sin, the temptation finds more or less inward sympathy, but there is no guilt incurred unless the evil suggestion is cherished or tolerated. The will has yet to be challenged, and upon its decision depends entirely whether the tempter is to be successful or not. If the will says 'No' to the temptation, the tempter is foiled and defeated, and the soul comes off more than conqueror. . . .

"Holiness makes none so secure that he cannot sin, but it gives him to possess all the elements of strength and stability. Though the warfare may be long and severe, yet, by abiding in Christ, victory may be constant and complete" (*New Testament Holiness,* pp. 17-19).

Samuel Rutherford: "The devil is but a whetstone to sharpen the faith and patience of the saints. I know that he but heweth and polisheth stones all the time for the New Jerusalem."

The distinction between the two may be set forth in the following statements:

Temptation comes unsolicited and undesired, while sin must have the consent of the will.

Temptation comes with divine permission, but sin brings divine condemnation.

Temptation may have definite beneficial results, but sin is always injurious.

None can deliberately sin without being eternally the worse for it; the wound, though healed, leaves the warrior weaker for the experience. Every victorious conflict leaves a stronger soul. 'Each victory will help you some other to win.'

We conclude with a quotation from Dr. R. T. Williams: "The sanctified person has a great advantage over the unsanctified in the matter of temptation. Not in the number of temptations, as it is possible that Satan will try harder to break down a sanctified life; and, too, the sanctified person is opposed and persecuted more by the people, even in some cases apparently good people, than the unsanctified person is.

"The advantage in favor of the sanctified is in the inner condition of the soul. The justified are on God's side, they are saved, they hate sin, they are living for the next world. They are not of this world, but they are fighting the carnal mind. In conversion the carnal mind is conquered but not destroyed. There is therefore a struggle not only with outside influences but a fight to keep this inner enemy down and conquered. This fallen nature, this inbred sin, throws its weight of influence with any desire that would tend to lead one wrong. This sinful self is against God and the efforts of the justified man to obey God.

"The sanctified man does not have this alien enemy within him to take sides against him in the battle with temptation. His fight within is only with a human nature. Instead of a carnal nature within him to aid the enemy without, he has the Holy Ghost enthroned within without a rival, having a pure heart filled with God. It is consequently easier for him to live the Christian life and be an overcomer" (*A Neglected Theme*, pp. 78, 79).

### QUESTIONS ON THE TEXT

1. It is not a sin to be tempted. Prove this.
2. Show where temptation gives place to sin.
3. State three distinctions between temptation and sin.

**(3) The Presence of Infirmity and the Absence of Sin**

AS with temptation, so it is with infirmity—we must distinguish between this and sin. At this point there is much confusion. The trouble arose with Augustine, and following him, Calvin, and later the general Calvinistic schools of thought, all of whom so crudely confound the carnal nature within the believer with the essential human nature that they fail to distinguish between the things which vitally differ.

The *Confessions of St. Augustine* will indicate this line of thought, especially in Book X. To Augustine, human nature is irrecoverably bad. Not even the Calvary work of the Son of God can liberate it from its corruption in this life. A bad dream is an indication of a bad heart. Pleasure in taking food is sinful, and even the love of music is wrong (see *Confessions of St. Augustine,* Bk. X).

This, of course, is extreme; but it is out of this teaching that the modern "must sin" theory has evolved, insisting that, constituted as we are since the Fall, sin is inevitable, but through our believing, though persistently sinning, "Calvary covers it all." Such teaching we cannot endorse. Until we have learned to distinguish between the infirmities of our humanity and the sins resulting from carnality, we have failed in our comprehension of one of the most vital distinctions in the spiritual life.

Rev. John Fletcher: "An infirmity is a breach of Adam's paradisical perfection, which our covenant God does not require of us now; and evangelically speaking, a sin for a Christian is a breach of Christ's evangelical law of Christian perfection; a perfection this, which God requires of all believers.

"An infirmity, considering it with the error which it occasions, is consistent with pure love to God and man; but a sin is inconsistent with that love: an infirmity is free from guile, and has its roots in our animal frame; but a sin is attended with guile, and has its roots in our moral frame, springing either from the habitual corruption of our heart, or from the momentary perversion of our tempers: an infirmity unavoidably results from our unhappy circumstances, and from the necessary infelicitous weakness of our present state; but a sin flows from the avoidable and perverse choice of our own will: an infirmity has its foundation in an involuntary want of light and power; and a sin is a willful abuse of the present light and power we have. The one arises from involuntary ignorance and weakness, and is always attended with a good meaning, a meaning unmixed with any bad design or wicked prejudice; but the other has its source in voluntary perverseness and presumption, and is always attended with a meaning altogether bad; poor at least, with a good meaning founded on wicked prejudices."

Rev. John Wesley: "Question: Do you affirm that this perfection excludes all infirmities, ignorance, and mistake?

"Answer: I continually affirm quite the contrary, and have always done so.

"Question: But how can every thought, word, and work be governed by pure love, and the man be subject at the same time to ignorance and mistake?

"Answer: I see no contradiction here. A man may be filled with pure love and still liable to mistake. Indeed I do not expect to be freed from actual mistake until this mortal puts on immortality. I believe this to be a natural consequence of the soul's dwelling in flesh and blood. For we cannot now think at all, but by the meditation of these bodily organs, which have suffered equally with the rest of our frame. And hence we cannot avoid thinking wrong, till this corruption shall have put on incorruption.

"We may carry this thought further yet. A mistake in judgment may possibly occasion a mistake in practice. For instance, Mr. DeRenty's mistake touching the nature of mortification, arising from prejudice of education, occasioned that practical mistake, his wearing an iron girdle. And a thousand such instances there may be, even in those who are in the highest state of grace. Yet where every word and action springs from love, such a mistake is not properly a sin; however, it cannot bear the rigor of God's justice, but needs the atoning blood.

"Question: But how can a liableness to mistake consist with perfect love? Is not a person who is perfected in love every moment under its influence? And can any mistake flow from pure love?

"Answer: I answer, 1. Mistakes may consist with pure love. 2. Some may accidentally flow from it. I mean love itself may incline us to mistake. The pure love of our neighbor springing from the love of God, 'thinketh no evil,' 'believeth and hopeth all things.' Now this very temper, unsuspicious, ready to believe and hope the best of all men, may occasion our thinking some men better than they really are. Here is a manifest mistake, accidentally flowing from pure love" (*Plain Account of Christian Perfection*).

Rev. J. A. Wood: "Question: Does Christian perfection exclude the infirmities of human nature?

"Answer: It does not. Freedom from these is not to be expected in this world. We must wait for deliverance from these until this mortal puts on immortality. These infirmities, so numerous and various, are the common inheritance of humanity. They are not sins; they are innocent; and although they may be our misfortune, they are included in the 'all things' which, by the grace and blessing of God, shall work together for our good. Although Christian perfection does not admit of any outward or inward sin, properly so called, yet it does admit of strong convictions of numberless infirmities and imperfections, such as slowness of understanding, errors of judgment, mistakes in practice, erratic imaginations, a treacherous memory, etc. If it be claimed that these innocent infirmities need the blood of Atonement, praise the Lord, the blood of Jesus meets every demand.

"Question: Is it important to distinguish between inbred sin and the innocent infirmities of fallen human nature?

"Answer: It is; otherwise we may on the one hand blame and afflict ourselves needlessly; or, on the other, excuse ourselves from blame when we are really culpable. An intelligent, faithful Christian will wisely discriminate between them, and seek the extirpation of the one, and patiently endure the burdens of the other. Mr. Wesley says, 'Let those who do call them sins beware how they confound these defects with sins, properly so called' (*Plain Account*).

"Inbred sin is a carnal principle or root remaining in the unsanctified heart, sending up sprouts of bitterness which cling to the desires and appetites. It is the source of moral evils, such as envy, pride, stubbornness, malice, anger, jealousy, unbelief, fretfulness, impatience, revenge, covetousness—everything opposed to the will of God.

"Human infirmities are various and numerous, such as mental aberrations, sophistical reasonings, treacherous memory, erratic imaginations, involuntary ignorance, and all those frailties and defects which may co-exist with the very best intentions.

"St. Paul recognizes this distinction; he writes to Timothy, 'Them that sin rebuke before all, that others may also fear,' and yet he writes to the Romans, 'We that are strong should bear with the infirmities of the weak.' Here are two plain commands; the first, not to bear with sins, and the second, to bear with infirmities.

"Many who reject the doctrine of Christian perfection confound infirmities and sins. Infirmities may entail regret and humiliation, but not guilt. Sin always produces guilt" (*Perfect Love*, pp. 65, 66).

Dr. Daniel Steele: "Infirmities are failures to keep the law of perfect obedience given to Adam in Eden. This law no man on earth can keep, since sin has impaired the powers of universal humanity. Sins are offences against the law of Christ, which is epitomized by John, 'And this is the commandment, that we should believe on the name of his Son Jesus Christ, and love one another' (1 John 3: 23).

"Infirmities are an involuntary outflow from our imperfect moral organization. Sin is always voluntary.

Infirmities have their ground in our physical nature, and they are aggravated by intellectual deficiencies. But sin roots itself in our moral nature, springing either from the habitual corruption of our hearts or from the unresisting perversion of our tempers.

"Infirmities entail regret and humiliation. Sin always produces guilt.

"Infirmities in well-instructed souls do not interrupt communion with God. Sin cuts the telegraphic communication with heaven.

"Infirmities, hidden from ourselves, are covered by the blood of Christ without a definite act of faith, in the case of the soul vitally united with Him. On the great Day of Atonement the errors of the individual Hebrew were put away through the blood of sprinkling, without offering a special victim for himself. 'But unto the second [tabernacle] went the high priest alone once every year, not without blood, which he offered for himself, and for the errors of the people' (Heb. 9: 7). Sins demand a special personal resort to the blood of sprinkling and an act of reliance on Christ.

"Infirmities are without remedy so long as we are in this body. Sins, by the keeping power of Christ, are avoidable through every hour of our regenerate life. Both of these truths are in Jude's ascription, 'Now unto him that is able to keep you from falling [into sin, or as the *Vulgate* reads, *sine peccato,* without sin] and present you faultless [without infirmity, not here, but] in the presence of his glory with exceeding joy.' Jude understood the distinction between faults, or infirmities, and sins. In this scheme of Christian perfection, faults are to disappear in the life to come, but we are to be saved from sins now.

"A thousand infirmities are consistent with perfect love, but not one sin.

"Thus we see on undisputed authority we may be conscious of human weakness yet well pleasing to God" (*Mile-Stone Papers,* pp. 44-47).

### QUESTIONS ON THE TEXT

1. Show the difference between temptation and infirmity.
2. Show the difference between infirmity and sin.
3. What was Mr. Wesley's position here?

### (4) Purity and Maturity

AS we have already seen, entire sanctification is a work of purification (pages 48-59), and this experience is by no means stagnant, but facilitates growth in grace (pages 69-73). Some, however, find it difficult to reconcile these two ideas, contending that a soul entirely delivered from sin would have reached the climax of spiritual experience and would be incapable of further development in this world. "Moreover," they argue, "the great Apostle Paul made no such profession. Indeed, he definitely declared, 'Not that I have already attained, either were already perfect, but I follow after.'" What a pity it is that so many are content to speak so glibly instead of pausing for a while to think seriously. Did Paul here say that he had not attained heart purity? Just what was it that Paul had "not already attained," and in what sense did he declare himself "neither already perfect"? Let the context be carefully read for the answer (Phil 3: 7-15).

The key to the problem lies in the fact that there is a distinct difference between purity and maturity; one is the heritage of faith, while the other is only the result of growth.

Rev. Thomas Cook: "There are various degrees of impurity, but, strictly speaking, there are no degrees of purity. According to Webster, the word 'pure' means 'entire separation from all heterogeneous and extraneous matter, clear, free from mixture; as pure water, pure air, pure silver or gold.'

"The word in the New Testament which is most frequently translated 'pure' occurs in some of its forms nearly seventy times... The idea is that that which is pure consists of one thing; it is uncompounded, without mixture or adulteration; it has all that belongs to it and nothing else. Gold that is free from alloy, unmixed with any baser metal, we call pure gold; milk that contains all that belongs to milk, and nothing else, is pure milk; honey that is without wax is pure honey. In like manner, a pure heart contains nothing adverse to God. Where there is mixture there cannot be purity. By purity of heart we mean that which is undefiled, untainted, free from evil stains, without earthly alloy. ... Purity is the removal of whatever God could not admit into His immediate presence, and fellowship with Himself; in other words, the abolition of sin itself.

"By maturity we mean all this, and much more. The error of confusing purity of heart with maturity of Christian character lies at the base of nearly all the objections made to instantaneous and entire sanctification. Identifying and confounding these have occasioned most of the difficulties we find among Christians in reference to this doctrine.

"The Scriptures always discriminate between purity of heart and ripeness and fulness of Christian virtues. The one is the work wrought within us in a moment by the omnipotent power of the sanctifying Spirit, and the other a natural process involving culture and discipline. Purity has reference to kind or quality, but maturity has respect to degree or quantity. . . . Holiness is both a gift and a process, and as such is both instantaneous and gradual" (*New Testament Holiness; pp.* 39, 40).

Rev. J. A. Wood: "Identifying purity and maturity as the same makes serious confusion, and is the occasion of nearly all the objections made to instantaneous sanctification. Christian purity is a present privilege and duty, and differs from maturity, which is largely a subsequent attainment, subject to the laws of growth, involving time and a progressive religious life.

"Christian maturity is indefinite and comparative. There are 'babes,' 'young men' and 'men full age' in a state of entire sanctification. There is a difference in entire sanctification in its beginning, in its infancy, and in its maturity as an advanced, established and confirmed state of purity. One just fully sanctified, and the other so grown and developed as to be 'rooted and grounded in love.'

"Maturity is not a condition of admittance into heaven, while purity is. The heart may be cleansed from all sin, while the Christian graces are immature, and the cleansing is a preparation for their rapid, unhindered and symmetrical growth.

"Maturity can be predicated only of age, time, culture, discipline and growth, in which, after the heart is fully cleansed, the process of enlightenment, enrichment, adornment, and endowment with love and power may be carried forward more easily than ever before, as the destruction and

death of sin gives free scope to a life of righteousness"
(*Mistakes Respecting Christan Holiness*, pp. 71-73).

"Is there a distinction between purity and maturity?

"There is, and a very important one. Identifying and confounding these lie at the base of nearly every objection made to an instantaneous sanctification; and has occasioned many strange notions, and much confusion upon this subject.

"Purity has respect to moral cleanness or freedom from the defilement of sin. 'Wash me, and I shall be whiter than snow.' Health is not manhood. Maturity has respect to moral stature and strength—to adulthood. 'The fullness of the measure of the stature of Christ.'

"Purity, in the light of gospel provisions, is a present privilege and duty. 'Be ye holy.' Maturity is a question of time, and is subject to the laws of growth and development. 'Grow in grace.'

"Purity, being instantaneous, may be received at once. 'Believe on the Lord Jesus Christ, and thou shalt be saved.' Maturity is a gradual, progressive ,and indefinite development. 'Take heed,' and 'add to your faith virtue,' etc.

"No Christian is cleansed into maturity, nor do any grow into purity. The Bible nowhere promises maturity as a work of God by faith, but purity it does. Even 'a babe in Christ' may be cleansed from all inbred sin and become a pure Christian; but a 'babe in Christ' becomes 'a young man,' and 'a father,' by growth and development, and not by cleansing power.

"It must be seen that there is a difference between purity or entire sanctification, in infancy—as just received—and in maturity, as an advanced and confirmed state of purity, 'rooted and grounded in love.' There are 'babes,' 'young men' and 'men of full age' in a state of entire sanctification.

"There are two classes of commands and figures in the Scriptures in regard to Christian character and duty. One contains commands and figures enjoining and illustrating growth in grace and maturity; the other class enjoins and illustrates Christian holiness or purity.

"Maturity is nowhere made a condition of entrance into heaven, while purity is. Millions of Christians die in immaturity and are saved: they have been made pure, which is the moral qualification for heaven" (*Perfect Love,* pp. 84, 85).

The distinction between purity and maturity may be set forth as follows:

Purity is the entrance into Canaan—maturity is the possession of the land.

Purity is received—maturity is acquired.

Purity is the work of a moment—maturity is the harvest of years.

Purity is always received by faith—maturity is often reached through pain.

Purity has to do with quality—maturity has to do with quantity.

Purity fits the soul for heaven—maturity acquires material for reward.

Purity brings fellowship—maturity develops experience.

## QUESTIONS ON THE TEXT

1.  What was Paul's position with regard to heart purity?

2.  Discuss the answer to the previous question in the light of Phil 3: 7-15.

3.  Show maturity in contrast to purity.

# 12

## Dangers

### WHAT THE SANCTIFIED SOUL MUST AVOID

THE experience of sanctification has its peculiar dangers. The Psalmist speaks of a "terror by night," an "arrow that flieth by day," a "pestilence that walketh in darkness," and a "destruction that wasteth at noonday" (Psalm 91).

Whether each of these is to be taken as having its spiritual counterpart may be a question for discussion. There is, however, a "noonday" experience of grace.

> "Where the flowers bloom for ever
> And the sun is always bright."
>
> (See Isa. 58: 10.)

This "noonday" experience has its "wasting destruction" or, in New Testament phraseology, the soul knowing the experience of life "in the heavenlies" finds the necessity for "wrestling, not against flesh and blood, but against the principalities, against the powers, against the world-rulers of this darkness, against the spiritual hosts of wickedness in the heavenly realms" (Eph. 6: 12). There are "wiles of the devil" against which he must learn to "stand" (Eph.

6 : 11), for he now finds that life in the Holy Ghost is not a vacation but a vocation indeed.

We are to beware "Lest any man should beguile us with enticing words" (Col. 2 : 4, 18) ; and to take heed "lest as the serpent beguiled Eve through his subtilty, so our minds should be corrupted from the simplicity that is in Christ. . . . for Satan himself is transformed into an angel of light" (2 Cor. 11 : 3, 14).

It is the main business of the Satanic powers, often using human means as their instruments, to wreck the sanctified life. If the temptation to sin does not avail, an attempt is frequently made along the line of religion by forcing the soul to unreasonable extremes, seeking to turn faith into presumption and faithfulness into fanaticism. An example of this is to be found in our Lord's wilderness temptation (see Matt. 4 : 1-11).

1.   We must learn to distinguish between *faith* and *presumption*. In the early days of spiritual experience, especially when the soul is on the alert to catch and obey the slightest whispers of the Holy Ghost, there is need for care lest we should be found doing the unreasonable thing in the name of the Lord and inadvertently bringing discredit.

Faith springs out of the abiding God life in a wholly yielded soul—presumption arises from a mind not kept in perfect subjection to the Holy Ghost.

Faith rests on the Word of God, the promises of which are prayed over and appropriated when divinely applied—presumption opens the Bible at random, catches up some phrase wrenched from its context, and hastily applies it without divine authority.

Faith initiates—presumption imitates (see Ex. 14 : 21-29 ; Heb. 11 : 29).

Faith leads to certain victory—presumption always ends in defeat, disaster, disappointment and despair.

2.   We must differentiate between *faithfulness* and *fanat-*

*icism*. Fanaticism is the twin brother of presumption. Into what wild extremes so many dear souls have gone! Satan can turn into a precipice of danger every solid rock of blessing on which you stand.

Christian perfection is interpreted as sinless perfection. Divine healing is seen to mean the sinfulness of simple remedies and the denouncing of all medical science. The baptism with the Holy Spirit becomes associated with some spectacular spiritual gift which is the only authentic sign of its reception.

The leading of the Spirit becomes a whimsical matter which runs into all kinds of excesses. It is possible to have "a zeal of God, but not according to knowledge" (see Rom. 10:2). We need "senses exercised to discern both good and evil" (see Heb. 5:12-14).

### QUESTIONS ON THE TEXT

1. What is meant by a "noonday" experience?
2. Show that this "noonday" experience has its "wasting destruction."
3. Show the distinction between faith and presumption.
4. Show the difference between faithfulness and fanaticism.

# = 13 =

## Erroneous Views

**(1) THE SIMULTANEOUS THE-ORY. (2) THE DEVELOPMENT THEORY. (3) THE DEATH AND POST-MORTEM THEORIES. (4) THE "HOLY IN CHRIST" THEORY. (5) THE "SIGNS" THEORY.**

---

### (1) The Simultaneous Theory

THE doctrine of entire sanctification has not been without its contending theories. We shall name five, and deal with them in order.

By the *simultaneous theory* we mean that teaching which opposes Second Blessing truth by declaring, "We get it all at once."

1. The theory stated.

"All true believers are not only saved from the dominion of sin but from the being of inward as well as outward sin, so that it no longer remains in them" (Count Zinzendorf, quoted by Rev. John Wesley in his sermon on 'Sin in Believers').

"The moment a believer is justified, he is sanctified wholly."

"Entire sanctification and justification are in the same instant, and neither is increased nor diminished."

[138]

"As soon as any one is justified, the Father, the Son, and the Holy Spirit dwell in his heart; and in that moment his heart is as pure as it ever will be" (Count Zinzendorf, quoted by Rev. John Wesley, *Wesley's Works*).

Count Zinzendorf, of the Moravian Church, seems to have been the father of this teaching.

2.   The theory tested.

(a)  It is contrary to the plain teaching of the Word of God.

In the Scriptures two distinct works of grace are quite differently represented (pages 24, 34, 35). Various groups and individuals are represented as needing and receiving a Second Work of grace.

Ex., The disciples at Jerusalem; (John 17: 16, 17; Acts 1: 4; 2: 4).

The converts at Samaria (Acts 8: 5-17).

Saul of Tarsus (Acts 9: 1-20).

The household of Cornelius (Acts 10; 15: 8, 9).

The church at Corinth (1 Cor. 3: 1-4; 2 Cor. 13: 7-11).

The church at Thessalonica (1 Thess. 1; 4: 3-8; 5: 23, 24).

The church at Ephesus (Acts 19: 1-5; Eph. 1: 13).

(b)  It is contrary to the received teaching of the church of God. Mr. Wesley said: "The doctrine that there is no sin in believers is quite new in the church of Christ. It was never heard of for seventeen hundred years; never till it was discovered by Count Zinzendorf. I do not remember to have seen the least mention of it, either in any ancient or modern writer; unless perhaps in some of the wild, ranting Antinomians. . . . I cannot, therefore, by any means receive this assertion, that there is no sin in a believer from the moment he is justified; first, because it is contrary to the whole tenor of Scriptures; secondly, because it is contrary to the experience of the children of God; thirdly, because it is absolutely new, never heard of in the world till yesterday; and lastly, because it is naturally attended with the most fatal consequences, not only grieving those whom God hath not grieved, but perhaps dragging them into ever-lasting perdition" (Sermon on "Sin in Believers").

Rev. William Bramwell: "An idea is going forth, that 'when we are justified we are entirely sanctified,' and 'to feel the evil nature after justification is to lose pardon.' . . . You may depend upon it, this is the devil's great gun. We shall have much trouble with this and I am afraid we cannot suppress it" (Letter to a friend).

Rev. J. A. Wood: "The theory that the soul is entirely sanctified at regeneration involves the whole subject of Christian sanctification in inextricable difficulties. The following are some of them:

"If sanctification is complete at justification, then every man who enjoys religion is entirely sanctified.

"If sanctification is complete at conversion, then every Christian, to be truthful, should profess entire sanctification.

"If all who are converted are entirely sanctified, then all the directions in the Word of God to seek holiness, sanctification, or perfect love, are given exclusively to sinners.

"If sanctification is complete at justification, then converts are not to seek for any further cleansing.

"If sanctification is complete at justification, then ministers have no right to urge Christians to 'go on unto perfection,' or to 'cleanse themselves from all filthiness of the flesh and spirit, perfecting holiness in the fear of God.'

"If justification and entire sanctification are inseparable, then all who feel the fruits of the flesh are in a state of condemnation.

"If a state of entire sanctification is consistent with the struggles of pride, unbelief, impatience, jealousy, and anger (the common experience of newly justified believers), must we not infer that these must go with us to heaven? as it must be admitted that entire sanctification fits the soul for heaven.

"If sanctification is complete at conversion, then every man who is not entirely sanctified is a child of the devil.

"If entire sanctification is complete at justification, it is so in opposition to the experience of the whole church of God; and, with slight exceptions, the whole Christian world has been seriously mistaken during two thousand years.

"If all that are regenerate are wholly sanctified, then whoever is convicted for full salvation, and groaning after it, is at once to infer that he was never converted, or that he is now backslidden. Thus would this heresy, if received, perplex and harass with perpetual difficulties and discouragements the very members of the church who are most deeply concerned to possess all the mind that was in Christ.

"A system involving such difficulties cannot be received as the truth of God, and should be regarded as anti-scriptural, and avoided as dangerous heresy" (*Perfect Love,* pp. 27, 28).

Rev. C. W. Ruth: "That justification and sanctification are experienced simultaneously; that whoever is justified is also sanctified. Those holding this theory may be heard to say they 'got all when they were converted.' But this theory is contrary to Scripture and to universal experience. Every command, exhortation, prayer, and promise in the Bible touching the subject of sanctification is for Christians—never for sinners. If Christians are sanctified when justified, why should sanctification be subsequently enjoined upon them? . . .

"Who ever heard of a minister inviting a sinner to seek sanctification?" (*Entire Sanctification a Second Blessing,* p. 21).

(c) It is contrary to the general experience of the people of God.

Rev. C. W. Ruth: "Not only is this theory contrary

to all Scripture, but contrary to all human experience.
Every truly converted soul has felt the motions and stir-
rings of carnality in his heart, subsequent to pardon, manifesting itself in fear, anger, unbelief, pride, self-will,
despondency, etc. We venture to assert that no young convert has ever gone six months from the place of his conversion without finding some of these things in his heart,
which is evidence that the roots of carnality were still within.
Again, no young convert has ever thought of testifying to
sanctification as an experience unless in a second blessing
meeting" (*Entire Sanctification a Second Blessing*, p. 22).

(See testimonies in the closing chapter.)

### QUESTIONS ON THE TEXT

1. What is to be understood by the simultaneous theory?
2. In what relationship did Count Zinzendorf stand to this theory?
3. State the simultaneous theory.
4. Test the theory by the Word of God.
5. Test the theory by the received teaching
of the church of God.

## (2) The Development Theory

BY the *development theory*
we mean that teaching which opposes Second Blessing truth
by declaring, "We grow into it."

The necessity for and possibility of growth in grace has
already been shown (pages 69-73). There can be no successful Christian experience without a continued development to the last day of our earthly pilgrimage. No

authenticated teacher of Scriptural holiness will question this, yet all will unite in declaring that growth has no sanctifying power. It is a trite but true saying, "We grow in, not into holiness of heart."

Yet how persistently and how glibly this theory is propounded; clearly without an effort to grasp its implications and honestly think it through. When honestly faced, three great factors will be found to be distinctly against it.

(1) The fact of *time*. Just how long must we grow ere sin really dies: Men "grow" for years, but no matter how long the growth process may be, they become no less conscious of the fact of indwelling sin.

But I want purity now. I may die at any moment. I cannot wait to "grow," even if I knew how much time it would require. Surely God must have a quicker method.

(2) The fact of *nature*. Just what will grow? And what will the growth accomplish?

Growth is simply the development and expansion of what already exists. Whoever heard of the development of roses to kill weeds? Whoever even suggested a fattening of the patient to destroy a malignant cancer? Even so, the "Old Man" will never grow himself "dead." He must be definitely destroyed.

(3) The fact of *experience*. The "growth theory" has no witnesses. Many will say, "I am growing" and "with all my failures I am better than I used to be" but none will dare to say, "Along the growth line, I have arrived." The most that the growth theory can offer is a protracted hope which never materializes.

Rev. John Wesley: "Enquiring how it was in all these parts we had so few witnesses to full salvation, I constantly received one and the same answer: 'We see now we sought it by our works; we thought it was to come gradually; we never expected it to come in a moment, by simple faith, in the very same manner as we received justification.' What wonder is it, then, that you have been fighting all these years as one that beateth the air?" (*Wesley's Works*).

"You may obtain a growing victory over sin from the moment you are justified, but this is not enough. The body of sin, the carnal mind, must be destroyed, . . .and this is done in a moment. To talk of this work as being gradual would be nonsense, as much as if we talked of gradual justification." (*Journal of H. A. Rogers*).

Dr. William Jones: "Another popular error entertained by many prominent scholars of this age is the notion that this state of entire purity is attained by growth. All growth is accretion. In all the phenomena of growth the vital forces proceed according to the general law of appropriation. All cleansing is by elimination—by removal. The processes and purposes of growth are entirely different from the processes and purposes of cleansing. Growth is for the enlargement of the organism, for maturity and fruitage. Christian growth is for character-building, for usefulness in the Master's vineyard—growth is a complex process, and involves the obedience and co-operation of a responsible being; it requires time in which the active forces may produce their desired result.

Cleansing is a vital part of man's salvation; and salvation, in all its stages, is God's own personal work and is done at once. Neither time nor growth can in any sense enter as factors into man's salvation. But growth is not conceivable without time, though time is never a worker" (Sermon, Personal Fellowship and Divine Cleansing," in *The Double Cure,* pp. 41, 42).

Dr. Asbury Lowery: "Some will have it that growth is equivalent to getting sanctified. Not so . . . growth implants no new quality in growing matter. It only develops the qualities belonging to its substance. . . . There may be better or worse specimens, but no difference in properties. On the other hand, saving grace produces a new creature. 'Old things pass away, and, behold, all things become new.' Note also, growth does not cure disease in animals, nor remove rottenness from vegetables. How often do we see decay and growth going on in the same tree. Wherever there is a bruised spot, or dead bit of integument, growth can never overcome it, nor put the smallest measure of life into it. The same is true of animal substance. Growth and disease progress side by side, with no counteraction of one by the other. By parity of reasoning it is impossible for the process of growth in grace to work corruption out of the soul, or infuse a new element of life into it. It is contrary to the law of growth to change anything. . . . Hence there can be no such thing as growth into holiness, for that would imply a change of kind which is contradicted and rendered impossible by the immutable **law** of growth" (*Possibilities of Grace,* pp. 231-233).

Dr. Daniel Steele: "Growth in grace, while accompanied by increasing power to abstain from actual sin, has no power to annihilate the spirit of sin, commonly called original sin. The revelation of its indwelling is more and more perfect and appalling as we advance from conversion" (*Love Enthroned,* p. 104).

Dr. F. G. Hibbard: "It has long appeared to us that many who are seeking after entire holiness mistake the duty of a gradual growth in grace, and the knowledge of our Lord Jesus Christ, for a gradual growing out of sin. They seem to think that the two mutually involve each other, and that as they must always grow up into Christ in all things, so they must by degrees grow out of the bondage, guilt, and pollution of sin.

". . . Now to all such we would say one word of admonition—there is no gradual growing out of sin. All that partakes of the proper nature of sin in you must be forgiven and washed away through faith in the blood of the Lamb. When this is done, it is an instantaneous work.

". . . Sin is not a thing to be grown out of, but a thing to be forgiven and to be cleansed away. . . . In this view of perfection (the improvement and maturity of the graces of the Spirit) there are degrees and progressive stages; but in the work of simply cleansing from all sin, both 'of flesh and spirit,' inbred and overt sin, there are no degrees, no progressive stages, but the work is complete at the first, and instantaneous as to time, performed by the Holy Ghost just at the moment when the burdened soul has faith to be made every whit whole" (*N. C. Advocate*).

Rev. J. A. Wood has the following: "Can a state of entire sanctification be secured by ordinary growth in grace?

"It cannot, for the following reasons:

"Growth in grace is neither a destroying, nor a washing, nor a cleansing, nor a crucifying process. Entire sanctification is a death, a washing, a purification. 'The blood of Jesus Christ his Son cleanseth us from all sin.'

"Growth in grace has respect to addition, to enlargement and development, and belongs entirely to the positive in Christian life—the graces of the Spirit. Growth is an increase or development of some living force: not a destroyer nor transformer of any living force. The idea of entire sanctification is that of purification, *i. e.,* the removal of an impurity or defilement. One is a destruction; the other is an enlargement.

"Growth in grace is a natural process, involving culture and discipline, and appertains to spiritual life. Sanctification is a supernatural and divine work wrought in the soul. Growth, the natural, gradual process of development, should not be mixed with the instantaneous, supernatural work of purgation and purification.

"In growth in grace, the soul is active and cooperative. Entire sanctification is something experienced, and not something done. The soul is passive, is the subject and not the agent of the cleansing, the same as it was in regeneration. Before and after both regeneration and entire sanctification the soul is active and co-operative.

"Growth never changes the nature of anything; hence a believer cannot grow pure, for the same reason that a sinner cannot grow into a saint—growth not changing the nature of things. A pure nature may grow, and an impure one may grow, and mere growth does not change the one or the other.

"Growth and development have no fixed relations to purity in any way. They have respect to size, or enlargement, and not to quality or purity; and hence, all changes by growth, or gradual processes, are in size or quantity, and not in kind or quality. Purity or holiness has respect to quality and not to quantity.

"Growth in grace is the same after entire sanctification as before. If growth in grace is a cleansing process, and is growth in purity, it must follow that when the soul is entirely sanctified there can be no further growth, since what is wholly pure can never become more pure" (*Perfect Love*, pp. 80, 81).

Dr. Samuel Chadwick: "Another mistake made by earnest Christians about holiness is that it comes by gradual growth in grace and a steady progress of spiritual discipline. They are always growing toward it, but they never get into it, always struggling and striving to attain but never entering into possession. The positive expectation is always seen to be afar off, and they die without having possessed. The hopeful future never becomes the positive now. The time never comes that calls for a definite step and a positive act of faith.

"But holiness does not come by growth, neither is it identified by growth. Growth is a process of life, holiness is the gift of abundant life. Growth is the result of health; holiness is health. Holiness implies a crisis, a new experience, a transformed life. It is not an achievement nor an attainment, but a gift of grace in the Holy Ghost" (*Way to Pentecost,* pp. 86-87).

There is no sin-destroying energy in growth.

### QUESTIONS ON THE TEXT

1. What do we mean by the Development Theory?

2. What three great facts will be found to be against this theory? Prove this.

3. Show just what growth can, and what it cannot, do in the believer.

### (3) The Death and Post-Mortem Theories

BY *death and post-mortem theories* we mean that teaching which opposes Second Blessing truth by declaring, "It is not possible in this life." The two outstanding theories are: The Protestant Theory of sin's destruction by the fact of death; and the Romish Theory of sin's destruction in the purgatorial flame.

1. Sanctification by the fact of *death.*

According to this teaching, death is man's sanctifier, or at least it is only in the atmosphere of death's presence that this sin-destroying work can be done. Here is an old-time relic of that Gnostic idea which saw in the body the seat of sin, and which could suggest no way of deliverance from sin but the severance of the spirit from the body. The only remedy was death. It is this error which John attacks in his first epistle.

The thought of death being a deliverer is repulsive. Death is not a friend, but an enemy, an intruder; a repellent monster trampling down the choicest blooms in this fair universe of God.

Two Scripture passages will help us here: Rom. 5 : 12, 17;
1 Cor. 15 : 26, 56.

Note these expressions: "Sin entered into the world, and
death by sin." "By one man's offence death reigned." "The
last enemy . . . is death." "The sting of death is sin."

Viewed in the light of this Sanctification-at-death Theory, these passages become illuminating. Death is seen to
owe its very existence to the fact of sin. Death is seen to owe
its power to reign to the fact of sin. Death's only sting is
seen to be the fact of sin. Death is seen as man's enemy to
the very last.

We wonder how much help grace needs from death in the
work of destroying sin?

Rev. John Wesley: "The whole comes to one point.
Is there, or is there not, any instantaneous sanctification
between justification and death? I say yes!" (Letter to
Charles Wesley, 1767.)

Rev. J. A. Wood: "Is not death a sanctifier?

"It would seem that many believe so. This may not be
said in words, but actions speak louder than words. The
greater part of believers defer their sanctification until
death, while death itself has no more to do with the believer's sanctification than with his justification.

"The Bible nowhere states or intimates that death sanctifies the soul. It nowhere exhorts Christians to rely upon
death for their sanctification. Christ and the apostles
placed no reliance upon death for that purpose.

"While the sacred writers speak often of the means, the
agencies, and the time of sanctification, they never name
death as its means, its agent, or its time.

"If death sanctifies the soul, then it, at least, is partially
our Savior; and thus the effect of sin (for 'death is by sin')
becomes the means of finally destroying it; that is, the effect
of a cause can react upon its cause, and destroy it.

"Death, in its very nature and circumstances, is entirely

unpropitious for the work of sanctification. If sanctification, as the Bible teaches, involves human agency, the free,
intelligent action of the mind, 'sanctified by faith,' 'through
the truth,' death is no process of cleansing the soul.

"If death sanctifies the soul, then the work is removed
from the ground of moral agency, and we have no responsibility in the matter. This would nullify all the precepts
requiring our agency to obtain personal holiness. That we
have a personal responsibility in our sanctification is evident.

"In so far as we can see, there is not a shadow of evidence
that dissolving the connection between the soul and body
will produce any effect upon the character or moral condition of the soul. The change produced by death is in our
physical state and mode of being, and a mere physical
change of state cannot relieve the soul of its pride, unbelief,
selfishness, and corrupt lusts. Change of character is God's
work, and is by grace, through faith, by moral means.

"Many appear to believe the old pagan dogma that the
body is the seat of sin, and that depravity pertains only to
the body, and that when the body dies, as the soul leaves
the body, it will be free from depravity. That the body is
degenerated, and possessed of deranged appetites and propensities, making it 'an instrument of unrighteousness,' is
admitted; but Christian sanctification has less regard to the
body than to the soul, which is the seat of inbred sin. The
carnal mind, or selfishness, pride, anger, covetousness, impatience, hatred, and all filthiness of the spirit, belong to the
soul and not to the body" (*Perfect Love*, pp. 177, 178).

2.   The theory of sin's destruction by the fires of *purgatory*.

This post-mortem theory has held multitudes in bondage,
and has been the instrument for bringing much wealth into
the coffers of the church.

Only fire can deal with the nature of sin, but God's Word

reveals a divine fire, to be applied here and now (see **Matt.** 3:11; Heb. 12:29).

**1.** What do we mean when we speak of the "death" and "post-mortem" theories of sanctification? What are these theories?

**2.** Show that death is not the sanctifier.

**3.** Show that purgatory is not the sanctifier.

**(4) The Holy in Christ Theory** BY the *"Holy in Christ" Theory* we mean that teaching which trims the corners of radical, full salvation truth by such sophistries as, "It is not what I am myself; it is what I am in Christ."

"In Christ." Here we have one of the great Pauline expressions which has become basic to evangelical doctrine, and to many it will seem strange that we should object to it here. It will soon be seen, however, how possible it is to twist a glorious Bible truth into a dangerous error, and thereby be deceived.

Rev. C. W. Ruth calls it: "The Calvinistic, Keswickian, Antinomian theory of repression and imputed holiness, as opposed to the Wesleyan theory of eradication of inbred sin and imparted righteousness" (*Entire Sanctification a Second Blessing,* p. 25). The difficulty here confronted is the almost inconceivable position of a limitation of the Atonement by an exaltation of Christ.

The expressions used by these brethren are often so ambiguous that the unwary are beguiled, and are apt to conclude that this holiness controversy is "merely a matter of terms" and that those who insist on a more drastic phraseology are only troublers in Israel who make "much ado about nothing."

Almost half a century ago Dr. William Jones rang out the warning in the National Camp Meeting: "There is a subtle and dangerous heresy vigorously propagated at the present time, which affirms that the sinful nature of man cannot be extirpated in this life.

"Those who entertain this doctrine affirm that the utmost the Holy Ghost can do for the soul is to repress hereditary depravity. They affirm that the Adamic nature cannot be crucified. . . .

"There is an unlimited difference between the terms 'repression' and 'destruction.' . . .

"The conception of holiness by repression is contrary both to human experience and to the Bible, and is antagonistic to the fundamental principles of philosophy. Holiness in man is the same in kind as holiness in God. Therefore as God is essentially holy, saved manhood must be essentially pure. . .

"He is nowhere styled as the divine represser. His name is called Jesus because He saves His people from their sins" (*The Double Cure,* p. 36, 37).

Since that day, this teaching has shown amazing development, and in dealing with it we must remember that among those who endorse it are many wonderful children of God. What they have is the best they know. We must keep in mind, therefore, that in dealing with the doctrine we do not attack the integrity of those who hold it.

1. The *truth.* There is so much about this teaching that is good that it is not easy for the uninstructed to detect the error.

a. Much is made of the person and passion of the Lord Jesus. They faithfully proclaim His deity, His death, and His high priestly intercession.

b. Essential emphasis is placed on the lost condition of the human race. Fallen, guilty and undone, the Calvary Atonement of the Son of God is declared to be the world's only hope.

c. Much is said about holiness, with the insistence that without it no man shall see the Lord. That holiness has Christ as its source and its center, and is ours only as we are in Him.

Thus far there is no difficulty. To such teaching as this not even the most fastidious could object.

2. The *error*. Now comes the error, which may be stated as follows:

Those abiding in Christ, and thereby partaking of His holiness, have, it is declared, two distinctly different natures which remain with them until the hour of death:

a. The divine life, imparted at regeneration, which cannot commit sin.

b. "The flesh," *i. e.,* the self life, our heritage from Adam, which is the seat of sin. Concerning this Adamic heritage three things are taught:

(1) It is the believer's constant humiliation. Like an incubus it holds the holiest soul, and from it there is no release. From those who hold this form of teaching, expressions like the following are frequently heard:

"This constant need of a deeper death to self."

"The power of corruption within every man, which to his last hour of life upon earth must defile his best deeds and give to his holiest efforts the nature of sin."

(2) In the believer it registers no condemnation.

In himself is corruption but the blood of Jesus Christ cleanseth from all sin, and by a divine imputation the merits of Christ are counted to him for righteousness.

(3) By the believer it involves continual suppression. The sinful nature must be checked, suppressed, subdued, but until this mortal puts on immortality, it can never die.

There is no real deliverance in this theory. It lacks the essentials of Bible salvation.

QUESTIONS ON THE TEXT

1.  What do we mean by the "Holy in Christ" theory?
2.  Discuss the expression "In Christ."
3.  How does Rev. C. W. Ruth describe this theory?
4.  What, then, is the almost inconceivable position which we face?
5.  State the truth in this theory.
6.  Show the error of this theory.

## (5) The Signs Theory

**B**Y the *"Signs" Theory* we mean that teaching which depreciates the faith position, insisting that the seeker must look for outward manifestation, generally an utterance in an unknown tongue.

Within recent years those sections of the Christian church which stood for the deeper experiences of grace have been torn with contention in controversy over that strange spiritual phenomenon. The battle has been fierce, both sides having their champions, and it would seem that at times neither side has distinguished itself by the manifestation of a superabundance of charity. The question calls for a frank discussion, based on open-minded inquiry into Scripture and history. This we shall endeavor to present in the section before us.

1.  The New Testament records a spiritual phenomenon which has become known within the church as *"the gift of*

*tongues."* This manifestation frequently accompanied the reception of the Holy Spirit.

We say "frequently" because this was not always the case, neither was this manifestation always of "tongues" alone.

The manifestations accompanying the reception of the Holy Spirit varied, but the central fact was always the same.

a. At Pentecost there were four (Acts 2: 1-4) : Wind, atmosphere, flame, tongues.

"A sound . . . as of a rushing mighty wind."

"It filled all the house where they were sitting."

"There appeared . . . cloven tongues like as of fire."

"They began to speak with other tongues."

The central fact of Pentecost lay beyond all these—"They were all filled with the Holy Ghost" (ver. 4).

b. At Ephesus there were two (Acts 19: 1-7) : Tongues, prophecy.

The central fact—"The Holy Ghost came on them" (ver. 6).

c. At Caesarea there was one (Acts 10: 44-48) : Tongues.

The central fact—"The Holy Ghost fell on all them which heard the word" (ver. 44).

d. At Samaria there was no sign at all (Acts 8: 14-17).

The central fact—"They received the Holy Ghost" (ver. 17).

In each case the experience sought was the same. Throughout the entire book there is no record of the seeking for "tongues." (Later we find this in the Corinthian church —1 Cor. 12-14—but the purpose of the Corinthian epistle was to discourage it. ) In each case the search was for—not the manifestation, but the fact—namely, the Holy Ghost.

Where "tongues" did accompany this bestowal it was the utterance of languages, the fact of which was recognized by those who heard (see Acts 2: 6-11).

This manifestation is recognized by Paul as having a

place among the nine "gifts" of the Spirit (see 1 Cor. 12: 4-11).

No one person possesses all nine. They are distributed at the will of the Spirit throughout the "body"—the figure used for the church.

a.   Among these gifts, the gift of tongues is evidently regarded by the apostle as not being of supreme importance.

Proof: In 1 Cor. 12: 4-11 the complete list of gifts, "tongues" is placed eighth in order. In Eph. 4: 8-13 the condensed list of gifts, "tongues" is omitted altogether.

b.   In the realm of spiritual gifts the Holy Spirit is sovereign, and makes distribution according to His own will (see 1 Cor. 12: 11).

c.   The people among whom "tongues" were most coveted and emphasized manifested the most shallow spiritual experience.

Corinth manifested two outstanding characteristics:

Carnality: So crude were its manifestations that the reader of the epistle blushes with shame.

Craze for sensationalism: So marked is the craze that the reader of the epistle immediately feels himself to be in the danger zone. The question of "gifts" is introduced into the epistle in response to inquiry and by way of warning.

2.   Some considerations concerning this manifestation for us today. Strangely enough, this tongues sign seems to disappear during seasons of stability and reappear at intervals of transition when the Spirit of God would seem to be at work.

It appeared, as we have seen, in the apostolic age, at Pentecost, and in numerous instances recorded in the Acts of the Apostles.

It has appeared at different periods throughout the years that have followed.

In the second century, among the Montanists. Protesting

against ecclesiastical domination, and preaching individual liberty and personal inspiration, they strove after a direct communion with God. They saw great revivals, coupled with what appeared to have been unwarrantable excesses. Trances, prophecies and tongues are recorded.

In the thirteenth century, among the Franciscans.

In the seventeenth century, among the Huguenots. They were subjected to rigorous persecution, out of which came what was later known as the "Church of the Desert." Continual experiences of the supernatural are reported, among which was "speaking in tongues."

In the nineteenth century. Numerous instances are recorded: Manifestations in London, the Irvingites, 1822; manifestations in Sweden, 1841; manifestations in Ireland, 1859.

In the twentieth century: Manifestations during the Welsh revival, 1904; manifestations of the modern "Pentecostal Movement."

On the basis of this we make a threefold suggestion.

a. Such extraordinary manifestations could originate in God. It would be utter folly to state rashly that any unusual supernatural phenomena must of necessity be from the devil. It is not for us to say what old thing God should or should not repeat, or what new thing He should or should not do. We must approach this subject from a totally different angle.

b. Such extraordinary manifestations could also originate in other sources.

The fact that they are extraordinary in no sense marks them as divine.

There are *subtle psychic forces* within the human personality which could account for much.

We are only just beginning to realize how deep and subtle our human nature is and what amazing forces we possess, which, unless understood, rightly directed, and divinely governed, may allure us into spheres which we do not understand, and leave us mental, spiritual and nervous wrecks.

There are *weird satanic forces* in the realm of the supernatural which need to be seriously taken into account. Such manifestations could be counterfeits of Satan (see Eph. 6:12).

c. Since then, the New Testament gives no encouragement to seek these manifestations, but emphatically declares the Holy Ghost to be Sovereign in His distribution of all spiritual gifts, and especially in view of the obvious dangers which surround it the only safe, sane and Scriptural attitude is to seek the baptism of the Holy Ghost and fire by a definite act of entire consecration and simple faith, leaving it to an all-wise God to distribute all else according to His own will.

God gives to His believing people the Holy Ghost, purifying their hearts *by faith*.

### QUESTIONS ON THE TEXT

1. What is to be understood by the "signs" theory?

2. Discuss the "gift of tongues" as a New Testament phenomenon.

3. Discuss the "tongues sign" as a manifestation since New Testament days.

4. What threefold suggestion may be made on the basis of all this?

# 14

# Christian Perfection

### (1) ITS POSSIBILITY.
### (2) ITS NATURE. (A) NEGATIVE. (B) POSITIVE.

---

## (1) Its Possibility

NO question has been more keenly debated, and probably none more misrepresented and misunderstood, than the question, "What is Christian Perfection?" At the word itself many have taken fright. Abhorring the thought of presumption and dreading the idea of fanaticism, they have loudly declared, "We are all human and shall be so long as we live. Therefore none can be perfect in this life." Now that sounds conclusive, that is, until it is squarely faced; then it becomes apparent that its logic is not so sound as at first it seemed. A good logician will define his terms. Let us do that with this sentence.

1. *"All Human."* Even that may not be quite so unfortunate as it sounds. What else could we be? What else shall we ever be? Humanity is not necessarily a synonym for sinfulness. On earth we are human on probation. Humanity's present trouble is its sinfulness, but are those blood-washed members of the race who rejoice in the fact that "the blood of Jesus Christ, his Son, cleanseth from all sin" to be regarded as enjoying no higher spiritual status than the rest?

a.  Our first parents were human, even before they sinned. Their humanity was God's best intention for the beings which He planned to create.

"Let us make man," we hear coming from the divine council chamber—not gods, not angels, just plain man. But that is not all. "Let us make man in our image, after our likeness: and let them have dominion . . ." (Gen. 1:26). It was that man who walked with God in Eden's garden. It was man, human, but in the image of God and after His likeness, exercising dominion and enjoying communion, but still man.

b.  Our Lord Himself became human. "The Word was made flesh, . . . and we beheld his glory . . ." (John 1:14). It is strange that flesh and glory should stand so close together.

"Forasmuch then as the children are partakers of flesh and blood, he also himself likewise partook of the same . . . For verily he took not on him the nature of angels; but he took on him the seed of Abraham" (Heb. 2:14, 16). Here are humanity and glory side by side; nay, one manifesting the other. Let it be remembered that while our Lord took our humanity at Bethlehem's manger, He did not take on Himself our sin until Calvary's cross.

But may we, in our humanity, be like either Adam or our Lord today? We think not. Ours is now a broken humanity by reason of the Fall, but a broken nature does not of necessity remain defiled.

Rev. John Wesley: "But surely we cannot be saved from sin, while we dwell in a sinful body. A sinful body? I pray observe how deeply ambiguous, how equivocal, this expression is! But there is no authority for it in Scripture. The word sinful body is never found there, and as it is totally unscriptural, so it is palpably absurd. For nobody, or no matter of any kind, can be sinful: spirits alone are capable of sin. Pray, in what part of the body should sin lodge? It cannot lodge in the skin, the muscles, the nerves, the veins, or the arteries; it cannot be in the bones any more than in the hair or nails. Only the soul can be the seat of sin."

2. *"None Perfect."* But who says so? And on what authority? Is it not strange that the Holy Spirit should use this word so frequently? It is used more often in Scripture to describe Christian experience than any other, occurring one hundred thirty-eight times, and more than fifty of these refer to human character under the operation of divine grace. Paul uses the word thirty-three times, and it is not difficult, even in the Old Testament, to find the record of lives, obviously human, yet declared by God Himself to have been perfect.

Rev. Joseph H. Smith: "We submit three reasons why we should treat of this subject of perfection:

a. "Man's mind is so constituted as to demand perfection. And this is most emphatically so in things of which he believes God is the author.

"Yes, even in arts and sciences of his own he has a perfect mark by which, for instance, he grades students up to 100 per cent. He rates commercial products according to certain fixed standards of purity, weight and measure; and awards premiums at the fairs and expositions accordingly. And most particularly is this true as to man's (and woman's) minds with regard to social and domestic relations of life. Here nothing short of a complete devotion and a perfect fidelity will satisfy the requirement of expectation. And in ethics it is the same; for not approximate but absolute truthfulness and honesty are the standard by which men at least judge their fellows and decry all graft and deception in public and business life.

b. "Men's hearts need and cry for a perfect solace and satisfaction. And when these hearts turn to Christ, is it not true that we all, either from instinct or intuition or a measure of inspiration, expect to find such a perfect satisfaction and salvation in Him?

"We think this is universally so. . . . The hearts of all true believers in Christ are born to long for and look for just what we shall trace in Paul as perfection. Anything less than a perfect alignment with God's will does not meet our expectation in Christ, nor satisfy what we feel is Christ's expectation of us.

"The Bible does unmistakably present such a perfection. Observe, we say such a perfection. And let us keep in mind that in any of the other lines of perfection to which we have alluded there is a distinct limit as to what it is that is perfect; and there is also a margin allowing for many other imperfections outside that limit. Thus, for instance, the boy who makes one hundred per cent, or a perfect mark in his mathematics, may still be a physical cripple, unable to walk. The wife whose perfection of love to her one and only husband is never questioned but can be proved in twenty different ways may nevertheless be an altogether unskilled seamstress or an inexperienced and an imperfect housekeeper. Christian perfection is like hers in that it is a perfection of the heart, though making no claim to perfection of the head or the hand. This may explain that very significant remark of a deeply spiritual man who said, 'One mark of perfection is patience with our imperfections.'

"For the perfection presented in the Bible is not a perfection of physical or mental state, nor of temporal circumstances or conditions, but rather a perfect acceptance of an adaptation to the probation that is involved in the imperfections of our lot.

"Thus, in a word, Christian perfection is limited to the perfection of that which Christianity contemplates for man while on earth and in the body" (*Pauline Perfection*).

The possibility of Christian perfection is seen in the Scriptures.

(1) It is commanded by God Himself (Gen. 17:1; Deut. 18:13; Matt. 5:48; 2 Cor. 7:1; 13:11; Heb. 6:1; James 1:4).

(2) Prayers are recorded for its accomplishment (1 Chron. 29:19; John 17:23; 2 Cor. 13:9; Col. 4:12; Heb. 13:20, 21; 1 Pet. 5:10).

(3) It is included in the plan of salvation (Isa. 26:3; Matt. 19:21; Col. 1:28; 3:14; 2 Tim. 3:16, 17).

(4) It is declared to be the grand purpose of the Christian ministry (Eph. 4:11-13).

(5) There are records of such an experience having been enjoyed (Gen. 6:9; 1 Kings 15:14; Job 1:1-8; Psa. 37:37; 1 Cor. 2:6; Phil 3:15; 1 John 4:17, 18; Heb. 10:14; Jas. 3:2).

### QUESTIONS ON THE TEXT

1. Why is the word "perfection" so frequently opposed?

2. Deal with the arguments: (a) "We are all human." (b) "None perfect."

3. Show the possibility of Christian perfection as seen in the Scriptures.

## (2) Its Nature
### (a) Negative

HERE two dangers meet us at the outset. On the one hand there is the possibility of setting the standard so high that men will despair of ever reaching it, while on the other hand we may bring it so low as to encourage presumption concerning the things of God.

Mr. Wesley: "If I set the mark too high, I drive men into needless fears: if I set it too low, I drive them into hell fire."

At this point it will be well for us to cover what to all students of this subject is well-trodden ground, so much so that it would seem impossible to state it with any degree of freshness. So many feet have walked this meadow that from it the grass seems almost gone. However, the statements, though old, are true, and for the sake of those who follow must continue to be made.

1.  It is not the perfection of *Jehovah* in His infinite majesty.

In this He stands alone, and to Him none can approach. He is omnipotent, omniscient, omnipresent, immutable and eternal, and these perfections are absolute, independent, unrivaled and underived. This of course implies freedom from all fault, mistake and error, and ignorance of every kind. No sane person claims a perfection such as that.

2.  It is not the perfection of *angels* in their high abode. Of these we know very little after all, but we do at least know that they are a higher order of spiritual intelligences than Adam's race, and in their unfallen condition surround the very throne of God. With unwearied wing they speed to the remotest part of this boundless universe, carrying out the commands of God. No mortal, rightly balanced, ever claimed a perfection such as that.

3.  It is not the perfection of *Adam* in his Eden home. His was a sinless soul and a deathless body. His mind had no memory of committed sin. Every power, spiritual, physical, mental and moral, was fresh from his Maker's hand. He had never seen an open grave; never felt a twinge of pain; never known a feeling of remorse. He knew no fear of the animal creation nor of the forces of nature. He needed no clothing, for in that unfallen condition his very body was bathed in light. Who today would think of claiming a perfection such as that?

4.  It is not the perfection of *Christ* while here on earth. "The Word was made flesh, and dwelt among us" (John 1:

14)—"flesh" in character like unto our very own. "Forasmuch then as the children are partakers of flesh and blood, he also himself likewise took part of the same" (Heb. 2: 14). "God sent forth his Son, made of a woman, made under the law" (Gal. 4: 4).

And yet is there not a difference? While we claim Him as one with us in our essential humanity, what man will dare to claim that in all points he is one with Him? Somehow we feel that the very fact that links Him to us at the same moment distances Him from us by a tremendous plus on our side and a great minus on His.

He "was made flesh." The "flesh and blood" of which He partook was as real as our own, so much so that in His physical nature all the human limitations are seen (Ex., Matt. 4: 2; 8: 24; 9: 36; 14: 23; Mark 3: 5; 10: 21; John 4: 6; 11: 33, 35; 12: 27; 19: 28).

His humanity was minus any personal memories of committed sin. All this we know.

Then the plus and minus is quickly reversed. In His essential humanity He was conscious of a unique divine relationship in His own right, while others can approach God only through Him (John 14: 6-9; 17: 1-5). No sane professor of Christian perfection ever claims that.

5. It is not the perfection of *redeemed souls* in glory. Having now left this mortal body and "put on immortality," they are no longer fettered by physical weakness, neither do they now know the strain of trial, the sting of temptation, the discipline of sorrow, the buffeting of circumstances, the threatening of death, nor the presence of sin. We are all conscious that while living here on earth it would be folly to claim that.

6. It is not the perfection of the *matured* in grace. Maturity takes time. It is the result of growth, development, discipline and long experience. All these have their part in producing the mature, well-balanced spiritual life.

Christian perfection, however, is not confined to white hairs,
bent backs and feeble steps. In fact, many who boast of the
length of time they have served the Lord are obviously far
from this experience now under consideration.

QUESTIONS ON THE TEXT

1. What does Mr. Wesley say about setting
the mark in Christian perfection?
2. Discuss Christian perfection from the
negative point of view.

## (2) Its Nature
## (b) Positive

AT this point it becomes
necessary to say something about the word itself, a study
of which will indicate a careful selection. Our English language is sometimes embarrassing by reason of its ambiguity,
but not so the Greek, where words and tenses often indicated
the slightest shade of thought, which in many instances our
translators either overlooked or found themselves unable to
express. An outstanding instance is this word "perfect."
Here two words used by the original writers are expressed
in our English version by the one word, and yet they so
widely differ as to cause endless confusion and to require
continual explanation. We shall examine both words.

1. Concerning *finality*. The word "teleios" indicates
something completed, accomplished, consummated, finished.
This word is not used concerning the believer as a completed
possession in this life, but as a process of development and
an end not yet attained. It is that long drawn out process
leading to perfection of growth in Christian character and
experience, and knows no finality here. It is used, for

instance, concerning the full Christhood in Eph. 4:13. "Till we all come in the unity of the faith, and of the knowledge of the Son of God, unto a perfect man [R. V., full-grown man], unto the measure of the stature of the fullness of Christ."

In this sense it is quite correct to say that no one is perfect, for "The path of the just is as the light of dawn that shineth more and more unto the perfect day" (Prov. 4:18). There is no finality to our spiritual development. In this sense we have not "already attained, neither are we already perfect" (Phil. 3:12).

2. Concerning *quality*. Here we find another word, "katartizo," which indicates adjustment and fitness resulting from an immediate act or crisis. It indicates the idea of repair and consequent readiness. This will be seen in the two following passages:

Matt. 4:21: "And going from thence, he saw two brethren, James the son of Zebedee, and John his brother, in a ship with Zebedee their father, mending their nets."

Eph. 4:11, 12: "And he gave some apostles; and some, prophets; and some, evangelists; and some, pastors and teachers; for the perfecting of the saints unto the work of ministering . . ." (Note, R. V.).

In God's great universe everything may be said to have its own measure of perfection. Even in material spheres this is seen. Nature gives us the sapling and the oak, the bud and the flower, the lamb and the sheep, the babe and the adult, all in their own degree beautifully perfect.

In workmanship a thing is regarded as perfect if it answers the purpose for which it was designed, whether it be a watch, a fountain pen, a baby's feeding bottle, or a steam engine. Watches do not write letters, neither do fountain pens give us time. Feeding bottles do not pull railroad coaches, neither do steam engines satisfy crying babies. There is a limit and a sphere for each, but if within that limit the purpose is realized, that is indicative of its perfection.

If perfection is acknowledged as within the range of possibility in every other department of life, why not the perfection of a saint?

Does God then have a standard for redeemed souls while here on earth? We answer, "Yes," Here it is: Mark 12: 30, 31.

Any soul by the power of divine grace may respond to that. In spiritual experience there may be much to be desired in respect to development, but there need be no lack as to devotion.

The three cardinal elements of Christian character are set forth in the New Testament as capable of perfection: Faith, 1 Thess. 3:10; hope, 1 Peter 1:13 (R. V.); love, 1 John 4:17, 18.

Mr. Wesley: "Christian perfection, therefore, does not imply (as some men seem to have imagined) an exemption either from ignorance, or mistake, or infirmities, or temptations. Indeed, it is only another term for holiness. There are two names for the same thing. Thus everyone that is holy is, in the Scripture sense, perfect. Yet we may observe that neither in this respect is there any absolute perfection on earth. There is no perfection of degrees, as it is termed; none which does not admit of continual increase. So that how much soever any man has attained, or in how high degree soever he is perfect, he hath still need to grow in grace, and daily to advance in the knowledge and love of God his Savior" (sermon on *Christian Perfection*).

"By perfection I mean the humble, gentle, patient love of God and our neighbor, ruling our tempers, words, and actions.

"I do not include the impossibility of falling from it, either in part or whole. Therefore I retract several expressions in our hymns which partly express, partly imply such an impossibility. I do not contend for the term sinless, though I do not object to it.

"As to the manner. I believe this perfection is always wrought in the soul by a simple act of faith, consequently in an instant. But I believe a gradual work both precedes and follows that instant.

"As to the time. I believe this instant generally is the instant of death, the moment before the soul leaves the body. But I believe it may be ten, twenty, or forty years before. I believe it is usually many years after justification; but that it may be within five years or five months after it, I know no conclusive argument to the contrary. If it must be many years after justification, I would be glad to know how many. And how many days, or months, or even years, can one allow to be between perfection and death? How far from justification must it be, and how near death?" (*Plain Account of Christian Perfection*).

Dr. Asa Mahan: "He is perfect in holiness whose love at each successive moment corresponds with the extent of his powers. 'If there be first a willing mind, it is accepted according to what a man hath, and not according to that he hath not.' Hence I remark that perfection in holiness does not imply that now we love God with all the strength and intensity with which redeemed spirits in heaven love Him. The depth and intensity of our love depends, under all circumstances, upon the vigor and reach of our powers, and the extent and distinctness of our vision of divine truth. In each and every sphere, perfection in holiness implies a strength and intensity of love corresponding with the reach of our powers and the extent and distinctness of our vision of truth in that particular sphere.

"The child is perfect in holiness who perpetually exercises a filial and affectionate obedience to all the divine requisitions, and loves God with all the powers which it possesses as a child. The man is perfect in holiness who exercises the same supreme and affectionate obedience to all that God requires, and loves Him to the full extent of his knowledge and strength as a man.

"The saint on earth is perfect when he loves with all the strength and intensity rendered practicable by the extent of his knowledge and reach of his powers in his present sphere.

"The saint in heaven will be favored with a seraph's vision and a seraph's power. To be perfect there, he must love and adore with a seraph's vigor and burn with a seraph's fire" (*The Doctrine of Christian Perfection,* pp. 8-9).

Rev. Thomas Cook: "Perfection signifies that spiritual completeness or wholeness into which the soul enters when the last inward foe is conquered and the last distracting force harmonized with the mighty love of Christ, every crevice of the nature filled with love and every energy employed in the delightful service of our adorable Savior.

"This implies not only complete deliverance from all spiritual pollution, but the possession of the unmixed graces of faith, humility, resignation, patience, meekness, self-denial, and all other graces of the Spirit" (*New Testament Holiness,* pp. 74, 75).

Dr. Harold W. Perkins: "By the phrase Christian or evangelical perfection we denote a spiritual state, mediated by the Holy Spirit, in which the believer in Christ has a full assurance of his redemption through the blood of Christ, and enjoys unbroken communion with the love of God" (*The Doctrine of Christian, or Evangelical Perfection,* pp. 6, 7).

Dr. Samuel Chadwick: "It is many years since I set myself to a scientific and earnest study of the New Testament on this subject. I had entered into an experience that I could neither define nor defend. I had to find reasons for the assurance of which I had no doubt. Books did not help me. I had no skill in Bible study, but with patient humility and much prayer I was led gradually into the light. I found in the Scriptures more than one angle of presentation for the same experience. The legal aspect expressed it in terms of law. The temple had a different vocabulary from the law court. Neither was complete without the other. The family completed both the court and the temple. Perfection in the court was acquittal without condemnation. Perfection in the temple was purity without defect, cleanness without stain. Perfection in the family was the perfection of love.

" 'There is therefore now no condemnation to them that are in Christ Jesus'—the law.

" 'The blood of Jesus Christ his Son cleanseth us from all sin'—the temple.

" 'Herein is our love made perfect . . . There is no fear in love: perfect love casteth out fear'—the home.

"No interpretation of perfection is complete that ignores any one of these three angles of interpretation.

"I shall never forget the excitement with which I discovered another word for perfection. The word for the perfection that is final is 'teleios.' That is the big word for perfection. It is used of Christ and His redeeming work which is all perfect. It is used also of the ultimate consummation of grace, and of perfect development. The word I discovered was 'katartizo,' which does not mean the finality of a thing, but its fitness. The uses of the word are illuminating. It is used of mending nets (Matt. 4: 21) ; to set in order as in music (Matt. 21: 16) ; to fit into perfect relationship (1 Cor. 1: 10) ; to adjust that which is dislocated (Gal. 6: 1) ; to complete that which is lacking (1 Thess. 3: 10) ; to frame together various parts of a machine (Heb. 11: 3). There is nothing very difficult to understand in this kind of perfection. Mending is done to repair damage and make fit again for use. Perfecting music is so arranging it that all discords are lost in the perfection of harmony. Limbs fitly joined work together in the unity of the body.

No one objects to perfection in the joints of arms, legs, and necks. Putting into joint a dislocated limb is making it perfect. The various parts of creation are perfectly fitted and framed together. When that which is lacking is supplied, the defective is made perfect. Threepence added to ninepence make a perfect shilling. That is what is meant by perfection. It is complete deliverance from everything that makes the soul unfit for, and unequal to, the will of God; the adjustment of life to perfect harmony, and the adaptation of all its powers to the purpose of God; and the supply of all grace, wisdom, power, and whatever else is lacking for efficient obedience to every demand in the fellowship of God in Christ. It is life so completely saved that there is no defect, no disorder, no discord" (*The Call to Christian Perfection*, pp. 30-32).

### QUESTIONS ON THE TEXT

1. Give the two Greek words used for "perfect" and show the distinction between them.

2. Answer the argument that perfection is not possible in this life.

3. What three cardinal elements of Christian character are set forth in the New Testament as capable of perfection? Prove this by Scripture.

4. Give the gist of the quotation from Mr. Wesley on perfection.

# 15

# The Perfect Life

## ITS DISTINCTIVE OUTWORKINGS

THE perfect life is, of necessity, unmistakable in its manifestation, and also in its restriction.

1. As to its *manifestation*. We call attention here to one of those outstanding New Testament passages, the importance of which is not generally recognized, namely, Matt. 5: 48: "Be ye therefore perfect, even as your Father which is in heaven is perfect."

The keyword is "therefore," and the force of the word can be realized only as we pause before it and turn it into the question, "Wherefore?" "Be ye therefore . . ." It is immediately evident that the verse is climacteric, relating itself to the entire chapter, which may be regarded as the concrete manifestation of the perfect life.

A life of *blessedness* is declared (ver. 1-16). Concerning this two thoughts are prominent.

First, this "blessed life" is dependent upon character. There are nine "beatitudes." Some count only seven.

Each beatitude is a spiritual quality.

Each of these spiritual qualities belongs to this world.

Hence, "purity of heart" (ver. 8) is as much a present tense experience as "poverty of spirit" (ver. 3) or "meekness" (ver. 5).

All these spiritual qualities have a distinct relationship the one to the other. It must be noted, too, that this pronouncement of "blessedness" is not a benediction merely, but the announcement of a distinct spiritual state.

Second, this character will react upon the world around. The blessed life is compared to salt—which, for the sake of a needy world, must not be allowed to lose its savor.

The blessed life is compared to light—which, because of the existing darkness, must not be hid.

Deep spiritual values are insisted on (ver. 17-48). The law is declared to have a permanent value, but with a new spiritual content. Now, instead of an outward letter regulating the actions, it is to be an inward spirit moving the soul. The righteousness of the believer is to "exceed the righteousness of the Scribes and Pharisees," otherwise he cannot in any case enter into the kingdom of heaven.

The Master then exhibits the wonders of the perfect life. By taking selected portions of that timeworn law distinctly universal in their principle, and holding them up to the light of His standard for men, He shows what Christian perfection really is.

The perfect life is a life of sincere intention (ver. 21-30). Its motives are purified and its thoughts are clean.

Anger is inward murder (ver. 21-26; 1 John 3:15).

Impure thought is inward adultery (ver. 27-30).

The perfect life is a life of sacred domestic relation (ver. 31, 32). Jesus did not believe in easy divorce, and admitted only one possible ground on which it could be valid.

The perfect life is a life of simple truthfulness (ver. 33-37). In speech there is no double meaning, crafty evasion or equivocation. The man is a man of his word.

The perfect life is a life of sweet demeanor (ver. 38-48).

Here are verses which have been a battleground of contention for centuries. They embody principles which are realizable only through the possession of that love which "beareth all things" (1 Cor. 13).

It "turns the other cheek" when smitten (ver. 39). Trusting God to vindicate and defend, it wins its enemies by kindness.

It lets the exactor have "the cloak also" (ver. 40). Foregoing, if need be, even its just rights, it seeks by the spirit of sacrifice to manifest the spirit of Jesus.

It goes with the unreasonable person "a second mile" (ver. 41). Helping the ungrateful under most undesirable circumstances, it manifests a cheerful spirit. It maintains and cultivates the compassionate spirit (ver. 42).

It returns blessing for cursing, good deeds for hate, and prayer for persecution, proving that it has capacity to endure and grace to manifest "more than others" (ver. 43-48).

All this is involved in the "therefore." It is the manifestation of the perfect life.

2. As to its *restriction*. This will be best seen in the following familiar article which has been so widely distributed in tract form:

## "OTHERS MAY—YOU CANNOT"

"If God has called you to be really like Christ, He may draw you into a life of crucifixion and humility, and put you on such demands of obedience that He will not allow you to follow other Christians, and in many ways He will seem to let other good people do things which He will not let you do.

"Other Christians, who seem very religious and useful, may push themselves, pull wires and work schemes to carry out their plans, but you cannot do it; and if you attempt it, you will meet with such failure and rebuke from the Lord as to make you sorely penitent.

"Others may boast of themselves, of their work, of their success, of their writings, but the Holy Spirit will not allow you to do any such thing, and if you begin it, He will lead you into some deep mortification that will make you despise yourself and all your good works.

"Others will be allowed to succeed in making money, or having luxuries, but it is likely God will keep you poor, because He wants you to have something far better than gold, and that He may have the privilege of supplying your needs day by day out of an unseen treasury.

"The Lord will let others be honored and put forward, and keep you hid away in obscurity, because He wants to produce some choice, fragrant fruit for His coming glory, which can be produced only in the shade.

"He will let others be great, but keep you small. He will let others do a work for Him, and get the credit for it, but He will make you work and toil on without knowing how much you are doing; and then to make your work still more precious, He will let others get the credit for the work which you have done, and this will make your reward ten times greater when Christ comes.

"The Holy Spirit will put a strict watch over you, with a jealous love, and will rebuke you for little words and feelings, or for wasting your time, which other Christians never seem distressed over. So make up your mind that God is an infinite Sovereign, and has a right to do as He pleases with His own. He will not explain to you a thousand things which puzzle your reason in His dealings with you. He will take you at your word; and if you absolutely give yourself to be His love slave, He will wrap you in a jealous love, and let the other people say and do many things that you cannot do or say.

"Settle it forever, then, that you are to deal directly with the Lord Jesus, and that He is to have the privilege of tying your tongue, or chaining your hand, or closing your eyes, in ways that He does not deal with others. Now, when you are so possessed with the living God that you are, in your secret heart, pleased and delighted over this peculiar, personal, private, jealous guardianship and management of the Lord Jesus over your life, you will have found the vestibule of heaven."

### QUESTIONS ON THE TEXT

1. Show the manifestation of the perfect life.
2. Show the restriction of the perfect life.

# 16

## Biblical Development

### (1) Holiness in the Old Testament

THE teaching of Scripture is always progressive. Beginning with a seed thought, it carries the reader through stages more or less defined, until maturity is reached. Remembering this would save us from many mistakes in our interpretation of revealed truth, and not least among that truth, in the subject of holiness.

As an example of the danger here, we relate the following. Some years ago we took up for perusal a book on the subject of full salvation in which, to our amazement, the author took the characteristics of the new birth as set forth in John's first Epistle and applied them to the life of one of the patriarchs recorded in the Book of Genesis. Then, because the Old Testament character did not measure up to the New Testament standard, he promptly declared that up to that period he could not possibly have known any saving relationship with God.

Now to any thoughtful mind that is obviously unfair, and had the writer been familiar with the most elementary

[178]

principles of sound exegesis he would not have made such
a glaring mistake. Every character must be judged by the
period in which he lives. It is said of Noah, for instance,
"Noah was a just man, and perfect in his generations"
(Gen. 6:9). There is the key, "in his generations." It is
only according to the light of his generation that he can be
measured when we say that he "was perfect . . . and walked
with God."

What we say of men, we may say also of words. A correct
exegesis of any word must be according to its thought content in the age in which it was used. The thought content
of a word in one age is not necessarily the same as that of the
same word in another age, therefore to take any word out of
its immediate historical setting and interpret it in the light
of an earlier or later day is to so "wrest the Scriptures" that
we do not "rightly divide the Word of truth."

In the process of years, words change. Some develop,
some deteriorate, while some take on an entirely new com-
plexion. Take, for instance, two words found in our English version of the Thessalonian Epistles:

1 Thess. 4:15: *"Prevent"*—meaning to precede, or to go
before.

2 Thess. 2:7: *"Let"*—meaning to restrain, or to hinder.

The danger, therefore, is twofold: To make their original meaning the fixed meaning for all time, thus limiting
their later use. To put into their earlier usage a later
thought content, thereby overloading their original use.

This must be carefully remembered in our word study on
the subject before us.

Dr. J. Agar Beet has reminded us that in both Testaments the words "holy" and "hallow" correspond exactly to
"saint" and "sanctify," and that holiness is the state resulting from the act of sanctification.

Says he, "That we have two families of words expressing
one idea results from the composite structure of our lan-

gauge in which a Latin super structure is built on a German foundation. From each of these languages we derive words conveying the idea of holiness" (*Holiness Symbolic and Real,* pp. 13-14).

The great truth of full salvation is so clearly woven into the texture of both Old and New Testaments that, turn where you will, some phase of it is not difficult to find. In promise, prayer, and precept; in symbol, statement and in-wrought personal experience, it is the grand theme of the entire book. Our purpose in this section, however, is not to deal with the subject in its wider relations, but to trace the development of the thought content of those leading words, holy and sanctify. We do so because of the assertion so often met, namely, that sanctification is merely to be set apart. We want the word to speak for itself in its numerous set-tings.

In the book of Genesis, the word holy does not occur, and the word sanctify is used only once, then with regard to the Sabbath (Gen. 2:3). Coming to the book of Exodus, how-ever, we find that throughout the remainder of the Penta-teuch the words are more conspicuous; then they appear again in the Books of Chronicles, Psalms, Isaiah, and Eze-kiel.

As used in the Old Testament, these words are to be gen-erally regarded as distinctly relative, and denoting devotion to deity. They are applied to persons, places, objects, sea-sons, and so forth, all of which Jehovah here regards as exclusively His own. They have no human owner, and none may touch them except at Jehovah's bidding. The underly-ing thought throughout is that of separation, the moral element not, as yet, having become a distinctive part, except, of course, as it is implied in the personal devotion of intelli-gent beings to God. In all, however, this thought is foremost —sanctification is complete separation unto God, and holi-ness is freedom from defilement. The words are used:

1. In relation to *persons*.

a. Concerning the firstborn (see Ex. 13:2; Num. 3: 12, 13; 8:16, 17; Deut. 15:19).

These are now not man's but God's. They are not even their own. They are holy in the sense that God has claimed them as His possession, and none may touch them except at His bidding.

b. Concerning the priests (see Ex. 19:22; 29:21, 24).

c. Concerning the entire nation (see Ex. 19:4-6; Lev. 11:44, 45; 19:2; 20:7, 8, 26).

By reason of His power displayed in the deliverance of the nation from Egyptian bondage, He now claims it as His own, "a peculiar treasure unto himself."

d. Concerning the Nazarites (Num. 6:5-8, 19-21).

2. In relation to *places*.

a. Concerning a temporary locality (see Ex. 3:5; 19: 23; Josh. 5:15), "holy ground" or "ground of holiness." Thus called because at that time it was regarded as standing in a specially defined relation to the God of holiness.

b. Concerning the sanctuary. Not the structure only, but also its furnishings (see Ex. 25:8; 26:33, 34; 29:44; Psa. 48:1; 99:9; Isa. 64:11). The outer section of the tabernacle was designated by the word "holiness," while the inner sanctuary bore the peculiar title "holiness of holinesses," translated in Heb. 9:3, "The holiest of all."

This same title is given to the brazen altar (Ex. 29:37). "So intense is the holiness of the altar that we read (three times), 'Whatsoever toucheth the altar is holy' (see Ex. 29:37; 30:29; Lev. 6:18).

"Holy" because of that "touch," it immediately ceased to be man's possession and must henceforth be used only for the purposes of God.

Holiness is also ascribed to the things inside the sanctuary (see Ex. 30:29); and to the bodies of animals offered in sacrifice (see Lev. 2:3).

c.   Concerning the city of Jerusalem (Psa. 48:1, 2).

3.   In relation to *seasons*.

a.   Concerning the Sabbath (see Gen. 2:3; Ex.20:8-11; 31:13-17).

b.   Concerning the feasts (see Ex. 12:16; Lev. 23).

"A holy convocation," lit, "a convocation of holiness." So called because the people were called together at the bidding of God and for the purposes of God. They had to do solely with holy things.

4.   In relation to *things*.

a.   The garments worn by the priests (see Ex. 28:4, 36; 29:6, 21).

b.   The anointing oil (see Ex. 30:31-33).

c.   The sanctuary vessels (Ex. 40:9).

d.   Things dedicated by vows to God (Lev. 27:2, 9, 14, 16).

5.   In relation to *Jehovah's name* (see Lev. 22:32; Ezek. 36:23).

### QUESTIONS ON THE TEXT

1. Show that the teaching of Scripture is always progressive.

2. What is the relationship between the words "holy" and "hallow," and "saint" and "sanctify"?

3. Show the meaning of the words "sanctify" and "holy" as used in the Old Testament.

## (2) Holiness in the New Testament

WHILE in the Old Testament words "sanctify" and "holy" we find a general limitation to the separation idea, other facts are to be recognized which ultimately result in a permanent deepening of the thought content of the word.

Distinct promises are made concerning inner spiritual experience.

That of heart circumcision (Deut. 30:6). That of heart cleansing (Ezek. 36:25, 26; Zech. 13:1). That of spiritual health (Jer. 33:3-9). That of an inwardly written law (Jer. 31:31-34).

Deep inward cravings are felt for a sustained personal contact with God. Not in all. Not necessarily in one all the time, but again and again as the Law Age proceeds, such indications are to be distinguished.

Example, Psa. 42:1, 2; 63:1; 84:2.

Desperate souls, leaping in advance of their fellows, entered into a life of definite blessing and close communion.

Of Enoch it is said that he "walked with God" (Gen. 5:24). Abram so contacted Deity as to receive a change of name and be given that mighty Abrahamic covenant (Gen. 12, and onward). Jacob, the supplanter, became Israel the prince with God (Gen. 32). Moses had amazing spiritual contact and knew God "face to face" (Deut. 34:10). Of Noah (Gen. 6:9), Job (Job 1:1), Asa (1 Kings 15:14), and others, it is declared that they were perfect. David is found confessing his inborn depravity and crying to God for a clean heart (Psa. 51), while Isaiah, suddenly conscious of and confessing his inward corruption, is assured that his "iniquity is taken away, and his sin purged" (Isa. 6:7).

Thus, opening the New Testament, we pick up again our two theme words "sanctify" and "holy," and find that they have now two distinct ideas, one having yet something of

the nature of Old Testament separation, while the other
has absorbed within itself the fuller and deeper thought
which struggled for expression in earlier days and at last
found its completion in the person of Christ and the fact
of Calvary, and in the outpoured Spirit of Pentecost.

Sanctification, then, has now two distinctive ideas, that
of separation and that of purification.

1.   The idea of *separation*. As Dr. Agar Beet reminds
us (*Holiness Symbolic and Real*), there is a very real sense
in which the writers of the New Testament take into their
teaching the Old Testament idea of sanctification.

In the Gospels, Old Testament passages are quoted and
endorsed, as, for example:

God's claim on the firstborn (Ex. 13: 2; Luke 2: 23).

The altar sanctifying the gift (Ex. 29: 37; Matt. 23:
17-19).

Jerusalem, the Holy City (Neh. 11: 1; Matt. 4: 5).

Sanctification of Jehovah's name (Ezek. 36: 23; Matt.
6: 9).

In the Epistles we find the separation idea incorporated
into church truth; thus, all believers are designated
"saints," and by reason of their saving relationship to Jesus
Christ are spoken of as "sanctified." They are "sanctified
in Christ Jesus," and "called saints" (see 1 Cor. 1: 2; Acts
9: 13, 32, 41; 26: 10; Jude 3).

This fact that they are "sanctified in Christ Jesus" and
spoken of in general as "saints" does not guarantee any
depth of personal sanctity, but simply indicates their separation from the world and their spiritual relationship to
Jesus Christ (see John 15: 18, 19; 17: 6,14-16). It is the
position of a justified soul, "a babe in Christ" (1 Cor. 3: 1).
"Being justified by faith, we have peace with God" (Rom.
5: 1). "There may be now no condemnation" (Rom. 8: 1),
but there is still "carnality," as 1 Cor. 3: 1-4 states, and the
remainder of the Epistle clearly indicates.

Some have chosen to call this "objective" holiness—a divine imputation because of a Christward relation. This idea of imputation is not without Scriptural sanction if regarded in its preliminary aspect, and not forced, to the detriment of its companion truth which we shall now take up.

2.   The idea of *purification*. The emphasis on the deepened thought content began with our Lord Himself (see John 17:9-19). In this prayer He deliberately limits His petition to His own people (ver. 9). Two outstanding facts will be noted:

a.   He acknowledges their "separation." "They are not of the world, even as I am not of the world" (ver. 14). There, at once, is the Old Testament idea—sanctification by relationship. But that, now, is far from being sufficient, for Calvary and Pentecost are at hand.

b.   He prays for their "sanctification." If, in the mind of the praying Christ, the idea of sanctification had no deeper thought content than that of the separated life, we have here one of the grossest examples of tautology to be found in any literature. Thus interpreted it would read, "They are already separated; separate them." Such an expression would not even make sense.

The marginal reading of verse 19 gives us at least a hint of the deeper meaning. "That they may be truly sanctified."

This being "truly sanctified" takes up into itself not merely the Old Testament separation fact, but also the fulfillment of its mighty promises and the satisfaction of its deep heart cravings.

Now, the promised heart circumcision could be performed. (Compare Deut. 30:6; Col. 2:11).

Now, the promised heart cleansing could be realized. (Compare Ezek. 36:25, 26; Zech. 13:1; Matt. 5:8; Acts 15:8, 9; 1 John 1:7-9).

Now, the promised spiritual health could be enjoyed. (Compare Jer. 33: 3-9; Rom. 6: 22).

Now, the promised inwardly written law could be realized. (Compare Jer. 31: 31-34; Heb. 8: 6-13).

The Master's prayer, "that they may be truly sanctified" (John 17: 19), finds a corresponding passage in 1 Thess. 5: 23, 24, where the apostle expresses what is virtually a prayer for the Thessalonian Christians that the God of peace Himself would "sanctify them wholly."

Again we say that if nothing more had been intended than sanctification in the Old Testament sense, or than its elementary New Testament idea of imputation, Paul also would have been guilty of the same tautology of which we spoke when referring to John 17: 19.

In this Thessalonian epistle, chapter one indicates the spiritual experience of the Thessalonian believers, a summary of which may be stated as follows:

They are recognized as being "in God" (ver. 1). They are a people for whom he is continually thanking God (ver. 2). They are a people whose experience left a fragrant memory (ver. 3: 4). They are a people in whom the Holy Ghost has produced much assurance (ver. 5). They are a people who exhibited joy in affliction, and became distinct samples of the grace of God (ver. 6). They are a people overflowing with missionary activity (ver. 7). They are a people who have made a clean cut separation from the world and things which concerned their past lives (ver. 9). They are a people who are thrilled with the Advent hope and look for their returning Lord (ver. 10).

It is to these souls that the apostle writes, suggesting that in their experience there is yet a "lack"; they need that "their hearts should be stablished unblamable in holiness" (ch. 3: 10, 13). He tells them, "This is the will of God, . . . your sanctification"; and "God has not called you unto uncleanness but unto holiness" (ch. 4: 3, 7). Then, after some very practical exhortations, he concludes, "And the God of peace himself sanctify you wholly . . ." (ch. 5: 23, 24).

It is evident, then, that to be "sanctified wholly" in the Pauline thinking is to recognize the Calvary provision for a complete destruction of the old nature, and on that basis to "reckon yourselves dead indeed unto sin and alive unto God" (see Rom. 6: 6-11).

## QUESTIONS ON THE TEXT

1.   What further facts are found in the Old Testament relative to the words "holy" and "sanctify" which result in a deepening of the thought content of the word?

2.   Show the two distinct ideas associated with the word in the New Testament.

# 17

## Symbolism

### THE SECOND BLESSING IN BIBLE PICTURES:
### (1) OLD TESTAMENT. (2) NEW TESTAMENT.

### (1) Old Testament

SOME suggestive volumes have been written on the subject of Second Blessing symbolism, setting forth the symbolic evidences of the second work of grace as found in the Scriptures. Some of these declared "symbols" have seemed to us to bear evidences of ingenious straining on the part of the writers to make them fit into a general Second Blessing scheme, and to be such as would not commend themselves to the thoughtful mind.

Let us settle it once for all that as honest exponents of God's Word we are not called upon to see Second Blessing holiness when it is obviously not there. Neither text nor type is ours to torture on the rack of pious imagination until it cries out just what we want it to say. The "workman that needeth not to be ashamed" must "rightly divide the word of truth" (2 Tim. 2:15).

There are, however, in the Scriptures what appear to be some well-defined foreshadowings of this second work of grace, and to them we shall do well to take heed.

Concerning ancient Israel's experiences, Paul wrote as follows:

"Moreover, brethren, I would not that you should be ignorant; how that all our fathers were under the cloud; and all passed through the sea, and were all baptized unto Moses in the cloud and in the sea; and did all eat of the same spiritual meat; and did all drink of the same spiritual drink: for they drank of that spiritual Rock that followed them: and that Rock was Christ. But with many of them God was not well pleased: for they were overthrown in the wilderness.

"Now these things were our examples [figures, types], to the intent that we should not lust after evil things, as they also lusted. Neither be ye idolaters, as were some of them; as it is written, The people sat down to eat and drink, and rose up to play. Neither let us commit fornication as some of them committed, and fell in one day three and twenty thousand. Neither let us tempt Christ, as some of them also tempted, and were destroyed of serpents. Neither murmur ye, as some of them also murmured, and were destroyed of the destroyer.

"Now all these things happened unto them for examples [types]; and they are written for our admonition, upon whom the ends of the world are come" (1 Cor. 10:1-11).

We may therefore claim New Testament authority for finding in the ancient incidents Spirit-pictures of some phases of the believer's life in God.

We have selected seven pictures which we think might reasonably be taken to represent the Second Blessing in symbol, in the Old Testament.

1. The *Levites* and the *priests* (Num. 3; Ex. 28, 29). The differences between the Levites and priests were marked. There was a difference of dress, of table fare, of approach to and waiting upon the tabernacle or temple. The priests went where the Levites did not and could not go.

There are priests and Levites in spiritual life today. There are followers of Christ who are clothed in the white linen of purity which others do not wear. They eat of heavenly fare that their brethren neither have nor believe in. They come boldly "into the holiest," that is hidden by a veil from the eyes of other followers of God.

Christ came to "purify the sons of Levi" (Mal. 3:3) and to make His people "a royal priesthood" (1 Pet. 2:9), "a kingdom of priests unto God" (Rev. 1:6).

It is better to be a priest than a Levite; better because it brings us into a higher religious experience than we had before; better because it gives easier and greater access to God; and better because it plants in the heart and writes on the face "holiness unto the Lord."

2. Dealing with *leprosy*. Leprosy, in the Bible, is a pronounced type of sin. The leper is the sinner. God's dealing with the leper in Jewish ritual is indicative of the divine method of dealing with those spiritually unclean.

This is seen in the two washings of the leper himself (Lev. 14:1-9).

Three things are to be noted here:

a. Two distinct "washings" or "cleansings" are recorded.

b. There is a distinct time interval between them.

c. The word of cleanness is not pronounced until the second cleansing has taken place.

This is also seen in two washings of the leprous garment (Lev. 13:47-59). Leprosy being a type of sin, the garment or robe of the leper is not without significance. The New Testament tells of redeemed souls who were "before the throne of God" because they had "washed their robes, and made them white in the blood of the Lamb" (Rev. 7:9-17).

a. Two distinct "washings" or "cleansings" are recorded.

b. There is a distinct time interval between them.

c. The word of cleanness is not pronounced until the second cleansing has taken place.

This is seen in the two anointings of the leper (Lev. 14: 10-20).

a. Two distinct applications are recorded.

He is touched with "blood." It is the blood of the "slain lamb." This can have only one meaning, which every spiritually enlightened soul will readily understand.

The blood of the slain Lamb (see John 1: 36; Rev. 1: 5; Heb. 9: 14; 13: 12; 1 Pet. 1: 18, 19).

He is touched with "oil." Oil, in the Scriptures, is a recognized emblem of the Holy Spirit.

b. There was a distinct time interval between them.

c. The word of cleanness was pornounced after the anointing with oil.

3. The *two chambers* of the sanctuary (Ex. 26: 31-33; Heb. 10: 19-22). The tabernacle was divided into rooms or sanctuaries. They have been variously called the first and the second, the outer and the inner, and Holy and Most Holy Place, or the Holy of Holies.

The brazen altar, with its sacrifice before the tabernacle, stood for Christ's suffering and death and so represented our justification. The laver with its pure water, standing between the altar and the tabernacle, symbolized regeneration.

The first room, or outer sanctuary, stood for the regenerated life. There stood:

a. The sevenfold candlestick, representing spiritual light.

b. The table of shewbread with its twelve loaves, representing spiritual nourishment.

c. The altar of incense, representing the ministry of prayer.

It was here that the priests accomplished the service of God, but one thing ever before their eyes suggested something better beyond; the "veil" hid the "holiest" from their view.

The second room, or "Holy of Holies," stood for the sanctified life. This inner shrine was distinguished by:

a. A deep quiet. No human voice was ever heard there, and except for the high priest's entrance on the Day of Atonement each year, no human foot ever trod its floor. The heavy folds of drapery excluded every earthsound. The "silence of eternity" remained unbroken there.

b. A divine light. Concerning this light there has been some difference of opinion. One writer speaks of "the abiding light." "A luminous glory," says he, "filled the room, and it was abiding. Unlike the lamp in the outer sanctuary, which burned high or low, this light continued in a steady, soft splendor all the while."

Another writer expresses a different idea. "Now this most holy place was dark inside. No lamp, no candle, no sunlight; all were excluded by the thick curtain. At certain seasons God would blaze out from between the wings of the cherubim, and thus the only light in the second veil was the Shekinah."

While these two writers differ as to when and how the light shone, they are agreed on this, that the only light which illumined the Holy of Holies was the light of God.

c. The divine presence. This, of course, is already suggested by the fact of the divine light, but it is essential to notice that standing there in the holiest of all were cherubim of beaten gold looking down on a bloodsprinkled Mercy Seat. There stood the Ark of the Covenant, in which were the tables of the law, Aaron's rod, and a pot of manna. That Ark symbolized the presence of God.

The "second room" is an outstanding portraiture of the sanctified life.

4. The *two crossings* (Ex. 14; Josh. 3). The Second Blessing is seen in the two crossings made by the children of Israel: one over the Red Sea, and the other over the River Jordan.

As the two crossings took place under the special direction of God, and as they are so markedly different, it is reasonable to believe that they are typical of different spiritual truths and experiences. This is seen in the following contrasts:

At the Red Sea the Israelites were fleeing from an enemy, and were delivered; at Jordan they were not in flight, but were drawn by the goodness and beauty of the land of Canaan, and entered into rest. The sinner has much to dread, but the believer is drawn on toward the experiences of holiness by the promise of rest, plenty, and victory.

At the Red Sea the children of Israel were in great haste; at Jordan we have evidence of calm and deliberate action.

Conversion is found in a hurry, but the blessing of sanctification comes invariably after deep reflection and full deliberation and conclusion of mind.

At the Red Sea the Israelites went down into the sea, a multitude of empty-handed and unarmed fugitives; at Jordan they went in fully armed.

How clearly here appears the state of the fleeing penitent seeking safety, and the consecrated Christian coming with all his powers to God, seeking a life of perfect rest and holiness.

At the Red Sea the children of Israel stepped into a dry and open path between the waters; at Jordan they had to place their feet in the water before the waves receded and the path became open.

In the way of pardon the path is clear. At such a time we are weak and could not face the difficulties before us; but in seeking the experience of sanctification our faith is naturally stronger. We claim the blessings by a strong faith before there is an indication or assurance of the great salvation.

There is a great difference in the emotional life after the two crossings.

At the Red Sea the Israelites were in transports. They sang, danced, struck the timbrel, and the burden of their song was short-lived. It soon gave way to murmuring; at Jordan there seems to have been an unutterable sense of peace, a calm, a holy joy, a triumph. As you read the description you cannot but feel the voiceless emotion of the multitudes. It was an hour too blessed and holy for noisy cymbals.

In conversion, the timbrel is frequently brought forth. But the crossing of the Jordan of death into Canaan of life is marked by a joy that is too profound for words; it is an experience full of glory, but unutterable.

5. The rite of *circumcision* (Deut. 30: 6; Rom. 2: 28, 29; Col. 2: 11). Here is another outstanding picture of a second work of grace.

To the Jew this metaphor was full of meaning—a physical operation with which the whole nation was familiar and with recognized spiritual values behind.

It was the seal of covenant relationship (Gen. 17: 10-14).

It was the sign of covenant blessing—the outward representation of a work to be accomplished within, and the symbol of a spiritual operation upon the heart.

Three things are taught us by the rite of circumcision:

a. There is a surgery of grace—an inward operation divinely wrought upon the heart which removes sin.

It is definite—a work wrought upon the heart. "The heart" in Scriptural imagery is the seat of sin.

It is drastic. To circumcise is to cut. In the spiritual surgery what is to the spiritual detriment is taken away.

It is divine. The "knife" is in the hand of God Himself. Only He can see the inward need, and only He can go within to do the work.

b. There is a special class of people on whom this operation is performed. God's own people. This is obvious for three reasons:

First, the nature of the metaphor. The act of circumcision is of necessity performed only on those previously born and still alive. Consequently, in point of experience, John 3 : 7 must precede Deut. 30 : 6.

Second, the people addressed. It was not the surrounding heathen nations, but Israel, the nation specially His own, and later the church, whom He addressed.

Third, the manner of the address. "The Lord thy God will . . ." God never spoke like that to any but His own.

c.   There is an assured result when this work is accomplished. An unadulterated love. "To love the Lord thy God with all thy heart . . ."

An unhindered life. "That thou mayest live."

6.   The *two kinds of service* (Ex. 21 : 1-6). That there should be two kinds of service rendered to God strikes the mind with surprise. That there is such a thing is plainly taught in the terms "servants" and "friends" used by Christ (John 15 : 14-16).

In this Exodus passage one man is seen in two relations to his master : first, as a bond servant, and, second, as a love slave. As a bond servant he stands for the regenerated man. The fact that he had been bought, that his life was one of service, and that he at the end of six years was free to leave his master is a faithful picture of the regenerated man.

In this passage we see the bond servant suddenly becoming a love slave by the act of making a voluntary gift of himself to his master. He is now no longer his own. He has literally given himself away. He has now no right to anything that was formerly his.

a.   It was an eternal gift. He said he would serve forever.

b.   He enters on a love service. He that doubts that there are two kinds of service, let him study the difference between a faithful servant and a devoted wife.

c.   He feels free to stay. To the world it looks like a life of hopeless bondage; but while there is law in it, it is the "law of liberty."

The bond servant is brought to the doorpost and his ear is bored through with an awl. By reason of this act there now remains no question as to whose he is. The mark in the ear indicating this voluntary, perpetual slavehood, brings upon him both jest and a life of servitude; but by this life he now comes into deepest intimacy with his master. So it is in sanctification, the blessing is obtained by the death route. The Cross now comes into view. The old man must die. The soul must be willing for its own measure of reproach, which will surely come.

7. The *highway* and the *way of holiness* (Isa. 35). There are two ways in the spiritual life leading to heaven. Not two ways leading in different directions which are contrary to each other, but both pointing and leading harmoniously. Regeneration is a highway. In the highway is a way—"the way of holiness."

## QUESTIONS ON THE TEXT

1. How far are we justified in taking things, incidents, and people as types?

2. Give the respective types drawn from the Old Testament, and show their spiritual values.

## (2) New Testament

THIS holiness symbolism is not confined to the Old Testament. We follow with six pictures from the New.

1. The *two rests* (Matt. 11: 28-30). This passage speaks of two rests for the soul. They are different "rests," obtained in different ways and at different times.

The first rest.

a.   It is offered to the unconverted.  The word "come" unmistakably teaches the fact of moral distance.

b.   This rest is "given."  "I will give you rest."

c.   It is obtained by coming to Christ.

The second rest.  What John Wesley called "the Second Blessing," his brother called "that Second Rest."  This is the "rest" of Heb. 4-5.

a.   It is "found."  The first rest was "given."

b.   It is obtained by consecration and faith.  "Take my yoke, . . ."; "learn of me . . ."

2.   Lazarus:  *Life*—then *liberty* (John 11: 20-45).

Lazarus dead is a type of the sinner.  Lazarus brought to life is a type of the regenerated man.  Lazarus set free is a type of the sanctified man.

3.   The *two baptisms* (Matt. 3: 11; Rom. 6: 3-5).  The Word of God has two distinct "baptisms," one of water, the other of fire.

The baptism of water has to do with the confession of sins, and is indicative of repentance. The baptism of fire deals with the inward man and destroys carnality from the soul.

This baptism is undoubtedly the Pentecostal experience. Water, of course, is the outward sign, but the spiritual fact may be known without the water ordinance, and the ordinance may be administered without the knowledge of the spiritual fact.

Baptism is not a synonym for "birth."  No person was ever "baptized" into existence.  In point of experience John 3: 7 must precede Matt. 3: 11.

4.   The *two touches* (Mark 8: 22-26).  The miracle on the blind man wrought in two touches is in perfect harmony with other teaching of the Word of God, and goes to establish the fact of a subsequent and perfecting work of grace.

The first touch brought sight.  However, it was defective

sight. Men were seen out of due proportion. After the first work of grace there is often man fear and man exaltation left in the heart.

The second touch brought perfect sight. He saw clearly. The second touch of grace realized in sanctification brings a clear and proper vision of things to the soul.

5. *In* the throne and *before* the throne (Rev. 3: 21; 7: 15). Those in the throne are the Bridehood company, Christ's reigning partners (see Phil. 3: 7-14; Rev. 20: 4-6). Those before the throne are tribulation saints who miss the Rapture at Christ's Second Coming, but in the period of suffering which follows, faithfully endure. They come in late and therefore miss the best.

6. The fact of *crucifixion* (Rom. 6: 6; Gal. 2: 20; 6: 14). Even more drastic than the thought of circumcision is the idea of crucifixion, again a spiritual experience, which can be known only to the children of God. It will be noticed that this crucifixion is said to be "with Christ," an identification which cannot be predicated of the sinner.

Here again "crucifixion" cannot be made a synonym for "birth," for none ever began to live by an act of "crucifixion," consequently John 3: 7 must precede Gal. 2: 20.


### QUESTIONS ON THE TEXT

1. List the types suggested in the entire chapter.

2. Deal with each one drawn from the New Testament.

# 18

## Objections

### PHILOSOPHICAL AND THEOLOGICAL QUIBBLES WITH THE DOCTRINE

STRANGE as it may seem, there are those within the Christian church who fight the teaching of deliverance from sin—and fight it bitterly, too. Christendom has split into contending camps on the holiness question.

The objections raised are not new. It is amazing to find what parrots intelligent men often are. They think things through in matters of business, but in things which concern the soul they will parrot stock phrases and repeat threadbare objections which, if they only took time to ponder, they would be ashamed to repeat. Here are some of them:

Says objector number 1: *"It is not an essential experience."* To which we reply: If God has made provision for it, and commanded that we should possess it, there is surely some distinct reason in the mind of God why we should have it.

Says objector number 2: *"It is not a Scriptural experience."* To which we reply: The man who makes such a statement either is ignorant of, or deliberately twisting, the teaching of his Bible. In command and promise, prayer and precept, testimony and teaching the Scriptures ring with the truth of holiness. There is nothing in the Scriptures to the contrary. No passage in any part of the Book, when read in the light of its context and historical setting, in any way contradicts this teaching, but all unite to declare either the need, the possibility or the possession of full salvation.

Says objector number 3: *"The standard is too high."* To which we reply: We admit that the standard as preached by some would so seem, but our concern is not with some extravagant talker but with holiness as it is taught in the Word of God. God's standard is reasonable. Here it is: "Thou shalt love the Lord thy God with all thy heart, and with all thy soul, and with all thy mind. This is the first and great commandment. And the second is like unto it, Thou shalt love thy neighbor as thyself" (Matt. 22:37-39).

Says objector number 4: *"The conception of the holiness of God and the sin of man is faulty and inadequate in humans; that is why some talk so glibly about holiness."* To which we reply: No human can ever adequately conceive either of the majesty of God in His holiness or of the depravity of man in his sin. Yet it was Isaiah's temple vision of these that drove him to cry for cleansing, and that cry brought an assured deliverance from the awful fact of corruption within (see Isa. 6).

Says objector number 5: *"This holiness idea engenders pride. A sense of sin is indispensable to a requisite humility."* To which we reply: Nothing could be farther from the truth. Who was more humble than our Lord? Yet He knew no sin. Who is more proud than the devil? Yet he is full of sin.

"When it can be shown that health leads to sickness, strength to weakness, light to darkness, wealth to poverty, virtue to vice, then, in the nature of things, this objection may be true. No Christian (other things being equal) has so clear and correct views of original and acquired depravity, of actual sin, of his dependence on Christ, of his numberless weaknesses and infirmities, as he who is made perfect in love" (Rev. J. A. Wood, *Perfect Love*, p. 234).

If the nature is freed from sin, then it is freed from pride, for humility is an essential part of the experience of holiness. There is, however, an essential difference between the consciousness of present sin and the recognition of original sinnerhood. This distinction will be seen by a comparison of 1 Cor. 4: 4 with 1 Tim. 1: 15.

> " 'Tis true I have no room to boast;
> When most I'm saved, I'm humbled most;
> Kept low by grace, but not by sin,
> My soul shall make her boast in Him."

Says objector number 6: *"This holiness experience is abnormal, leading to oddness, eccentricity and fanaticism."* To which we reply: Please give us reasonable proof. When and where has it happened? That fanatical persons have allied themselves with this cause cannot be denied, and that some well-intentioned people have been inclined to extravagant ideas is all too true. These things, however, are not holiness, neither are they the products of it. They are the unfortunate excrescences which unavoidably appear in any movement. They indicate lack of balance and control. They are the outcome of misconception as to what holiness really is.

There is another side, however, which is frequently overlooked. Among what other section of the Christian church have there been such stalwarts for God; sound, reliable, spiritually progressive men and women, as among those who have espoused the truth of full salvation?

Here are some conspicuous holiness "oddities," if any care to call them such; but who will dare? John Wesley, Charles Wesley, George Whitefield, John Fletcher, William

Bramwell, William Carvosso, George Fox, James Caughey, Bishops Whatcoat, Asbury, Hamline, Peck, Simpson, Foster and others; Dr. Fowler, Dr. Steele, A. B. Earle, William and Catherine Booth; J. A. Wood, Dr. Lowery, Inskip, McDonald, Frances Willard, Frances Ridley Havergal, Thomas Cook, Samuel Chadwick, beside the many other stalwarts of the grace who are still alive.

Take these and their work and influence out of the history of the church, and see how much remains.

Says objector number 7: *"This holiness business makes cliques, and tends to isolation."* To which we reply: In most cases it might be more correct to say that because of their testimony they are cold-shouldered and pushed into isolation. A faithful pastor who is loyal to the Word of God will find that he has no more devoted members in his church than those who enjoy the experience of full salvation.

Says objector number 8: *"Is it not strange that so many really good people in the church do not profess the experience?"* To which we reply: There are no more really good people in the church who do not profess the experience of holiness than there are morally good people in the world who make no profession of religion at all. This latter fact, however, is no argument against salvation, neither is it an argument against entire sanctification.

But this "really good" idea is only our human judgment after all. Then again, many believers sincerely desiring to do God's will are bound in their mental concepts by preconceived ideas learned from childhood. They are not sanctified wholly because they do not take the step of faith, but at heart they are better than their creed.

### QUESTIONS ON THE TEXT

1. Carefully list each objection given thus far.

2. Answer each objection in your own words.

**Objections**
(Continued)

$\mathcal{S}$AYS objector number 9: *"This high-flown profession of holiness is just plain modern Pharisaism, that is all."* To which we reply: By this we understand the critic to mean that wrapped up in this profession of holiness there is of necessity some element of hypocrisy. The term "Pharisee" has come to be regarded as a synonym for "hypocrite," and consequently here the parable of the Pharisee and the publican is frequently quoted.

Yet, the person who will honestly read this parable and then carefully listen to the testimony of a truly sanctified man will soon discover that the two have nothing whatever in common (see Luke 18: 9-14).

Note the drift of the parable:

"And he spake this parable unto certain which:

"Trusted in themselves." A truly sanctified man never does that.

"That they were righteous." A truly sanctified man never says that.

"And despised others." A truly sanctified man never does that.

Listen to the testimony of the sanctified man:

I thank God that:

Corrupt as I was—

He sanctified me wholly—

And He can do the same for you.

Says objector number 10: *"This teaching exalts sanctification at the expense of regeneration."* To which we reply: We fear that it is true that some have given such an impression, but these are not to be regarded as authenticated teachers of this great truth. The Word of God does not allow for known sin in any state of grace, and though "babes in Christ" may be "in Christ" though "carnal" (1 Cor. 3:

1-4), it is only that they might "go on unto perfection" (Heb. 6:1).

The experience entered at the new birth is far beyond what some have said concerning it. A safe conception of the "born again" experience may be formed on the basis of those seven characteristics of the new birth to be found in John's first Epistle.

Says objector number 11: *"If you were made good all at once, there would be no need to grow better."* Or, to put it in more direct theological language, "If this work were done once for all, there would be no need or possibility of growth in grace." To which we reply: It is at this point that growth really begins. No plant can thrive while a worm eats away at its root. With the soul, sin is that worm. Destroy it and growth is assured.

Says objector number 12: *"If carnality were really destroyed, one would never be able to sin again."* To which we reply: That would not be so great a tragedy as it seems, would it? But unfortunately it is not so. Sinful or holy, man is a free moral agent and is on probation so long as this life shall last. After sanctification he need not sin again. Provision is made that he should not—and also lest he should (see 1 John 2:1, 2).

Says objector number 13: *"If a soul were really delivered from all inward sin, it could not be tempted any more."* To which we reply: That is certainly not true. Adam, fresh from the hand of a holy God and standing in his original purity, was tempted by the devil. The Son of God Himself was "tempted in all points like as we." The fact of holiness puts a keener edge on the temptation, but it supplies also a new power to resist.

Says objector number 14: *"If sin should really cease, that would end the Christian warfare, and yet we are exhorted to 'fight the good fight of faith.'"* To which we reply: It does end warfare, on one side, but intensifies it on another. It ends the fight of Gal. 5 : 17, but increases the warfare of Eph. 6 : 12.

"When the heart is pure, Satan is not chained in hell, and a pure heart may have war with outside enemies, both offensive and defensive. After all sin is expelled from the heart, we shall have a warfare to keep it out. It is a mistake to suppose that the Christian warfare is confined to inward bosom foes. Satan goes about 'as a roaring lion,' whom we are to 'resist, steadfast in the faith.' Our blessed Savior was entirely free from sin, but He had warfare, and was 'tempted in all points like as we are, yet without sin.' 'The servant is not above his Lord' "(Rev. J. A. Wood, *Perfect Love*, p. 232).

Says objector number 15: *"If sin were really taken out, we should be immediately ready for heaven."* To which we reply: That is exactly so, in fact, we begin to live in its very portals, or as Bunyan called it, in "Beulah Land." We may go at any time, not merely as isolated individuals by the way of death, but as one great company, caught up·without dying to meet the Lord in the air (1 Thess. 4 : 13-18). For the present, however, we are most needed down here. We stand toward the world in the relationship of:

Salt—checking its corruption; and light—illumining its darkness (Matt. 5 : 13-16; Phil. 2 : 15, 16).

Our Lord prayed for His people, not that they should be taken out of the world, but rather that they should be kept from the evil one while in it (see John 17 : 15).

Says objector number 16: *"If all sin were destroyed, what further need would there be for the blood of Jesus?"* To which we reply: Such an objection does not indicate a very clear conception of the relation of the atoning blood to the believer's salvation. The blood is basic; it is the procurative cause, and also the only means of our approach. Our "boldness to enter into the holiest" is by the blood of Jesus (see Heb. 13 : 12; Eph. 2 : 13; Heb. 10 : 19).

"To say that the doctrine of Christian perfection super-
sedes the need of Christ's blood is no less absurd than to
assert that the perfection of navigation renders the great
deep a useless reservoir of water" (Rev. J. Fletcher, *Last
Check to Antinomianism,* p. 574).

### QUESTIONS ON THE TEXT

   1.  List the entire sixteen objections.
   2.  Deal with each objection in this section,
using your own method of expression.

# 19

# Controversial Scriptures

**(1) Old Testament**

THE opponents of full salvation truth not only bring against it the amazing stock arguments dealt with in the last chapter, but also seek to buttress their position by quoting from the Scripture itself. Usually, however, their quotations have two outstanding characteristics:

a. They are incomplete. An expression is taken from a verse or a verse from a paragraph without any regard as to context or historical setting.

b. They are incorrect. Often they are stock quotations, picked up from others and not the result of personal reading or original thinking. Sometimes a Scripture verse is used with the alteration (not necessarily intentional, but nevertheless vital) of what would seem on the surface to be a most insignificant word, but when carefully checked the importance is seen. Take for instance:

Gal 5:17: "For the flesh lusteth against the Spirit, and the Spirit against the flesh; and these are contrary the one to the other; so that we cannot do the things that we would."

Let the student compare this quotation with the actual reading in the Word of God, noting the words misquoted, and pondering over them until their significance is apparent.

These brethren usually harp upon the necessity of having a Scriptural basis for experience, and then go on to mutilate and misinterpret the most precious and vital portions of the Word of God, while, on the other hand, they bring in passages which to any thoughtful mind are obviously not connected with the subject in hand.

It will be well for us to take up the passages generally used, and thereby fortify the student against coming attacks.

1. *1 Kings 8: 46; 2 Chron. 6: 36:* "There is no man that sinneth not."

This sentence is a parenthesis in the prayer of Solomon at the dedication of the newly-erected temple, consequently the entire prayer should be read before any attempt is made to interpret the one sentence.

Assuming that this has been done, we will ask Dr. Daniel Steele, late professor of theology at Boston University, to explain this:

"We answer that Solomon, when correctly interpreted, as he is in the Vulgate, the Septuagint, and most of the ancient versions, gives no countenance to sin. All these read, 'There is no man that may not sin.' The Hebrew language, having no potential mode, uses the indicative future instead. The context must determine the meaning. The context is nonsense in the King James' Version, using an if where there is no room for a condition—'If any man sin, for every man sins.'

"Let me illustrate the absurdity of this translation. At the laying of a cornerstone of a state lunatic asylum, the governor, in his address, is made by the reporter to say, 'If any person in the commonwealth is insane—for every person is insane—let him come here and be cared for.'

"We should all correct the blundering reporter, and say, 'may become insane,' instead of 'is insane,' in order to make the governor talk sense. Correct the reporter, or translator rather, of Solomon, and let him talk sense also, and you will hear him say, 'If any man sin, for there is no one who is impeccable, who may not sin' " (*Difficulties Removed from the Way of Holiness,* pp. 8, 9).

2. *Eccles. 7:20:* "For there is not a just man upon earth, that doeth good, and sinneth not."

This passage has three reasonable interpretations, any of which is a sufficient answer to our critic:

a. The answer to the previous Scripture (1 Kings 8: 46) may be applied here also.

b. From another angle we would say, the statement here is positively true. This very fact is the basis of all evangelical doctrine. It is a statement of man's natural condition apart from grace. But while it clearly states that there is "not a just man upon earth," evidently meaning "just" by nature, it does not say that there is not a "justified" man on earth, nor a sanctified one, for this would not be true. The statement of this verse is abundantly confirmed by Rom. 3:23, and other New Testament passages.

c. Some have viewed the book of Ecclesiastes as the lament of a pessimist whose outlook on life is that of things "under the sun" (earthly), in contrast with the Ephesian Epistle, life in the "heavenly places" (spiritual). If this is allowed, the critic is answered again.

3. *Job 9:2:* "How should man be just with God?"

Job's question simply indicates the need of a basis for human justification in the sight of God, which is not in man himself. He can only be "justified freely by his grace, through the redemption that is in Christ Jesus" (see Rom. 3:23-28).

4. *Job 9: 20:* "If I justify myself, mine own mouth shall condemn me; if I say I am perfect, it shall also prove me perverse."

That is exactly what every accredited teacher of holiness would say. He never seeks to "justify himself," nor would he ever think of saying, "I am perfect." It is just because he knows that there is no perfection in human nature that he seeks and finds it in and through Christ.

5. *Psa. 14: 1-3:* "They are corrupt, they have done abominable works, there is none that doeth good. The Lord looked down from heaven upon the children of men to see if there were any that did understand and seek God. They are all gone aside, they are all altogether become filthy; there is none that doeth good, no, not one."

Just why this should be used against "holiness" any more than against "regeneration" we fail to see. It is simply a statement of man's depravity, making necessary the work of grace in his nature.

6. *Psa. 51: 5:* "Behold I was shapen in iniquity; and in sin did my mother conceive me."

Here again is a statement of inborn corruption, necessitating the work of saving grace.

7. *Psa. 119: 96:* "I have seen an end of all perfection; but thy commandment is exceeding broad."

Just another statement indicating human insufficiency. But neither the Psalmist nor anyone else has seen an end of divine perfection, nor of the perfection which God imparts.

8. *Psa. 130: 3:* "If thou, Lord, shouldest mark iniquities, O Lord, who shall stand?"

No one, for "all have sinned" (Rom. 3: 23). But what if instead of "marking iniquities" He should forgive them? (see Jer. 33: 8; 1 John 1: 9). This God proposes to do.

9. *Prov. 20: 9:* "Who can say, I have made my heart clean, I am pure from my sin?"

None but a hypocrite indeed. Such expressions as, "I have made, . . . I am pure . . ." are not the expressions of a sanctified soul. The sanctified man says, "I have trusted God to cleanse my heart, I am purified from my sin" (see Acts 15:8, 9).

10. *Isa. 64:6:* "But we are all as an unclean thing, and all our righteousnesses are as filthy rags."

That is exactly what we are as a race. That is our natural condition, hence the need of the Atonement and of personal cleansing.

11. *Jer. 13:23:* "Can the Ethiopian change his skin, or the leopard his spots? then may ye also do good that are accustomed to do evil?"

We find no difficulty here. It is simply a declaration of the sinner's inability to change his nature or his ways. This very fact is the basic need for the work of redemption and its personal application in the experiences of regeneration and entire sanctification.

12. *Jer. 17:9, 10:* "The heart is deceitful above all things, and desperately wicked: who can know it? I the Lord search the heart, I try the reins, even to give every man according to his ways, and according to the fruit of his doings."

Here again is a simple statement of man's heart condition by nature. Redemption is not even approached. It is the ground-work indicating redemption need.

### QUESTIONS ON THE TEXT

1. Show the two outstanding characteristics of the Bible quotations usually brought against full salvation truth.

2. Take up each passage given in this section and answer it in your own words.

## (2) New Testament

WE now consider "proof texts" which opponents of the doctrine take from the New Testament.

1. *Matt. 6:12:* "And forgive us our debts, as we also forgive our debtors." *Luke 11:4:* "And forgive us our sins; for we also forgive every one that is indebted to us."

This petition, using the word "debts" in Matthew's Gospel, "sins" in Luke, and "trespasses" in the general English form of the prayer, is part of what has come to be known as "The Lord's Prayer," although, strictly speaking, it is "the disciples' prayer," as taught by the Lord.

Dr. Adam Clarke: "The three terms, 'debts,' 'sins' and 'trespasses' certainly all mean the same thing, and are used not only to indicate certain wrong actions, but also the ethical and judicial relations of such actions, whether as respects their procuring cause, or their final results."

"The 'Lord's Prayer' is not so much a form of supplication to be presented to God as an embodiment of the substance of prayer, to be presented by the true worshiper to the divine compassion; and, brief as it is, it contains all that may properly enter into our prayers."

Says the objector: "If sanctified wholly, there would be no further need of the Lord's Prayer."

But why not? If it is, as Dr. Clarke indicates, a general prayer "containing all that may properly enter into our prayers," then for the person using it that portion having to do with his immediate need would become applicable.

The petition, "And forgive us our sins" need have no more immediate concern for the person conscious of a past already forgiven, a heart cleansed and a life in constant communion with God than "Give us this day our daily bread," uttered after supper before retiring to rest.

The use of the Lord's Prayer, with its fifth petition, has for the sanctified heart a threefold significance:

It is a reflective recognition of past sins so freely forgiven.

It is a grateful confession of present dependence on the grace and love of a forgiving God.

It is a constant self-reminder of our human weakness and limitation, which is free from actual transgression only as we are kept by the power of God.

2. *Rom. 7:* Read the chapter. This passage is a favorite with holiness critics.

Dr. Daniel Steele: "That fancied Magna Charta for the necessary existence of sin in the Christian heart prompting to sinful acts" (*Difficulties Removed,* p. 23).

Concerning it, various views are held, among which are:

a.  That it represents a real Christian experience. That is, it was the experience of the apostle himself and represents that of the child of God today. To this we reply:

We doubt whether Paul as a Christian ever knew such an experience. If he was saved on the Damascus road (Acts 9:6) and entered into the life of spiritual fullness three days later (Acts 9:7-20) what time would there be for him to know it?

The Scriptural standard of the new birth experience is far beyond this (see 1 John 2:29; 3:9, 14, 17; 5:1, 4, 10).

Believers everywhere who have really sought God's best have reported an experience far higher than this chapter indicates.

b.  That it represents the experience of a Jew under law.

Dr. Daniel Steele: "This was never designed to depict the ideal Christian life, but is rather the portrayal of the struggles of a convicted sinner seeking justification by the works of the Law" (*Love Enthroned,* p. 79).

Rev. John Fletcher: "St. Paul no more professes himself actually a carnal man in Romans 7:14 than he

professes himself a liar in Romans 3 : 7, or James professed to be a curser in James 3 : 9. It is the figure
hypotyposis, so-called in rhetoric by which the writers use
the present tense to relate things past or to come, to make
narration more lively. It is St. Paul's past in the present
tense."

c.   That the passage is to be divided:
   (1)   Verses 7-13 treat of the unregenerate experience.
   (2)   Verses 14-25 describe the regenerate experience.

Leaving the numerous opinions concerning the chapter,
we suggest that the key hangs right there on the front door
in verse 1. In fact, this is to be recognized concerning each
of the three chapters—6, 7, and 8. The key word for chapter six is the word "grace"—verse 1. The key word for
chapter eight is the word "Spirit"—verse 1. The key word
for chapter seven is the word "law"—verse 1.

We submit the thought that this seventh chapter of the
Epistle to the Romans is, in its original intention, a description of the Jew convicted of his need, and vainly trying to
find relief under law. As a secondary interpretation, however, it may be regarded as an apt portrayal of a child of
God convicted of his need of holiness, but not as a normal
portraiture of the Christian life.

3.   *1 Cor. 9 : 27:* "But I keep under my body, and bring
it into subjection: lest that by any means, when I have
preached to others, I myself should be a castaway."

This has nothing whatever to do with the sin question.
The mastery of the body here referred to must be distinguished from the divinely ordained way of dealing with sin.

Compare this verse with Rom. 6 : 6, noting the word
"body" in each and its distinctly different application.

In Rom. 6 : 6, "The body of sin"—lit., the totality of sin,
which "is to be destroyed."

In 1 Cor. 9 : 27, "My body"—the natural appetites of my
humanity which are to be "kept under."

One is the object of destruction, while the other is the subject of redemption (see Rom. 8:23).

4.  *1 Cor. 15:31:* "I die daily."

Here again the sin question does not enter. The context plainly shows that the idea in the apostle's mind is his daily exposure to possible martyrdom.

5.  *Gal. 5:17:* "For the flesh lusteth against the Spirit, and the Spirit against the flesh: and these are contrary the one to the other; so that ye cannot do the things that ye would."

In the previous section we hinted at a frequent misquotation of this verse. We have heard it very glibly quoted: "So that we cannot do the things that we would." Now Paul never said that, and in our interpretation of this passage we must bear in mind the entire drift of the Epistle of which it is a part.

The greeting of the Epistle will be found to differ from that of all the rest.

To the Romans:

Rom. 1:8: "First, I thank my God through Jesus Christ for you all, that your faith is spoken of throughout the whole world."

To the Corinthians:

1 Cor. 1:4: "I thank my God always on your behalf, for the grace of God which is given you by Jesus Christ."

To the Philippians:

Phil 1:3: "I thank my God upon every remembrance of you."

To the Colossians:

Col. 1:3: "We give thanks to God and the Father of our Lord Jesus Christ, praying always for you."

To the Thessalonians:

1 Thess. 1:2: "We give thanks to God always for you all."

2 Thess. 1:3: "We are bound to thank God always for you, brethren. . . ."

To the Galatians:

Gal. 1:6: "I marvel that ye are so soon removed from him that called you into the grace of Christ unto another gospel."

The distinction is clear immediately. On the one hand, "I thank my God," on the other hand, "I marvel."

Numerous expressions in the Epistle carry their own implication:

a. They were "removed from him that called them" (ch. 1:6).

b. They had been spiritually "bewitched" (ch. 3:1).

c. They had "begun in the Spirit," but were now living as though they expected to be "made perfect by the flesh" (ch. 3:3).

d. They were "turning again to the weak and beggarly element" (ch. 4:9).

e. They were becoming "entangled again in a yoke of bondage" (ch. 5:1).

It is these backslidden Galatians to whom the apostle writes, and in no instance does he identify himself with them in personal experience. Concerning himself he writes, "I am crucified with Christ . . . Christ liveth in me . . ." (ch. 2:20). Concerning the Galatians, he writes, "Ye cannot do the things that ye would" (ch. 5:17).

What has chapter 5:17 to do with a normal spiritual experience?

One writer has said: "We can no more measure a freed soul by the Galatian experience than we can measure a free nation by a nation in bondage."

6. *Phil. 3:12-14:* "Not as though I had already attained, either were already perfect: but I follow after, if that I may apprehend that for which also I am apprehended of Christ Jesus. Brethren, I count not myself to have apprehended: but this one thing I do, forgetting those things which are behind, and reaching forth unto those

things which are before, I press toward the mark for the prize of the high calling of God in Christ Jesus."

"There!" says our objecting friend, "Paul himself admits that he has not 'attained.' He says that he is still following after. Do you profess to have gone beyond that choice soul?"

No, we have not gone beyond Paul. We are just marching shoulder to shoulder with him, and his cry becomes ours, "Not that I have already attained, . . . but I follow after."

But wait a moment. Attained what? Follow after what? "The resurrection of the dead" (verse 11). Who but a fool positive would ever think of making such a claim? With the glorious truth taught in the passage it is not for us here to deal. Our only business at the moment is to show that the holiness critic is entirely out of order in using this passage for his destructive work. In this very chapter Paul makes it clear that there is a "perfection" which he claims to possess (verse 15). In the evangelical sense he claims to be "perfect," but in the resurrection degree he is yet to be perfected, and for this he "presses toward the mark."

7.   *1 Tim. 1: 15:* "This is a faithful saying, and worthy of all acceptation, that Christ Jesus came into the world to save sinners, of whom I am chief."

Dr. Daniel Steele: "This is another of the apostle's perverted texts. Our readers may be surprised to learn that Paul the aged, in the fullness of his faith, and love, and professed holiness (1 Thess. 2: 10) was at the time of writing this epistle actually outsinning all the sinners on the earth. This is the interpretation of some who search the Scriptures with the microscope to find proofs that sin must continue in the heart and crop out in the daily life of the best Christian so long as he is in the body. They emphasize the present tense, "of whom I am chief." Let us read the context and see whether Paul is describing his past or his present character:

"Who was before a blasphemer, and a persecutor, and injurious." Now it is a rhetorical usage for a writer describing past events to change to the present in order to render his narrative more lifelike and impressive. This is called the historical present tense, which need not be confounded with a real present, especially when the historian begins, as Paul does, by advertising the reader that he is narrating past events. The Spirit of inspiration assumes that his readers will exercise the same good sense in reading the Bible as they do in reading other books. St. Paul had been the chief, or a chief, of sinners. He is now the chief of saved sinners" (*Difficulties Removed from the Way of Holiness*, pp. 20, 21).

8. *Jas. 3: 2:* "For in many things we offend all."

Of whom does the writer speak when he says "we"? Is it of himself and the rest of the apostles, or has it to do with men in general? The context answers the question, and consequently deals with the objection.

9. *1 John 1: 8:* "If we say that we have no sin, we deceive ourselves, and the truth is not in us."

Dr. Daniel Steele: "I wish to notice the connection in which those words stand. The connection is this, 'If we walk in the light, as he is in the light, we have fellowship one with another, and the blood of Jesus Christ his Son cleanseth us from all sin. If we say that we have no sin, . . . the truth is not in us. If we confess our sins, he is faithful and just to forgive us our sins, and to cleanse us from all unrighteousness.'

"Now, if "we" here means the persons cleansed, just spoken of when it says 'The blood of Jesus Christ cleanseth us from all sin,' we must convict this inspired writer of a manifest contradiction in affirming that the same persons are cleansed from all sin, and yet are still living in sins. It is very much like saying that vaccination is a prophylactic against small pox, but if anyone tries it, and is cured, and

makes declaration of the fact, it is false. That is the absurdity to which John is reduced by that kind of exposition.

"He is addressing a class of men who believe there is no
sin in their souls. This is one fallacy of the gnostics—they
believe that these two principles of good and evil exist in
the world, run on parallel lines, and never touch. The sin
principle they believe to be only in the body, the envelope of
the soul, never staining the soul itself. The sin is all laid
off upon the body, and is only a seeming sin; the soul is not
a sinner and is unpolluted.

"A person may appear to be a great sinner, mixed up
strangely with sin, but he is not. The figure they used was
this: You may cast a gold ring into a pig pen, and have it
trodden down in the filth there, and it remains gold still;
the filth does not really touch or render the gold impure.
So the gold of their souls remained pure and holy, though
their bodies were full of sin, of drunkenness, of lust of all
iniquity.

"That is the class of men John had to deal with, a class
that sprang up in the age of the apostle; and to them he
says, If you say you have no sin that needs the Atonement,
that needs the cleansing blood of the Lord Jesus Christ, you
utter a falsehood and the truth is not in you. But if you
own up and make a clean breast of it, and confess that you
are a sinner before God, and flee to the great fountain of
cleansing, then what follows? We shall see. 'If we confess
our sins, he is faithful and just to forgive us our sins,' and
to go a step further, not only to forgive the sins that have
reference to the past, but to cleanse the nature from the sin
principle which is in it, 'from all unrighteousness'" (*Difficulties Removed from the Way of Holiness*).

To sum up, we say again that there is no passage in the
entire Word of God which, if read in the light of its context
and its historical setting, will not be found to teach either
the need, the promise, or the possession of full salvation.

## QUESTIONS ON THE TEXT

1. Take up the objections dealt with in this last section and deal with them in your own words.

2. Record any other objections which you have met, and answer them.

# 20

## The History of the Doctrine

**(1) THE APOSTLES TO WESLEY. (2) THE WESLEYAN PERIOD. (3) TO THE PRESENT.**

---

### (1) The Apostles to Wesley

THE history of the Holiness Movement is alive with interest. It has its origin in the Word of God, and finds its dynamic in the fact of Pentecost. Beginning with portraiture, prophecy, promise and precept in the Old Testament, it finds its fullness of expression in the New, and its unfolding in the history of the church.

The Old Testament is, of course, anticipatory, having expressions such as the following:

Ezek. 36:25: "Ye shall be clean; from all your filthiness and from all your idols will I cleanse you."

Joel 2:28: "And it shall come to pass afterward . . ."

Zech. 13:1: "And in that day there shall be a fountain opened. . . ."

Opening the New Testament, however, the style is noticeably different, and is found to indicate present blessing:

Matt. 5:8: "Blessed are the pure in heart . . ."

Rom. 6:6: "Knowing this, that our old man is crucified with him. . . ."

Rom. 6:11: "Likewise reckon ye also yourselves to be dead indeed unto sin but alive unto God. . . ."

1 Thess. 5 : 23 : "And the God of peace himself sanctify you wholly . . . preserved blameless . . ."

It was with this conscious heritage that the church began, but it has been through a checkered history that the truth has developed; sometimes corrupted, sometimes despised, sometimes seemingly dead, then manifesting itself in unexpected power and victory, ultimately to fall back into another lull; but throughout the changing years it has never been left without a witness, crude at times though the witness has been.

1.   The testimony of *fathers*. After the apostles, their successors took up the testimony, and such men as Polycarp, Clement of Alexandria, Cyprian, Theophilus, Gregory, Ignatius, Irenaeus, Tertullian, Origen, Clement of Rome, Chrysostom, Cyril of Jerusalem, and others became responsible for the torch.

2.   The testimony of *medieval times*. We use the term "medieval" in its widest sense, as indicating the period from the apostles to Wesley. During this period we may not expect to find an unbroken line of witnesses, clearcut in doctrinal expression and without other encumbrances as though we met them in an old-fashioned Methodist class meeting. Frequently we find only a flickering light, and sometimes what appears to be no light at all; but although it may lie wounded and bleeding, truth never utterly dies. Like its immortal Lord it startles its foes by coming back from the tomb in which it has been sealed, even more radiant than it was before.

Early in the Christian era there began to be manifest a noticeable corruption. The combat actually began in the days of the apostles themselves. In the Colossian Epistle Paul is seen coming to grips with what he terms "philosophy and vain deceit" (Col. 2 : 8, 18), while John takes up the fight with the Gnostic element which had already begun to creep in.

With the fathers, the light gradually failed. They were good men and suffered far more than we shall ever realize, but it would seem that the strenuous nature of the fight for the faith in general had the tendency at times to dim their emphasis on doctrines in particular.

Dr. Lowrey: "The fathers had a morbid spirit and reckless zeal that courted suffering and death. They were more anxious to die for Christ as martyrs than to die in Christ to all sin.

"But leaving the Gnostics and Christian fathers, in whose hands the Gospel doctrine of holiness began to be disfigured and covered with rust, we enter a prolonged period in which the great truth was buried for the most part in the ashes and debris of a fallen church. It was so intermixed with foul thought and practice that many, it must be confessed, who professed it, went, in some cases, to the extreme of shocking excesses.

"But while smoke can cover a crystal or diamond with a coat of obscurity, it cannot penetrate the substance. It is so with the subject of holiness. Though intermingled and soiled with the mistakes and pollutions of degenerate years yet, as a neglected jewel, it sparkled here and there among the dust and trumpery of medieval superstitions. There were, all along through the Dark Ages, individuals and societies who believed in a high type of Christian perfection, and strenuous efforts were made from time to time to graduate experience up to the ideal standard.

"The doctrine of Christian perfection during medieval times was represented chiefly by five classes of exponents, namely: Fanatics, Ascetics, Mystics, Pietists, and Evangelicals. This line runs from the apostles to Wesley. There are many divergences, more or less sound; but it is a continuous line which, like the railroads, have come up from the scrap iron of absurdity to the steel rail of well-defined faith" (*Possibilities of Grace,* pp. 19, 20).

We shall trace briefly this flickering light of full salvation through the darkened years, using as guide words the classes here suggested, with one addition which we think Dr. Lowrey has overlooked.

a. The *Fanatics*. They are not all dead, even yet. What a problem these people have created within the church! It is necessary, of course, to differentiate between the fanatic and the hypocrite. A hypocrite professes to be what he is not—and usually with some selfish end in view; but a fanatic devoutly believes all that he professes, the trouble being that he allows emotion to outrun reason, and thereby loses his spiritual balance. He is frequently driven to his extremes by the laxity of other religious professors around him; but while they lose the steady spiritual glow he, in his overwrought zeal, plunges into the wildfire of excess and thus mars what would otherwise have been a useful life. Strange as it may seem, these wildfire fanatics have been overruled in the divine economy, and while their extravagances are neither to be imitated nor condoned, they are often to be recognized as the only possible medium through which God could keep a light burning even though that light became a dangerous flare rather than a steady flame.

Such an one was Montanus, the founder of Montanism, back to whom the history of fanaticism may be traced. He appeared in Phrygia soon after the middle of the second century, and startled the drowsy church with the announcement that in him dwelt the Paraclete in a peculiar degree, and through him and his followers preparations were being made for the return of the soon coming Lord and the setting up of the kingdom. With him were two women, known as "prophetesses" who, in trances and ecstasies, poured forth their "messages."

Strangely enough, amid all this confusion, Montanus is said to have kept straight on his doctrine so far as salvation was concerned, and here, in such a hotbed of extravagance,

God saw to it that the precious truth of Christian perfection should be sheltered until more congenial surroundings could be found.

b.   The *Ascetics*. Dr. Lowery: "Asceticism is another form of half truth and blurred holiness. This type of piety on its right side may be traced back to the Gospel itself: 'If thine right hand offend thee, cut it off; if thine eye offend thee, pluck it out'; and to Paul, who says, 'I keep under my body, and bring it into subjection.' But this needful discipline was soon pushed to shocking extremes in the form of sour asceticism.

"The first and worst type of this morbid sanctity, and that which gave rise to all the austerities and monastic orders of Romanism, took its rise in Egypt in the second century.

"But ethical discipline, resembling the hygienic exercise of the body, is, undoubtedly, a Christian duty, and cannot be dispensed with in the race for the highest perfection. 'Exercise thyself unto godliness,' is the Christian regimen. This virtue has been practiced in all ages of Christianity, and out of it has grown, not legitimately, but by perversion, the hybrid of extreme asceticism. We say extreme, for it must be confessed that the purest specimens of the Christian life have been found among the Ascetics. But this Christian duty has been abused, and, therefore, from Origen down, has taken on the aspect of self-torture.

"Asceticism is founded upon the idea of a perpetual conflict between the flesh and the spirit. Adopting practically the heathen and Gnostic notion, that sin is located in the body, they wage war upon its members, and aim to crucify its natural and innocent appetences. And as they cannot get rid of the body till they die, the Ascetics have at all times been obliged to put in a caveat against salvation from all sin in this life. This makes their teaching inconsistent. In one paragraph they are quite on a plane with Wesley and

Fletcher; in the next they drop down among the brethren who tell us that a bit of sin is necessary to preserve our humility. How absurd! A deposit of death to keep us alive!

"Among the Ascetics who held to sublime holiness with the remains of some sin may be named Macarius, of Egypt; Nilus, a Greek disciple; and Marcus Eremita. The faith of these men, like Fenelon, Madame Guyon, DeRenty, like Chalmers and Edwards of later times, rose to the verge of full salvation, and yet, like St. Augustine, and the whole Calvinistic school, they were fettered with the servile belief that concupiscence or some sin must remain till death" (*Possibilities of Grace,* pp. 22, 23).

Here, then, we see the beginning of the corruption of the truth which has developed on the one hand into the Roman heresy, and on the other into numerous more subtle ideas which have been styled evangelistic; but through it all the witness has persisted.

c. The *Mystics.* "Mysticism" is a queer combination of truth and error. By it many have been allured into a maze from which they have never emerged into clear light; and yet, withal, by a strange divine overruling, some of the choicest saints of the ages have been found among these people, and through their instrumentality the truth of Christian perfection has been preserved.

Concerning Mysticism Dr. Lowrey writes: "This form of marred truth figures largely in the ancient struggle for attainment of sublime holiness. Like Asceticism, it took its origin in Egypt in the second century, under Ammonius Saccas, a native of that country. He attempted to lift a lofty standard of sanctity by forming a coalition between the Egyptian, Platonic, and Christian philosophies and religions—another foolish attempt to blend truth and error, light and darkness—the first instance of Broad-Churchism. From this cockle and wheat sprung Mystics, which have since ramified into various sects.

"The Mystics did not differ much in their austerities and aim from the Ascetics, only they were more extreme and, in some cases, more absurd. And yet as the underlying principle of Mysticism was personal sanctity, it could not perish. On the theory of the immortality of truth and the necessary survival of the fittest, it has outlived every change, defied all persecution, and transfused itself into every spiritual type of religion, from Ammonius, of the second century, to Wesley, of the eighteenth. Its vital element was early incorporated into all that was good and true in Catholicism, and from Catholicism it has been transferred into the Pietism of Germany, the Moravianism of Bohemia, the Quakerism of England and America, and finally into the Methodisms that now belt the world. Luther himself was a Mystic and commended Mystic theology. The germinal principle of Mysticism was in Fenelon, Madame Guyon, De Renty, Thomas a'Kempis, William Law, Spener, Peter Bohler, and largely in Wesley and Fletcher.

"Mysticism was based on the great truth that there is a hidden sense in the text of Scripture which the carnal mind cannot perceive. No doctrine is more absolutely true. But some of them rode this splendid hobby to destruction. They ran it into hallucination and vagary, and found sense where there was nothing but nonsense. The bottom fact, however, was a truth which has been most hallowing in all ages. For it must be confessed that this principle of superior enlightenment by an unction from the Holy One is Scriptural and, as such, has been aimed at and coveted by all the spiritual and holy from the days of Christ until now.

"The misfortune of the church in all periods has been, not so much the loss of truth, as the corruption of truth; not the extinction of the sparks and embers of the holy fire, but the covering of them with error and superstition. And the duty of the church today is not to discover and put forth a new doctrine, but to burnish up the old; not to coin a new currency out of other and richer minerals, but to rub off the tarnish and dirt from the very fine gold that lies neglected and trampled under foot all around us. The great mission of the ministry is the universal propagation of this faith, and a revival of a corresponding experience" (*Possibilities of Grace,* pp. 24-26).

d.   The *Pietists.* With the Reformation came a tremendous awakening, but so far as personal holiness was concerned it was merely a beginning. Out of the controversy, however, came the expression of that deep-rooted desire for likeness to God; hence in the seventeenth century came the rise of "Pietism," a movement in Holland and Germany led by one named Spener.

The essential mark of Pietism was the quest for individual holiness. It was the necessary reaction against a type of religion that was rigidly doctrinal but laid no stress on a high spiritual attainment in the present life. The Pietists laid stress on devotion rather than doctrine. "The real proof of one's standing in grace and justification by faith lies in love and obedience in the passion for practical holiness." It was necessary and possible for the regenerate to fulfill all the divine commands. There seems to have been no uniform doctrine of perfection among the Pietists, but the movement represents at least an awakening in the direction of the teaching of full salvation now soon to be proclaimed by that great apostle of truth, John Wesley.

e.   The *Quakers.* While in Holland and Germany the Pietists were reviving the teaching of personal holiness, a movement in the same direction was being felt in England. George Fox, Isaac Penington and others were receiving what was felt to be divine revelation concerning the "inner light." These men were not satisfied with reformation teaching but with deeper insight insisted that the holiness taught by the Lutheran school demanded another emphasis; it was not imputed but real.

Thus, on many sides, came signs of awakening, until at last the great evangelical revival burst upon the world.

### QUESTIONS ON THE TEXT

1. Show the distinctive difference between the expressions of the Old Testament and those of the New on the subject of holiness.

2. Trace the trend of doctrinal history from the apostles to Wesley.

## (2) The Wesleyan Period

WITH the opening of the eighteenth century came the new era of clear teaching on the subject of Bible holiness; yet not even this period may be claimed as a steady witness to the experience, for even since Wesley there has been much to regret. Yet it has never been allowed to sink so low as in those earlier years, for the great evangelical revival did something for the cause of holiness which the passing of the years has not been able to erase.

John Wesley was born at Epworth parsonage on June 17, 1703, and died at the ripe old age of eighty-eight years, having been for sixty-five years before the public eye. Of him it is said that, "he was carried to his grave by six poor men, leaving behind him nothing but a good library of books, a well-worn clergyman's gown, a much-abused reputation, and—the Methodist Church" (*Wesley and His Century,* Fitchett, p. 9).

Yet Wesley's legacy to the world was tremendous. Without his contribution we should have been poor indeed. Around him were gathered very ordinary people, mostly poor, many of them having been lifted from a life of squalor and sin; but out of these he fashioned a church and sent it forth on the same great business of evangelism, emphasizing one great fact—salvation from all sin, for all men, in this life.

Two years before his death Mr. Wesley wrote, "This doctrine is the grand depositum which God has lodged with the people called Methodists; and for the sake of propagating this cheifly He seems to have raised us up" (*Letter to R. C. Brackenbury, Esq.*)

Many names are worthy of note in connection with early Methodism (the student should see *Wesley's Veterans,* 7 vols.) ; but the outstanding characters of the period, so far as full salvation is concerned, are three whose names have been a blessed memory to every succeeding generation. They are:

John Wesley—preacher and traveler, chief exponent of full salvation truth, and founder of the Methodist Church.

Charles Wesley—also a preacher, but chiefly a hymnwriter and the chosen channel of God to embody the truth of holiness in hymns for the Methodist Church. These hymns are the church's choice heritage, although to many they are nothing more than a relic of a past day.

John Fletcher—that, for the sake of convenience, was the English form of the name which he adopted—was a clergyman of the Anglican Church ; a scholar, a saint, and a skilled apologist of full salvation truth, as his writings, especially *Checks to Antinomianism,* will show.

The result of this evangelical revival was twofold:

1. *Nationally.* Affecting the entire land, it brought a moral change into the country at large. Sin was rampant. Darkness was upon the people. Revolution was in the air. Soon, however, a change was recognized, for the entire land underwent a moral clean-up such as only a divine visitation could bring. At this same period France plunged into atheism and red revolution, but by the grace of God, under the instrumentality of Wesley, Britain began to throb with the

urge of a mighty religious awakening, the effects of which have never wholly worked themselves out of the national life.

Dr. Fitchett: "Wesley may challenge the judgment of mankind by the test of the mark his work has left on the history of the English-speaking race. His contribution to that history may be compressed into a single sentence. He restored Christianity to its place as a living force in the personal creed of men and in the life of the nation. It was a change profound and wonderful, carrying in itself the pledge and the secret of a thousand other changes. For more than fifty years—from the moment he broke through all ecclesiastical conventions and preached on the moors at Kingswood to the rough miners, down to the moment speech failed on his lips in the death chamber at City Road—Wesley was the greatest force in England. And he was a force for all that Christianity means" (*Wesley and His Century*).

2. *Ecclesiastically.* Wesley's monument is the Methodist Church—and that is a miracle in itself.

Dr. Fitchett: "In the case of Wesley, many of the ordinary elements of power were visibly lacking. He was to the day of his death a poor man, if only because he gave away everything he possessed. He was, at the moment when his career takes the scale of history, a clergyman without a charge, a leader without a party, a preacher with every pulpit in three kingdoms shut against him" (*Wesley and His Century*).

Today that church belts the globe and wherever Christ is known the name of Wesley is soon known also.

### QUESTIONS ON THE TEXT

1. Tell the story of the revival under Wesley.

### (3) To the Present Day

THE revival under Wesley was by no means an isolated event. It was rather a source-event. That is to say, within it were forces destined to affect both localities and generations far beyond its immediate range. It would be safe to say that there is no evangelical force today, whatever its peculiar emphasis, which is not indebted, directly or indirectly, to the Wesleyan source.

There are, however, distinct channels which must be named as direct resultants of this event because of their emphasis on Wesleyan doctrine. Every land has its own part in the story, but here we can take up only that which concerns the British Isles and America. We join these two countries because in Wesley they possess a mutual heritage; for while it was in the former country that the stream of blessing began, it was from the latter that it flowed back, and that with renewed emphasis. The campaigns of American holiness evangelists and teachers such as James Caughey, C. G. Finney, Inskip, McDonald, Amanda Smith, and others, backed by the writings of Daniel Steele, Asa Mahan, J. A. Wood, T. C. Upham and others, were used to establish full salvation testimony in Britain when again it seemed likely to die, so that today there is a mutual indebtedness in the two countries which neither can disregard.

1. Holiness in the *British Isles*. We place Britain first for chronological reasons; for it was here under Wesley that the work began, and from this center it spread. We shall trace in barest outline what have seemed to be the outstanding influences for Second-Blessing holiness in that land.

a. The influence of original Methodism. This was discussed earlier in the chapter.

b. The influences within Methodism. While standing nominally for the doctrine of the Second Blessing, the Methodist Church as a whole has now ceased to teach it. Yet within its borders the light still burns; faithful ministers and laymen here and there, often at personal cost, are bearing a loyal witness to the Savior from all sin. The two principal centers avowedly standing for this truth are Cliff College and the Southport Convention.

c. The influences without Methodism. These are numerous. The largest body is the Salvation Army. William and Catherine Booth, the founders of this organization, were clear and uncompromising exponents of this interpretation of New Testament teaching, and where its officers are truly spiritual it is still a power for Second Blessing holiness and its most effective gathering is the holiness meeting.

Beyond this, however, are other smaller but no less effective agencies which, during recent decades, have been raised up to propagate the truth. For many years the chief interdenominational center was Star Hall, Manchester. The fame of its marvelous conventions became internationally known. In Scotland, the Faith Mission was established in 1866 and is still sending out its pilgrims two by two, both in Britain and in Canada, with the message of full salvation. There also the Pentecostal Church of Scotland has borne a loyal witness, later to become affiliated with the Church of the Nazarene.

Among the churches in general has been the witness of the Pentecostal League of Prayer. (This is not to be confused with modern Pentecostalism.)

Contemporary with these are such agencies as the International Holiness Mission, with its British and South African work; the Emmanuel Church, Missionary Bible School and foreign agencies; the Calvary Holiness Church; and numerous other local and independent works.

Mention should also be made of the holiness missionary societies, among which are: The Japan Evangelistic Band, The Japan Rescue Mission, The World Wide Evangelistic Crusade, and a representation of the Oriental Missionary

Society which, of course, is American in its origin, but international in its scope.

2. Holiness on the *American continent*. On the American side this testimony has worked itself out through numerous avenues: churches, associations, camp meetings, conventions, tabernacles, colleges, Bible schools, missionary organizations, and the like.

a. The witness of Methodism. It began thus: Wesley had visited Georgia, but being himself without a conscious heart experience had returned to England a disillusioned and disappointed man. Then came Wesley's spiritual transformation and the beginning of Methodism in Britain. Whitefield visited America and did good work.

In 1760 Methodists from Ireland arrived, settling in New York and Maryland, and reaching out into Delaware, Pennsylvania, and Virginia. Another company also landed from County Limerick, and were soon busy in the work of establishing American Methodism.

In the British conference of 1769, held in Leeds, John Wesley said, "We have a pressing call from our brethren in New York (who have built a meeting house) to come and help them. Who is willing to go?" Joseph Philmore and Richard Boardman volunteered, and two months later we hear Philmore on the steps of the Old State House in Philadelphia "delivering a Methodist sermon." Other Methodists came out, among them Francis Asbury, and soon revival was in the air.

Then came the Revolution. Every English preacher except Asbury left the country, and Asbury went into retirement, leaving the Methodists a disorganized, leaderless company.

In 1783 peace was signed, and Asbury, with a few local preachers, is again seen. Wesley, seeing the need of separate Methodists in a separated America, ordained Dr. Thomas Coke as its first bishop and, with Richard Whatcoat and Thomas Vasey, sent him to America. Dr. Coke rode a thousand-mile circuit to meet his preachers.

In 1784 a conference was held, and the Methodist Episcopal Church came into being, Francis Asbury being elected by acclamation to work with Dr. Coke as Bishop. Until that time Asbury had been only an itinerate preacher. On Christmas day Dr. Coke called him to the altar rail and made him a deacon, the next day he again called him forward and made him an elder, the next day he laid his hands on his head and called him bishop; and so in Baltimore, with sixty preachers and a membership of two thousand seventy-six, American Methodism was officially born.

(For more details see *See These Banners Go,* Mead).

Those were days of wonderful blessing. Concerning them much could be written, did space permit.

Bishop Asbury wrote: "For the past two years, amid innumerable trials, I have enjoyed almost inexpressible sensations. Our Pentecost is come in some places for sanctification. I have good reason to believe that upon the eastern shore four thousand have been converted since the first of May last, and one thousand sanctified" (*Journal*).

Rev. Henry Boehm's Diary: Writing of Bishop Asbury he says: "There were one hundred forty-six converted and seventy-six sanctified during the day. During the meeting there were reported 1,321 conversions and 916 sanctifications. At sunset they reported 339 conversions and 122 sanctifications."

"Here we have the work of God plainly stated in the old Methodist way by the venerable Father Boehm, the sainted centenarian of American Methodism, who was an eye witness and participator in the meetings he reports. It is no wonder that Bishop Asbury wrote in his *Journal,* 'Our day of Pentecost is fully come'" (*Perfect Love,* pp. 152, 153).

This, like other spiritual waves, at length subsided and formalism came in, but in 1847 the testimony of holiness again began to revive, and in western New York the Nazarite Movement began to manifest itself.

Within Methodist circles bitter antagonism and ruthless opposition developed, focusing itself against Benjamin T. Roberts in the Genesee Conference. This warrior for the faith later became the founder of the Free Methodist Church.

The East Coast revival. About this time New York began to feel the throb of Second Blessing holiness teaching through the witness of Mrs. Phoebe Palmer. She and her husband, Dr. Palmer, opened their home for a holiness meeting each Tuesday evening for more than forty years. From practically every part of the country and from many other countries people are said to have come to these services. Dr. and Mrs. Palmer traveled extensively in America, Canada, and in Europe, preaching and teaching this truth.

Associated with this period are the names of a number of mighty men. Bishop Hamline, Dr. George Peck, Dr. F. G. Hibbard, Dr. Nathan Bangs, Dr. Jesse T. Peck, Dr. T. C. Upham, Rev. John Inskip, Rev. William McDonald, Rev. C. G. Finney, Dr. Asa Mahan, and others.

b. The witness beyond Methodism. Holiness may have been the sacred trust of Methodism; it certainly was; but it was no more a Methodist prerogative than Christ and salvation were the exclusive property of the Jewish people. Spiritual forces cannot be localized, and although Methodism led the advance, the time was coming for the bursting of bands and the breaking of barriers.

First, there was the organization of the National Association for the Promotion of Holiness, which had its roots in Methodism.

Concerning this we give the historical sketch presented by its president, Dr. C. W. Butler, in the Association report, 1932-1936.

"About the close of the Civil War in this country many

godly souls in different Christian communities became greatly concerned over the lack of spiritual power in the church of their day and the prevailing worldliness, and in different sections of the country special meetings were held for the promotion of vital spirituality, or holiness. Some very devout Methodist preachers were especially burdened in spirit because of the waning interest of their church in the doctrine and experience upon which it was founded, and for the spreading of which God seemed to have raised them up. Evangelistic fervor and spiritual power were being displaced by formality and worldliness. John S. Inskip, the illustrious first president of our organization, writing about this condition said: 'It was conceded by all candid minds that something must be done to excite among professing Christians a deeper interest in this momentous theme, *i. e.*, holiness. The prevalence of worldliness and formality seemed to call loudly for a special effort on the part of those concerned for the extension and ascendancy of evangelical religion.'

"These Methodist preachers came together from time to time for consultation and prayer, and were quite clear as to the great need of a revival of the preaching and experience of holiness in the church; but as to the methods of promoting such a revival, they were not clear. But a message from heaven came to that godly man, W. B. Osborne, of the New Jersey Conference, and, unable to restrain himself, he took the train to New York and hastened to the study of John S. Inskip, and with a soul full of holy passion and fire said, 'I feel that God would have us hold a holiness camp meeting.'

"Inskip was ready for that message, and together they fell on their knees and cried to God for wisdom and guidance. They prayed, waited, wept, and believed, and heaven opened and the glory came upon them as God revealed His pleasure to them; and they rose, clasped hands, and with hearts full and eyes streaming pledged their eternal fidelity to God and holiness. And then and there the National Association for the Promotion of Holiness was born.

"When they separated it was settled that a holiness camp meeting should be held, and by the grace of God there would be at least two tents there. It had also been agreed that other brethren who were like-minded concerning this great doctrine should be invited to meet with them for consultation as to when and where this meeting should be held. This brought together in the city of Philadelphia, Pennsylvania, on June 13, 1867, that company of noble and godly men— including the venerable Dr. Roberts of Baltimore, who was made chairman, and Rev. John Thompson of the Philadelphia Conference, who was appointed secretary—who waited upon God under a profound sense of the importance and responsibility of the subject in hand until the divine plan was revealed to them. 'It was the most fraternal and religious business meeting any of us ever attended,' writes Inskip. There was one continued earnest invocation for the light and aid of the Holy Spirit. The considerate and deferential manner of everyone who spoke on the occasion was so marked as to convince all present that God had taken the affair into His own hands and would lead us on to victory.

"Under the guidance and illumination of the Holy Spirit certain things were settled at that meeting. To inaugurate a camp meeting movement had already been decided. John S. Inskip and William Osborne settled that. But when and where to hold the first meeting was discussed in the Philadelphia gathering, and Vineland, N. J., was unanimously chosen. Then came the question of the name. It was not to be an ordinary camp meeting. They had a specific object in view, and that was to spread Scriptural holiness, not among Methodists only, but among all believers, and not only in one particular section of the country, but throughout the land. They cherished the largest catholicity of spirit, and resolved to invite all evangelical denominations to join with them at once in the great undertaking before them. They had faith for a nation-wide holiness revival. So they adopted the name 'National Camp Meeting,' and were careful to set forth the fact that the object of the meeting was the promotion of holiness among believers. This did not mean that the conversion of the unsaved was not to be sought after. The multitudes who were saved in their camp meetings proved this. It did mean, however, that the great outstanding object these men had in view was the sanctification of those who had already been justified. And they knew also, as John Wesley said after he had obtained the experience, that 'the more explicitly and strongly believers are pressed to aspire after full salvation as obtainable here and now by simple faith, the more the whole work of God will prosper.' Hence, they determined that the camp meeting which was to inaugurate a great revival movement should be distinguished from all other meetings of like character in that it was a national, interdenominational meeting for the specific purpose of promoting holiness among believers and, thereby, the success and prosperity of the church of Jesus Christ in all departments of soul-saving activity.

"The National Association for the Promotion of Holiness is now the corporate name of the organization which came into being at the national camp meeting of 1867."

This association has been the instrument in developing some of the mighty leaders in the interdenominational ministry of this doctrine, among whom should be mentioned: John S. Inskip, William McDonald, Charles J. Fowler, Joseph H. Smith, Henry C. Morrison, Edward Walker, Seth C. Rees, Phineas F. Brasee, C. W. Ruth, and others.

In 1910 the Missionary department of this Association was organized for the spread of Scriptural holiness in foreign lands, and has developed its work especially in China, Africa, and India.

Concerning the early days of this movement Rev. J. A. Wood writes:

"Never, perhaps, since the days of primitive Christianity, has there been a more general manifestation of the Spirit and power of God to purify human hearts and save sinners than at the services of this Association.

"The great gatherings at Vineland, Manheim, Round Lake, Oakington, Des Plains, Hamilton, Urbana, Moundsville, Landisville, Cedar Rapids, Wesley Grove, Clear Lake, Old Orchard, Sacramento, Salt Lake, and San Francisco will never be forgotten. . . . The comparatively low religious life of the whole American Protestant Church at the close of the war felt the impulse and has been benefited by the revival of Christian holiness" (*Perfect Love,* pp. 274, 275).

In the last ten years the Association held thirty-four national camp meetings in at least fifteen states, besides tabernacle meetings on both shores of the continent.

Colleges and Bible schools followed the organization of the National Association.

Worldly tendencies in the educational system and the denominational schools began to concern the leaders of this spiritual awakening. This led to the founding of colleges with the emphasis on holiness evangelism. At the same time, these leaders of the new movement recognized the imperative need of definite theological training for the young preachers, both male and female, which led to the organization of Bible training schools to offset the lack which was felt to exist in the theological seminaries.

Distinctive holiness churches also began to appear. These are now both numerous and strong. Their founders recognized, as did Wesley in the beginning, that only organization could conserve the work, and so set themselves to spread and preserve the doctrine along denominational lines. Added to these must be recognized the many independent holiness tabernacles throughout the country, whose leaders are now drawing closer together in their determination to spread the truth. To this end an Association of Holiness Tabernacles has been formed.

Holiness literature should also be mentioned here. The books written on this subject have become an extensive library, while the holiness periodicals are far too numerous here to record.

## QUESTIONS ON THE TEXT

1. Name the streams flowing from the Wesleyan source.

2. Show where this work began, and trace the development in that land.

3. Give a brief survey of the development of the holiness testimony within the United States.

# 21

## Witnesses

### PERSONAL TESTIMONIES
### OF RECOGNIZED AUTHORITY

WE have reserved this final chapter in which to give the testimonies of some of the leading exponents of this truth. In this field we find our wealth to be our embarrassment, and are reluctantly compelled to select only a mere handful out of the mass of material which offers itself. It would not be difficult to pack an entire volume with the direct and definite testimonies of men and women of repute who have enjoyed this experience and rejoiced to declare it. We select a few out of those best known.

1. *John Wesley:* Strange as it may seem, there has been much controversy concerning Wesley's own enjoyment of this experience. Some have gone so far as to declare that while Wesley preached this blessing he never actually gave testimony to the possession of it. We submit two quotations, which we think to be sufficient evidence. Further, we suggest that as an honest man Wesley could not have taught the experience for so many years without personal participation.

"I was unusually lifeless and heavy till the love feast in

the evening; when, just as I was constraining myself to speak, I was stopped, whether I would or no; for the blood gushed out of both my nostrils, so that I could not add another word. But in a few minutes it stayed, and all our hearts and mouths were opened to praise God. Yet the next day I was again as a dead man; but in the evening, while I was reading prayers at Snowsfields, I found such light and strength as I never remember to have had before. I saw every thought, as well as every action or word, just as it was rising in my heart; and whether it was right before God, or tainted with pride or selfishness. I never knew before (I mean not as at that time) what it was to be still before God. Tuesday 25. I waked, by the grace of God, in the same spirit; and about eight, being with two or three that believed in Jesus, I felt such an awe and tender sense of the presence of God as greatly confirmed me therein: so that God was before me all the day long. I sought and found Him in every place; and could truly say, when I lay down at night, 'Now I have lived a day' (*Wesley's Journal*, Dec. 23-25, 1744).

"Many years since I saw that without holiness no man shall see the Lord. I began following after it and inciting all with whom I had any intercourse to do the same. Ten years after, God gave me a clearer view than I had before of the way to attain this; namely, by faith in the Son of God. And immediately I declared to all, 'We are saved from all sin, we are made holy by faith.' This I testified in private, in public, in print; and God confirmed it by a thousand witnesses. I have continued to declare this for about thirty years, and God has continued to confirm the word by His grace."

2. *John Fletcher:* Rev. John Fletcher, a minister in the English Episcopal Church, was vicar of Madely. His saintliness was outstanding. At his funeral John Wesley said: "A man so inwardly and outwardly devoted to God,

so unblamable in character in every respect, I have not found in Europe or America; nor do I expect to find another such on this side of eternity" (*Letter,* dated June 19, 1771).

"I will confess Him to all the world; and I declare unto you in the presence of God, the Holy Trinity, I am now 'dead indeed unto sin.' I do not say, 'I am crucified with Christ,' because some of our well-meaning brethren say, 'By this can only be meant a gradual dying'; but I profess unto you that I am dead unto sin, and alive unto God. He is my Prophet, Priest, and King, my indwelling Holiness; my all in all" (in *Journal of Hester Ann Rogers,* p. 136).

3. *Adam Clarke:* Dr. Adam Clarke was the great commentator of Methodism, and one of the most scholarly men of his day.

"I regarded nothing, not even life itself, in comparison of having my heart cleansed from all sin; and began to seek it with full purpose of heart. Soon after this, while earnestly wrestling with the Lord in prayer, . . . I found a change wrought within my soul, which I endeavored through grace to maintain amid the grievous temptations and accusations of the subtle foe" (Quoted, *Perfect Love,* p. 160).

4. *George Fox:* "I knew Jesus, and He was very precious to my soul; but I found something in me that would not keep patient and kind. I did what I could to keep it down, but it was there. I besought Jesus to do something for me, and when I gave Him my will, He came into my heart, and cast out all that would not be sweet, all that would not be kind, all that would not be patient, and then He shut the door" (Quoted from *Streams in the Desert,* p. 360).

5. *Mrs. Hester Ann Rogers:* Mrs. Hester Ann Rogers was the wife of a Methodist preacher. Her name has come down to us as one of the most saintly women of her day.

"On the morning of February 22 I awoke poorly in body,

and felt a strange hardness in my heart, and a great backwardness to private prayer. Satan told me if I prayed it would be a solemn mockery. But I cried out, 'Lord, help me,' and fell instantly on my knees. My intercourse was now opened with my Beloved, and various promises presented to my believing view. Shall I ask now small blessings only of my God? Lord, make this the moment of my full salvation. Baptize me now with the Holy Ghost and fire of perfect love. Now enter Thy temple and cast out sin forever.. . . . In Thee I behold and feel all the fullness of Godhead mine; I am now one with God. Sin . . . inbred sin, . . . no longer hinders the close communion, and God is all my own" (*Men and Women of Deep Piety,* p. 400).

6. *Mrs. Phoebe Palmer:* Mrs. Palmer has been called "The Hester Ann Rogers of America." She was a leading figure in the early days of the American holiness movement.

"For a long time after her conversion Mrs. Palmer found her heart hungering for a deeper work of grace. Searching the Scriptures for light, she became convinced that 'This is the will of God, even your sanctification' (1 Thess. 4: 3), and that 'God hath not called us unto uncleanness, but unto holiness' (1 Thess. 4: 7). She began to seek earnestly for the experience. When she finally saw that it was obtainable not by struggling, but by simply putting herself into the hands of the Lord and believing His promises, she entered into that second rest which remains for the people of God" (*Men and Women of Deep Piety,* p. 371).

"It was at this point that the covenant was consummated between God and my soul that I would live a life of faith; that however diversified life's current might roll—though I might be called to endure more complicated and long-continued trials of my faith than were ever before conceived of, or even brought to a climax, where, as with the father of the faithful, commands and promises might seem to conflict— I would still believe, though I might die in the effort. I would hold on in the death struggle. In the strength of Omnipotence I laid hold on the Word, 'I will receive you!' Faith apprehended the written word, not as a dead letter but as the living voice of the living God. The Holy Scriptures were intensified in my mind as the living oracles—the voice of God to me as truly as though I could every moment hear Him speaking in tones of thunder from Sinai. And now that, through the inworkings of the Holy Spirit, I had presented all my redeemed powers to God, through Christ, how could I doubt His immutable word, 'I will receive you'?

"O with what light, clearness and power were the words invested, 'Sanctify them through thy truth; thy word is truth.'

"Yet, though I knew that it could not be otherwise than that God did receive me, my faith was at once put to the test. I had expected that some wonderful manifestation would at once follow as the reward of my faith, but I was shut up to faith—naked faith in a naked promise.

"The next step, faith, in regard to the divine acceptance of all, had also been distinctly taken. And now, as I plainly saw the third step, clearly defined in the Word, I took the advanced ground—confession.

"Giving God the glory due to His name, I exclaimed, 'Through Thy grace alone I had been enabled to give myself wholly and forever to Thee. Thou hast given Thy word, assuring me that Thou dost receive. I believe that Word! Alleluia! the Lord God Omnipotent reigneth unrivaled in my heart. Glory be to the Father! Glory be to the Son! Glory be to the Holy Spirit forever!' O, into what a region of light, glory and purity was my soul at this moment ushered! I felt that I was but as a drop in the ocean of infinite love, and Christ was all in all" (*Forty Witnesses,* pp. 304-305).

7. *Amanda Smith:* Black of skin, but one of God's

choicest saints. It was while listening to the preaching of
John Inskip that the simplicity of faith dawned on her
mind; and in a moment she had trusted God to do the
work.

"I seemed to go two ways at once—up and down. Such
a wave came over me, and such a welling up in my heart.
Oh, what glory filled my soul! The great vacuum in
my soul began to fill up and I wanted to shout, 'Glory to
Jesus!' . . ." (*Men and Women of Deep Piety*, p. 411).

8. *Catherine Booth:* Known to the world as "The
Mother of the Salvation Army." Mrs. Booth's testimony is
full of interest. It was some time after her marriage that
she entered into this experience. Her chief failing had been
irritability, and she longed for a constantly sweet disposition. She devoted all she could of two days to waiting before
God. The word, "Now are ye clean through the word I have
spoken unto you," was applied to her heart, and as her confidence waxed bold, she was enabled to reckon herself to be
"dead indeed unto sin."

"I did not feel much rapturous joy, but perfect peace—
the sweet rest which Jesus had promised to the heavy laden.
I have understood the apostle's meaning when he said, 'We
who believe do enter into rest.' Two or three very trying
things occurred on Saturday, which at another time would
have excited impatience, but I was kept by the power of
God through faith unto full salvation" (*Men and Women
of Deep Piety*, p. 36-37).

9. *George Muller:* The name of George Muller is known
throughout the world as the founder of those marvelous
orphanages at Bristol, England, where, in response to a daring faith, God has sent an unceasing supply to meet the
constantly recurring need. Read, if possible, the book *A
Million and a Half in Answer to Prayer.*

In an address given to ministers and workers, after his
ninetieth birthday, Mr. Muller said:

"I was converted in November, 1825, but I only came into the full surrender of heart four years later, in 1829. The love of money was gone, the love of place was gone, the love of position was gone, the love of worldly pleasures and engagements was gone. God, God, God alone became my portion. I found my all in Him. I wanted nothing else.

"By the grace of God this has remained, and has made me a happy man, an exceedingly happy man, and it led me to care only about the things of God. . . . This change was so great that it was like a second conversion."

10. *Bishop Warne:* This saintly Methodist bishop, so recently gone to his reward after faithful service in India, was known and loved by many Methodists in the United States.

"Now after years of study and hearing the testimony of many, it is clear to me that during those years as a boy I had prayed myself through to the abiding life which I now believe to be the experience of Scriptural holiness, which, as I understand it, is such a freedom from sin, self-will, and selfishness, and such a passionate love for Jesus, that it makes the heart long, above all things, for His approval, companionship, guidance and blessing, and that gratefully and joyfully gives Jesus in all things the pre-eminence" (*Warne of India,* Bishop Badley).

11. *Joseph H. Smith:* Rev. Joseph H. Smith is one of the best-known holiness evangelists of his day. To his helpful expositions he adds his testimony :

"My early apprehension and appropriation of this second crisis in Christian experience was largely due to the very favorable condition amidst which I was converted. In a church that was always in revival atmosphere and activities, its pastors for many years had rung clear and strong in preaching and testimony of entire sanctification. More than a dozen weekly class meetings were held by leaders who witnessed to this experience. Every Sabbath afternoon a general holiness meeting was conducted by the pastor, and was attended by many from other churches, as well as this. In fact, this centrally located Methodist church in Philadelphia was known as a 'hotbed of holiness.'

"The very night of my conversion there was placed in my hand a copy of J. A. Wood's book on *Perfect Love.* The eager appetite of my new life set me devouring its contents, and I read until long after midnight; and at 1:27 o'clock on the morning of January 30, 1874, I made this record in my diary, 'I am converted. My sins are forgiven. I am justified. I am now after something else: I guess that is what they call being sanctified.'

"Then all the ardor of my first love was spent in pursuit of holiness. The first day I made four distinct strides in advance thereunto. And each day some, till nearly five weeks had passed; when I told the Lord that I did not know how to get it, and asked Him these four questions: Will I pray more? Will I study more? Will I fast more? Will I pay more?

"Just then the Spirit used a little home incident to cross out for me all those big 'I's' and showed me it was nothing that I could do but that He who had let me in out of the dark and cold would Himself lift me up to the rest that remains to the people of God. That was a Friday night. All day Saturday over a busy desk I was looking up—Sabbath in six usual services, I was still looking up—Monday morning, early at the office, I supplied what had been missing from my prayer hitherto and said, 'Lord, wilt Thou lift me up now?' And He sweetly answered, 'I will, my child.' Faith at once embraced my cleansing through the Blood. The Holy Spirit came closer and entered more deeply than before, and gently announced, 'I am come to abide.' That Monday night, in a general testimony meeting at the church, I witnessed to the occurrence and stated that my joys today have been as much beyond those of the last five weeks as those were greater than all the pleasures I had in the world before. This was sixty-three years ago—I am still on the witness stand" (written especially for this handbook by Brother Smith).

12. *Bishop W. F. Oldham:* "I was hungry for salvation. A brother came to me after the meeting and said, 'Will you not come to our class meeting tomorrow evening at a brother's home?' I promptly said that I would, although I had not the faintest idea what a class meeting was. But I was in that state that if he had said, 'Come to the Timbuctoo,' I would have agreed.

"I was at the class meeting the next night, and had a chair at the end of the room. I saw that the leader of the class meeting was saying to each one, 'Now, brother, tell us how it is with you,' and then the brother would rise and give his experience. I saw that the leader was getting nearer and nearer to me, and I was greatly disturbed. When he stood in front of me and asked that question, I said, 'I know nothing about this matter, but I am here to learn.' So the leader appealed to all the people there to 'pray for this young brother.' They all knelt and prayed for me, and then and there I was converted to God, and His peace came into my soul.

"I lived in that state for many years and was a fairly fruitful Christian. I wanted to work for God, and one moonlit night, sitting on a rock, God spoke to me and said, 'I want you for my service.' I then began to prepare. Dr. James M. Thoburn said, 'I want just such a man as you are in Calcutta. Come and attend the university and also teach in our boys' school.' But I felt that there was something in the American type of education which I needed. So the way opened up, and I came to America for my training. As I was sailing to America I was a sick man, and was the only passenger on a slowgoing vessel. The captain regaled me with many stories of the storms that he had passed through.

He told of one terrific storm that swept in great distant circles about his ship, and in the morning he awoke to find the deck of his ship covered with birds. They had flown away from the terrific perimeter of the storm and taken shelter on the ship which was in comparative quietness. I thought this was a good illustration of the Christian life that is kept in perfect peace while the storms of life are surrounding and threatening—a place of perfect calm. I had always felt that there was such a state of experience for the Christian.

"I was fairly successful in the work of the Lord, as a pastorate in Pittsburgh where I took in six hundred members, will testify; yet all this time I was prejudiced against the experience of holiness. I had heard some teachers of the doctrine who seemed to me to be too critical. I was then a somewhat arrogant young man. I found out afterwards that these people were better than I thought they were, but this prejudice remained. Yet all the time I was hungry for something which I did not possess.

"In the years that followed, the church made me this and that, and then made me a bishop, and I was sent to my old field in Malaysia. At Singapore an adjustment of work made it necessary for the pastor of the English church to go to another place, and I arranged to take the English services. One day I announced that at the week-night service I would talk on 'The Higher Christian Life.' I do not know why I used this phrase, for I had always resented the idea of any Christian life being higher or lower. My wife said to me, 'William, what do you know about the higher life?' I replied, 'I do not know anything, but I am going to find out.' The first night there were forty present, the second night, eighty, the third night, one hundred and over, showing that many other hearts beside my own were hungry for this full salvation. After I had spoken several times on the subject of holiness, one night I said to my audience, 'The things that I have been teaching on this subject I know nothing at all about by experience, but I am determined to know.' So I walked down to the altar as a seeker of full salvation. The whole audience seemed to follow me to the altar. Ministers and workers of all denominations were present kneeling beside me, Baptists, Presbyterians, and others, as well as my own church. And there I consecrated my all to God, and He sanctified my soul. I lost consciousness for ten or fifteen minutes, and I awoke to find my soul filled with His peace and glory. That experience has been with me all these years in various kinds of service and under varying circumstances, and it abides tonight. Glory to God!

"You ask me what difference this full salvation has made. I reply:

"1.   That there is a deeper sense of the immediate presence of God in my life.

"2.   There is a deep quietness of soul—a calmness of heart free from restlessness.

"3.   There has come a great sympathy and love that reaches out to every human being. There is no one on earth that I am not willing to meet and help. I am willing that all the world shall know that there is one man who believes and knows that Jesus Christ can save from all sin" (Bishop Oldham's testimony).

### QUESTIONS ON THE TEXT

1.   Go through these testimonies, and state what strikes you the most in each.

2.   Gather at least three other testimonies of well-known servants of God who professed this blessing.

3.   Write your own testimony. Try to be definite and brief.

# Index of Quotations

# Index of Scriptures

Th